Trust in Black America

Trust in Black America

Race, Discrimination, and Politics

Shayla C. Nunnally

NEW YORK UNIVERSITY PRESS

New York and London

NEW YORK UNIVERSITY PRESS
New York and London
www.nyupress.org

References to Internet websites (URLs) were accurate at the time of writing.
Neither the author nor New York University Press is responsible for URLs
that may have expired or changed since the manuscript was prepared.

Library of Congress Cataloging-in-Publication Data
Nunnally, Shayla C.
Trust in Black America : race, discrimination, and politics / Shayla C. Nunnally.
p.   cm.
Includes bibliographical references and index.
ISBN 978-0-8147-5865-6 (cl : alk. paper) — ISBN 978-0-8147-5866-3 (pb :
alk. paper) — ISBN 978-0-8147-5930-1 (ebook) — ISBN 978-0-8147-5931-8
(ebook)
1. African Americans—Attitudes. 2. African Americans—Psychology.
3. African Americans—Socialization. 4. Trust—Political aspects—United
States. 5. Trust—Social aspects—United States. 6. Political socialization—
United States. 7. United States—Race relations.   I. Title.
E185.615.N86 2011
305.896'073—dc23   2011028197

New York University Press books are printed on acid-free paper,
and their binding materials are chosen for strength and durability.
We strive to use environmentally responsible suppliers and materials
to the greatest extent possible in publishing our books.

Manufactured in the United States of America

c   10 9 8 7 6 5 4 3 2 1
p   10 9 8 7 6 5 4 3 2 1

Contents

Preface and Acknowledgments

Having grown up in Petersburg, Virginia, I came to understand race easily. For my elementary and secondary education, I attended predominantly black public schools in the city. In a yesteryear, pre-1965, I would have attended an all-black, segregated school, but in the context of a city that had approximately an evenly split population between whites and blacks. Nevertheless, this racial context was different from the one in which I grew up. As the Petersburg City Public Schools integrated, many whites left the city, and by the time I attended school in the 1980s and 1990s, my school experience occurred in the context of a city population that had become predominantly black. The surrounding counties in the southeastern part of Virginia were either predominantly white or were more evenly split between a black and white population, and the schools mirrored this demography.

Although I had attended school in the same public school system as my father, my reality encompassed one in which I understood that my school represented a legacy of many southern public schools once segregation became unconstitutional—hyperconcentration of blacks in inner-city schools. As far as college, nevertheless, I made the conscientious decision to attend a historically black university to engage in a cultural and educational experience like the one I had in my formative years. It is in these contexts that I became exposed to diverse black perspectives and lifestyles that have informed the bases of my inquiries into race and trust in this book.

In the face of the world, my and other black students' solidarizing experiences as black students in the South included facing the prejudice that came with attending school at predominantly black educational institutions. In college, especially, daily conversations among students could be heard about how to navigate leaving a predominantly black context and face the "real world." Could we navigate the "real world" easily, or would we have trouble navigating the "real world" because we lived in isolated, black environments? It is through these experiences in these black institutional contexts that I also have gained some foreground and exposure to diverse messages about navigating race in one's daily life and possibly trusting through a racial lens, whether intraracially or interracially, to overcome the complexities of racial discrimination in racially insular and racially diverse communities.

Through a large faculty grant at the University of Connecticut, I have been able to field a national survey among blacks, whites, and Latinos in the United States. Therefore, I am grateful to the University of Connecticut and the Department of Political Science (Howard Reiter and Mark Boyer) and the Institute for African American Studies (Jeffrey Ogbar and Olu Oguibe) for offering additional monetary and resource support to help me field the survey. I also thank Jack Barry, Yazmin Garcia, Lin Li, Juhem Navarro, Chaka Uzondu, all current or former graduate students at the University of Connecticut, who assisted me with or chatted with me about my research, as I finished this project. Thank you, Destinee Chambers, for assisting me with revisions of my references. Very importantly, thank you to my executive editor at NYU Press, Ilene Kalish, for believing in the full scope of my project and being a most cordial and supportive editor during this process.

I wish to thank Niambi Carter, Victoria DeFrancesco-Soto, Melissa Harris-Perry, Monique Lyle, Monica McDermott, Chris Parker, Efren Perez, Howard Reiter, Evelyn Simien, Matthew Singer, Alvin Tillery, Heather Turcotte, and Keith Yancey, as they read various drafts of the manuscript or offered comments in different stages of the project. Very special thanks go to my graduate adviser and mentor, Paula McClain, who has shepherded my professional growth and who has been very supportive during my development of this project. Thank you to my mentor, Melissa Harris-Perry, who, along with Jarvis Hall, first introduced me to political science as a discipline of study in my undergraduate studies at North Carolina Central University (NCCU) and who encouraged me not to think of political science as merely a springboard for law school. To them, I am grateful for encouraging me to apply to graduate school in political science and, ultimately, for introducing me to my career. Especially, thank you Melissa, for encouraging me early in my studies to center black people in my political inquiries. I give special thank-yous to my former professors Joseph Aicher and the late Jeffrey Elliot, for supporting me as an undergraduate and encouraging me to strive toward the best in all that I did at NCCU and beyond. Thank you, Tyson King-Meadows, for believing in the tradition of Eagles soaring and encouraging me to do the same in the profession.

Thank you, Evelyn Simien, for all your continuing support and encouragement, as I navigate the profession. Special thanks go to Alvin Tillery, who, as another exceptional mentor, guided me through my dissertation writing and the writing culminating in the production of this book. Thank you Khalilah Brown-Dean, Melanye Price, and Robert Rusher for all your support, as I adjusted to New England. I wish to thank Nikol Alexander and Julia Jordan-Zachery, for your emotional support throughout my various revisions of this project. I also wish to thank a host of colleagues at the University of Connecticut for their continuing support and side chats, all of which made writing more creative and fun.

As well, I wish to thank several friends, who have laughed with me and at me, whenever I really needed to laugh—Everette Catilla, Andrea Chapman, Shirron Dobie, Jamorya Funderburk, Sataria Joyner, J. Alan Kendrick, Belinda Morrison, Maurice McNeil (and the McNeil family), Kenya Overton, Warren Richards, Farrand Violette, and Anisha Wilson. Thank you, as well, to a host of friends from Virginia, North Carolina, and Connecticut who have offered their support over the years. Most importantly, I wish to thank my mother, Gladys Nunnally, and my father, Sterling Nunnally, and other extended family members for their endless support. Through their love, guidance, and support of me charting my own path over the years, I have been driven to pursue my goals. To my ancestors, thank you for extending to me spirituality to build endurance during this effort.

— Part I —

Understanding Race and Trust

Introduction

Race, Risk, and Discrimination

The Significance of Race and Risk in America

In July 2010, American television media revealed seemingly controversial footage of Shirley Sherrod, a black American woman and U.S. Department of Agriculture (USDA) Rural Development agent in Georgia, speaking about her being unable to treat a white farmer fairly. The videotape featured Sherrod's March 27, 2010, speech delivered to a Douglas, Georgia, chapter of the National Association for the Advancement of Colored People (NAACP) for its twentieth annual Freedom Fund program.[1] The video clip initially had been released online by Andrew Breitbart, a conservative blogger affiliated with BigGovernment.com, in order to show Sherrod's and the NAACP's racist attitudes toward whites,[2] as it appeared that Sherrod described how she considered denying a white farmer access to government benefits.

At the time, the story seemed shocking and newsworthy. Fox News anchors suggested that the video clip exemplified a black bureaucrat in President Barack Obama's administration practicing reverse discrimination against whites. Indeed, in their perspective, Sherrod represented ideals that were being incorporated into the agenda of the nation's first black president. Critics asked how a civil servant could deny benefits to others based on their race. The alleged controversy also lay in the paradox of a civil rights organization promoting racial discrimination. Some charged that the NAACP was hypocritical because, as a civil rights organization, it invited a "racist" speaker, despite its professed challenges against racism; here, it seemed as if the NAACP endorsed a speech by a civil servant who supposedly upheld discrimination against whites.

In effect, Breitbart's video snippet started a national media frenzy that characterized Sherrod as a racist, ill-willed civil servant who was "out to get white people." The ramifications of the snippet were great, as the brouhaha over it led to calls for Sherrod to be fired, and eventually, she was asked to resign her post. The NAACP president, Ben Jealous, also denounced her speech. But, as the eventual release of and attention to the full-length video of the speech showed, the allegations of Sherrod's "racist acts" were not true and, in fact, were unfounded.

As the news story developed, the actual travesty lay in the fact that the video snippet did not capture Sherrod's *full* speech. In fact, in the unedited, full video of Sherrod's speech, she actually challenged the NAACP audience to think about supporting justice for all, despite their personal discrimination experiences and misgivings about historical racial discrimination and mistreatment of people (by whites, in particular). Sherrod's own father had been lynched by whites in the Jim Crow South in 1965, and the perpetrators were never brought to justice. In her entire speech, she actually encouraged a standard of justice that centers on seeking greater good and not seeking racial retribution for one's personal, past racial discrimination experiences. Sherrod even questioned her own intentions toward the white farmers, as she stated, "I was struggling with the fact that so many black people had lost their farmland, and here I was faced with having to help a white person save their land. So I didn't give him the full force of what I could do. I did enough."[3]

In its entirety, Sherrod's speech actually relayed her personal triumphs of overcoming her own prejudices to aid a white farmer in saving his farm land. As the Sherrod news story continued to unfold before the public's view, the white farmer and his wife, whom Sherrod assisted in saving their farm, appeared on news interviews to add veracity to Sherrod's claims about assisting them in their time of need. They even praised her for helping them keep their farm land. Ultimately, the truth revealed a gross mischaracterization of Sherrod, and the out-of-context scope of the video prompted a national controversy without any substantiating evidence. Sherrod was branded a racist for no evidentiary reason.

Soon the television media attempted to redeem Sherrod's character, as they invited her for guest appearances to speak about the matter from her perspective. Eventually, the NAACP president apologized to her, and the secretary of agriculture, Tom Vilsack, both apologized and offered Sherrod another job with higher rank. President Obama also called to offer his regrets for the incident and to encourage her to rejoin the USDA. Sherrod respectfully declined.

What is a simple moral of this story? "Don't judge a book by its cover. . .

without reading its *full* content." But, in the broader scheme of things, this vignette sheds light on a deeper, more troubling aspect of American society: that people judge one another on the basis of race and that people distrust decision-making because of the perception that members of other racial groups will seek racial expediency and ill-will toward people not in their own racial group.

Sadly, our nation's history has an indelible imprint of race affecting the status of humanity, equality, and participation of people in American society. Frankly, such racist decision-making has had dire consequences, especially and most frequently for nonwhites. Such vagaries of race and perceived zero-sum gains of one racial group at the expense of another, lead people to assess actions, intents, and the risks of discrimination on the basis of the race of the actor making the decisions. Just as the Sherrod episode implies, people think about race with respect to whether it will disproportionately affect outcomes in their disfavor. Underlying these sentiments is the extent to which race influences how people are perceived as being trustable to fulfill actions on others' behalves and the extent to which people perceive the probability of discrimination as a negative risk to their interests and well-being on the basis of their own racial group membership.

This relationship among race, risk, and inequitable experiences of democracy is the focus of this book—*racial (dis)trust*. With the tables turned differently from the Sherrod story, which focused on the perception that whites were being mistreated and that they were implicitly distrusting of a black woman bureaucrat's decision-making, this book entertains how race influences trust from black Americans' social and political perspectives. This book also explores how race influences blacks' assessments of whites and other nonblack groups as far as their roles in racial discrimination and trustworthiness in social and political aspects of blacks' lives. In this sense, this book offers a historical and contemporary look at how race and trust intertwine in (black) Americans' social and political perceptions.

One way in which we see the significance of trust in America is with respect to United States currency. The face of the penny, for example, states simply across its top, "In God We Trust." The image of President Abraham Lincoln rests below it, and the word "Liberty" is engraved to the left. Trust is not entrusted in America, nor is it even entrusted in President Lincoln. Instead, the penny implies that trust is a divine relationship shared between people and God. But people make trust go around, and moving from one's faith in a higher being to connecting with others depends on how people view each other and their relationships. Trust has everything to do with how we think about people. Moving from the celestial conception of trust to one that underscores human relationships, we must ask, "In whom do we trust?"

In America, much of how we think about people also depends on their *race*. What is race? *Race* is a social construct. In the United States, people's physical characteristics have been categorized into pseudoscientific racial categories that assigned biological significance, with sociopolitical consequences. Embodied in the construction of race are group-based interests that perpetuate conflict and social stratification (Omi and Winant 1994). Historically, race has operated as a physical characteristic that affected people's welfare under uncertain circumstances. It also intensified their exposure to discrimination depending on their specific racial group.

Race also governs the *way* that people engage(d) in social, political, and economic conflict (Omi and Winant 1994). For black people, *who* is black[4] and *how* black people have been treated in America are connected to their race. Even when considering trust with respect to the United States' penny: Lincoln's likeness on the coin, his trials to unite the nation during the Civil War, his eventual greatness for reuniting the nation, and his pursuit of liberty relate to the subjugation of blacks in much of American history because of their race. Historically, the construction of race in the United States has physically, symbolically, and psychologically marginalized black Americans (and other nonwhite groups) to an otherized group classification, especially vis-à-vis whites. This has operated to deny blacks and others their human, civil, and political rights. Whites' power domination over black Americans, additionally, historicized black-white relationships in a way that created power imbalances favorable to whites and that created uncertainty between the two groups over individuals' commitment to white-dominating practices. Race, thus, is not benign: it has and continues to operate malignantly. Its sociohistorical development and contemporary effects, thus, have ravaged the full scope of humane possibilities.

To this degree, there are unknown probabilities of risks associated with people's racial group and their likelihood for being perpetrators or victims of racial discrimination. With respect to trust, this means that *in whom* people trust and *where* people trust has real political and social consequences. Because of the racial hierarchy in the United States, this means that there is a *racial calculus of trust*. Where people are situated in this hierarchy (as whites or nonwhites) affects how they perceive this racialized trust calculus. For nonwhites in particular, I argue that historical and contemporary experiences with race increase the extent to which they rely for their trust calculations on the race of the trustee (the person who is to be entrusted).[5] But, as I elaborate later, respective racial groups and their group members' experiences with race are not the same, and diverse racial experiences are what affect variations in people's trust. In particular, racial experiences are what I offer inform and reduce black Americans' trust in others, making them one of the least trusting groups in America.

For blacks, I argue that enhanced socialization about historical race relations, black culture, and the effect of race on their living conditions influences how they perceive and relate to black and nonblack group members. Socialization that emphasizes group-specific mistrust should increase the likelihood that blacks perceive nonblacks in more negative, uncertain, and distrusting ways. Personalized experiences with race in contemporary society also inculcate information about racial groups and their relationships with blacks, and these experiences also influence trust assessments. It is the nexus between perceived risk, uncertainty, racial discrimination, racial socialization, and the psychological processing of race that I believe is core to the examination and explanation of black Americans' (dis)trust. This approach is important for the study of trust because it elucidates the effect of undemocratic racial experiences on racializing trust. Therefore, with the significance of race and the risk of discrimination in black Americans' lives, we must ask the question, "In whom do blacks trust?" Most importantly, this question must be analyzed explicitly with respect to this group's racial circumstances. In this vein, the focus of this book, as I describe in more detail later, is to explain the aforementioned interrelationships of these racial circumstances with respect to blacks' trust.

The remainder of this chapter establishes the historical racial experiences that blacks have had and how these experiences have contradicted theoretical foundations and conceptions of both democracy and trust. The chapter also provides more discussion about the focus of the book and situates its study of blacks' trust within the larger literature and debates about trust. It provides a cursory overview of the theory of *discriminative racial-psychological processing* that I offer to describe how race influences blacks' trust. In addition, this chapter describes the methods that I use to operationalize the theorized relationships that I see between race and trust. To conclude the chapter, I provide an overview of the book chapters, all of which examine in various ways trust in black America.

Racialized (Dis)trust? Race and the "Unmaking" of Democracy

For hundreds of years in America, blacks' unique experiences with slavery and de jure and de facto discrimination have stood in stark contrast with democratic principles envisioned for the foundation of the nation. Historically, every constitutional right assured American citizens was either denied or understood to be applied differently to blacks. In law and society, physical characteristics (as they were associated with blacks' racial phenotypes) prescribed both behavioral expectations and behavioral prohibitions.

During the era of slavery, psychological descriptions of black temperament accompanied the physical descriptions of the black body, as slave traders and slave owners attempted to define blacks' labor productivity as being ripe for them to be enslaved persons (Johnson 1999; Roberts 1997). Scientific racism also infiltrated social, political, and economic thought, and it created multiple distinctions and stratifications of the "Negro" as subordinate and inferior to whites (Gossett 1997).

Racialized behavioral descriptors thus normativized behavioral expectations for blacks, and "acting" properly in certain "places" defined whether blacks "appropriately" followed slavery and Jim Crow etiquette and, thus, could be "trusted" to perform their generally perceived role as being property or second-class citizens. The confinement of the "Negro's place" to the bottom rung of the socioeconomic ladder and the racial hierarchy continued well through the mid-twentieth century, thus codifying racial etiquette between blacks and whites (Litwack 1998; Woodward [1951] 1999, 1974). Part of defining blacks' "place" involved restricting "black behavior" in ways that further institutionalized the link between race, behavior, social customs, and law (Crenshaw et al. 1995; Key 1949).

The mores about race had to be learned and transmitted across generations of black Americans. With Jim Crowism emphasizing etiquette that both black and white children had to learn in order to maintain racial equilibrium in the South and across the country (see Ritterhouse 2006), black social, political, and economic actions depended on racial knowledge about blacks' "place" in order for them to avoid racial harm. In contemporary American society, race still structures behavioral expectations and actions both intraracially and interracially, encapsulating what scholars refer to as the "performance of race" (Willie 2003), as people assess whether people as racial group members comply with racial expectations and cultural norms and "act" like other members of their racial group.

Even historical linguistic characterizations of blacks' and whites' behaviors suggest how much their behavior either substantiated a racial hierarchy or contradicted it, making it all the more evident that both groups' behaviors were interpreted to qualify how much they could be trusted to "stay in their place" in historical American race relations. For example, whites who supported black interests were referred to as "negrophiles," whereas those that did not were referred to as "negrophobes." More common epithets reduced whites who sympathized with black interests to "nigger lovers" and "race traitors." Thus, slavery and Jim Crow governed carte blanche the historical probability, risks, and benefits of black Americans' interactions with whites in social and political contexts.

With respect to the behavior of American political institutions and their (white) actors, we also see evidence of how distrust was institutionalized and normativized among black Americans. The era that generally symbolizes the tenuous relationship between African Americans and the U.S. government has been called "The Nadir," the low point during which the government retracted its protective advances on behalf of blacks during the Reconstruction era (Logan 1965). Institutionalized, asymmetrical power relations between blacks and whites affected how these two groups interacted with one another historically, as whites were constructed as a dominant group over blacks and other nonwhites. With white-group interests being integral to white domination, nonwhite interests were often subordinate, if not excluded, based on what was thought to be in the best interests of whites.

Organized terror against black Americans (e.g., in the form of actions by the Ku Klux Klan and other antiblack groups) and state-sponsored unequal protections for black Americans by whites (or even by blacks who held a negative view of the value of black life) also signaled how much people inside or outside political institutions could be trusted to act on behalf of blacks' interests and protection. Even blacks who internalized racism could act in ways that were adverse to black interests (Woodson [1933] 1999). Moreover, blacks who did not challenge their subjugated status in society were referred to as "good," whereas those who contested their status were referred to as "bad" (Hartman 1997).

Many whites also distrusted blacks because they feared blacks' ability to overthrow institutions that benefited white-group interests (Woodward [1951] 1999, 1974; Key 1949). Conversely, many blacks distrusted whites because of their power to oppress and disempower them socially, politically, and economically (Bay 2000; Hartman 1997; Haney López 2006; Omi and Winant 1994; Woodward 1974).

Massive resistance to desegregation in the South and elsewhere during the mid-twentieth century also made the route toward blacks' inclusion a piece-meal experience for blacks. As opposed to government acting as an agent to promote trust, as Putnam (1993) prescribes, in the United States, the government propagated racial discrimination against African American citizens and other nonwhites, denying them equal access to citizenship, equal access to the franchise, and equal protection of the law. It was not until the passage of the Civil Rights Act of 1964, which codified into law that public accommodations could no longer be segregated and that customs associated with racial etiquette and racialized spaces were supposedly dismantled. Despite the codification of racial equality, blacks still have had to face the uncertainty of being racially discriminated against by people who retained antiblack attitudes. Such racially uncertain conditions also perpetually remind(ed) blacks about the prospective costs of racial discrimination, especially in black-white interactions. (Of course, this entails that blacks must be aware of these historical black-white relationships.) Thus, historicized relationships between blacks and whites are meaningful for analyzing African Americans' contemporary trust because those relationships offered very little room for trusting, then and possibly even in today's society.

Moreover, racial attitudes toward black Americans by other historically discriminated groups also can be negative or perceivably competitive in ways that can inhibit cross-group relations (Mindiola, Niemann, and Rodriguez 2002; McClain 2006; Sigelman and Tuch 1997; Bobo and Hutchings 1996). Civil rights violations by ordinary citizens (white and nonwhite) thus also taint social relationships between racial groups—social relationships that the trust literature would argue should be meaningful for enhancing trusting relations between citizens and government, writ large.

The psychological effects of abuse by the state and civilians during the pre-1960s era contributed to blacks' development of insular communities to respond to and provide agency to black Americans' circumstances (Lewis 1991). But, on the downside, black intragroup relations were complicated by out-group racial subjugation, color-line favoritism toward lighter-skinned black Americans, race-class intersections and dualities, racialized gender stratifications, and even negative psychological conceptions about fellow blacks that informed the politics of blacks during the late nineteenth to mid-twentieth centuries (M. Hill 2000; Orr 1999; Gaines 1996; Higginbotham 1993; Cross 1991). Thus, even how black in-group members identify with and treat other in-group members can be complicated by the negative orientations learned about blackness and incorporated into their racial belief system (Cross 1991; Allen, Dawson, and Brown 1989). Such intraracial attitudes, aside from those of nonblacks, also can reduce blacks' trust in other blacks.

After passage of state-induced protections of black Americans' civil rights and voting rights in the 1960s, black Americans still experience racial discrimination, although these experiences vary (Feagin 2000; Broman, Mavaddat, and Hsu 2000; Hochschild 1995; Sigelman and Welch 1991). African American parents also continue to teach their children about race in America through a socialization experience known as *racial socialization* (Demo and Hughes 1990). It is through this experience that black children become familiar with what it means to be black in America historically and contemporarily, who are their fellow racial group members, how to interact with other racial group members, how to deal with racial discrimination (McAdoo 2007), and as I argue, even whom to trust.

Furthermore, despite whites' developing increasingly liberalized views about race and racial policies (Schuman et al. 1997), the racial divide in public opinion remains prominent even today (Kinder and Sanders 1996). Whites with negative attitudes about blacks either subscribe to principled opposition to blacks who are viewed as possessing comportment that is at odds with American values, or they harbor racial antipathy toward blacks, castigating them as social and political outsiders (Sears, Sidanius, and Bobo 2000).

Blacks' racial consciousness about their plight as members of a low-status group continually informs their sociopolitical realities and interests (Tate 1993; Dawson 1994), making race a probable factor in reducing or increasing their social and political trusts. With increasing real and perceived political and economic competition between blacks and other nonwhite groups such as Latinos and Asian Americans (Kim 2000; Bobo and Hutchings 1996; McClain and Karnig 1990), race and the risk of racial discrimination potentially affect contemporary trust relations among these groups, as well. Blacks' racial experiences, therefore, warrant a fuller understanding of how historically institutionalized racism, contemporary racial attitudes, and perceptions of intergroup relationships affect their trust in present society.

In sum, I argue that historical and contemporary racial experiences promote(d) *distrust* among Americans and *distrust* of their government. So "distrust," *not* "trust," has been the basis on which race relations have been institutionalized in America. Blacks' historical discrimination experiences, moreover, have become the foci of explanations for their contemporary low-level political and social trusts compared to other racial groups (Abramson 1977; Walton 1985; Rahn and Transue 1998; Brehm and Rahn 1997; Putnam 1995, 2000a). This proposed link between history and today's society makes trust a major concern and intellectual site for the study of black political and social behavior. Analyzing trust through the lens of race, therefore, becomes an important endeavor in the study of trust in political science and becomes an important part of explaining blacks' distrust.

Based on blacks' experiences with race, evidence suggests that, in principle, trust and democracy did not function in American politics in the way that normative theories about trust would predict. For one, we would expect democratic societies and governments to treat all their citizens equally, without regard to race. We also would expect that the trust between citizens and government is color-blind. But, contrary to normative expectation, neither the American government nor everyday citizens have treated all citizens equally or beneficently with respect to their race. Historically, as I have described, race has excluded people and segregated their coordinated actions. Legal and social sanctioning prescribed segregated social, political, and economic networks. As a consequence, even social capital is racialized (Mansbridge 1997; Orr 1999; Hero 2007). Given the historical risks and suboptimal benefits of blacks' experiences with other citizens and government, we can see clearly that trust in America does not have a foundation for it even to be considered "color-blind." But much of the literature on trust treats it as if it is. Because racially marginalized groups such as African Americans have had undemocratic experiences at the behest of government (Hero and Wolbrecht 2005; Tillery 2005; Hochschild 2006; Franklin and Moss 2007), this also begs the question of why they would even trust at all in whites (and other nonblacks) and in any institution in their social or political environments that historically discriminated against them.

Ipso facto, race and racial discrimination have broken down trust in American democracy by segregating racial groups in ways that make it difficult to facilitate coordinate actions. This is contradictory to what Putnam (1993) suggests such coordinating actions should do in enhancing trust. Overlooking the significance of race in the breakdown of democracy and what it means for trust in general, therefore, is an egregious error in the approach of trust studies, especially in political science. This is because it ignores the extent to which race affects Americans' lives generally and blacks' lives more specifically.[6]

Thus, as Melissa Williams (1998) suggests, we must consider what trust entails for historically marginalized groups such as black Americans. Studying race and trust helps us to understand the limitations of normative expectations about trust in American democracy. In recognizing differences in racial discrimination experiences and racial and political socialization experiences, we also can test whether dissimilar racial predispositions enhance or reduce blacks' trust. This, likewise, will allow us to account for variation in black sociopolitical attitudes.

Based on the premise that racial discrimination breaks down trust in a democracy, this book provides a comprehensive analysis of blacks' political *and* social trusts in order to determine the effect of race on their trust. It also invites the study of race and trust, or *racialized trust*, through an interdisciplinary perspective that builds on political science, history, and psychology literatures. To broach the subject of the connection between race and trust, several foundational inquiries animate this study. How can we explain the continuing disparate levels of trust (social and political) among blacks, especially in modern times when blacks have been included more equitably into American society? Are there different manifestations of race in blacks' lives that account for how they trust others? Do the ways that blacks internalize race affect how they externalize race in their trust? These inquiries also inform the theory of *discriminative racial-psychological processing* (described in greater detail in chapter 2), which I submit to describe how blacks internalize race and externalize it in their social and political trusts.

Focus of the Book

As I have described previously, this book is about blacks' trust and how they psychologically process race in their social and political trust assessments. Because race is one of the foremost ways in which we perceive people in the United States (Omi and Winant 1994; Dyson 1996; Bonilla-Silva 2001), I am principally interested in determining how race is socialized, internalized, and externalized in blacks' trust (as trustors) in others as members of racial groups (as trustees).

This text revisits Abramson's (1972) notion that blacks' (dis)trust is socialized. It provides a contemporary analysis of how information learned from both political and racial socializations inform black Americans' trust attitudes. Moving beyond Abramson's focus on parent-child socialization messages about politics, this book contributes to the literature on trust and African American politics by positing that black Americans' trust varies depending on their racial socialization about blacks' status in society, their racial attitudes, and their perceptions of social or political actors' race in different contexts. More specifically, in my submission of a theory of *discriminative racial-psychological processing*, I aim to explain black Americans' (dis)trust.

This theory centers race as the causal mechanism that not only explains African Americans' distrust but also differentiates black trust attitudes. More specifically, I offer to complicate how we think about the way race functions in blacks' trust. For example, trust measures commonly ask people simply, "Who do you trust?" or "How much do you trust people in general?" Given the continuing influence of race on blacks' lives, these questions should ask more directly, "In *whom* (black, white, Asian American, or Latino) do you trust?" and "*Where* (neighborhoods, workplaces, shopping places, and religious institutions) do you trust in others (as members of racial and ethnic groups—black, white, Asian American, or Latino) more or less?" Thus, we must measure how people's trust varies depending on the trustee's race and the context of the trust evaluation.

As I elaborate later, my theory of *discriminative racial-psychological processing* submits six ways to measure variations in blacks' racial and trust perceptions: (1) their racial socialization experiences, or learning about the effect of race on their lives, (2) their racial homogenization of racial group behavior, or perceptions of racial stereotypes, (3) their perceptions of racial uncertainty, or the likelihood of being racially discriminated against, (4) their personal experiences with racial discrimination, or the frequency of lived, racial discrimination experiences, (5) their racialized trust variation across racial groups, or differentiation in trust based on the race of the person to be trusted, and (6) their racial-contextual perceptions of racial groups, or their perceptions of racial groups in social and political spaces. I anticipate that racial socialization messages that emphasize negative intergroup relations and negative racial attitudes will reduce blacks' social and political trusts. I also hypothesize that, with respect to trusting black, white, Asian American, or Latino social or political actors, blacks will be more trusting in their own group members than in other racial groups. However, blacks who are socialized negatively about their fellow group members and possess negative attitudes about them will be less trusting of their group members, as well.

In all, as a comprehensive study of blacks' trust in both political and social contexts, this book examines the following: (1) *what* black Americans learn about race and intergroup interactions, (2) how information learned about race affects black Americans' racial predispositions and understandings about their place in society, (3) how racial predispositions influence *who* (other black group members and other racial groups) blacks trust and *how much* (the intensity level of trust) blacks trust others, (4) *where* blacks are more willing to trust others (in social and political contexts), and (5) *how* these several factors influence blacks' trust. While much of the trust literature in political science obscures how race functions in trust perception, especially with respect to black Americans, herein I address the nexus between race and trust by offering the following research inquiries:

1. How does race influence blacks' social and political (dis)trust?
2. How does socialization specifically about blacks' discriminatory historical experiences affect their (dis)trust in both social and political spaces?
3. Can we attribute blacks' (dis)trust to *historical* discrimination experiences alone? That is, how do *contemporary* experiences with racial discrimination affect their (dis)trust?
4. Does socialization about race influence racial attitudes and the perceived likelihood for discrimination?
5. Does racialized distrust lower social and political trusts?
6. What are the psychological consequences, if any, of a democratic government and society discriminating against its own citizens?
7. How do we reconcile the value of trust in democracy when people have racially discriminatory social and political experiences that defy normative expectations for trust and government?

Why Study Blacks' (Dis)trust?

Conceptually, this book challenges the way political scientists define what is political by suggesting that we study political *and* social spaces. This is because race has an all-encompassing effect on people's lives. For blacks, especially, race and racial discrimination against them led them to mobilize politically for full integration into society. The research herein also elucidates the racialization of (dis)trust as a major vestige of racial construction and racism. This suggests that blacks (and others) distinguish trust on the basis of race and their status in the American racial hierarchy. Consequently, people become protective (and perhaps sometimes overly protective) of their social and political relations in ways that may or may not be beneficial to them in the long run.

In the study of trust, we have come to understand the qualities of being *trustworthy* or *trusting* of others as major social and political assets. However, once trust is broken, it is hard to restore (Hardin 2004; Solomon and Flores 2001). Thus, being *trusted* is a scarce and fragile resource (Messick and Kramer 2001).

With trust's potential reward, it is foundational and adhesive for society and democracy (Warren 1999; Putnam 1993; Rahn and Transue 1998).

Normatively, the trust literature expects that people who are trusted more and trust others more stand to participate more freely in democratic processes and, subsequently, to reap the benefits. When citizens trust one another and political institutions, they should sustain positive relationships with others and their government, and their government should become more accountable to them. There also should be a greater good of *trust* in the proper functioning of democracy: the more citizens trust, the better democracy should function, and vice versa (Brehm and Rahn 1997; Putnam 1993, 2000a).

Notwithstanding *trust* being an important aspect of democratic theory, *distrust* also is rooted in the founding of the American political system (Hardin 2004, 2006; J. Braithwaite 1998; Warren 1999). For the Framers, self-interested behavior of unscrupulous political actors could contradict the best interests of common good on behalf of the nation (Hardin 1998, 2004, 2006; V. Braithwaite 1998). The U.S. Constitution, consequently, includes a separation of and check on powers among the branches of government, because of the Framers' distrust in human behavior. Trust and distrust, then, are counterbalancing forces in American democracy. But when is there an unhealthy balance of distrust? When people distrust others to the point that they find them to be suspicious, in the context of political or social spaces, people fear or underexplore the full range of human relations.

Distrust, then, can inhibit the full benefits of humanity, especially if people are less willing to build relationships or to consider public goods regardless of race. At the same time, distrust can protect people from prospective racial discrimination and race-related risks. Because trust is such a valuable commodity for interpersonal and intergroup relations, understanding black Americans' (dis)trust assists us in considering the implications of normativized racial distrust and ways to repair psychological injuries that loom because of historical and contemporary racial discrimination. Studying blacks' distrust helps us consider ways to improve blacks' equitable experiences of both humanity and democracy.

Data for the Study

In order to provide a comprehensive examination of black Americans' trust, I analyze national public-opinion data from two sources: the *2000 Social Capital Benchmark Survey* (SCBS; Robert Putnam, principal investigator; national sample, N = 3,003) and the *2007 National Politics and Socialization Survey* (NPSS; Shayla C. Nunnally, principal investigator; N = 1,021).

The SCBS was in the field between July and November 2000. Using random-digit dialing, the telephone-interview survey includes data from two sample sources in the continental United States: (1) a national sample with a sample size of 3,003 and (2) a community sample of forty-one communities with a sample size of 26,230. The combination of the two samples gives the survey an overall sample size of 29,233. For the analysis herein, I analyze only the national sample survey.

The SCBS includes measures of political, social, and racial trusts. As a national survey, it also includes a multiracial sample with an oversampling of black and Latino respondents (N = 3,003 respondents; n = 501 black and n = 502 Latino respondents). The racial-attitudes measures in the SCBS, however, are limited. Unfortunately, there are no stereotype measures, and most important, there are no measures of racial or political socializations to test some of the relationships proposed in the theory of racial-psychological processing. Therefore, I developed and fielded a national survey of black, Latino, and white respondents—the NPSS.

The NPSS was administered in affiliation with SurveySavvy and Marketing Systems Group, a survey and market-research firm that I contracted to administer the survey. The survey was placed in the field December 26, 2007, through January 2, 2008. The NPSS has tremendous "added value" for the study of trust. For one, the 2007 NPSS includes many measures found in the 2000 SCBS, including measures of racial trust, social trust, and political trust that offer more recent data collected on these measures. Second, the NPSS includes measures on racial socialization that also offer updated data on measures found in the 1979–1980 National Survey of Black Americans (NSBA; James Jackson 1991). Third, the NPSS complements the SCBS by giving the principal investigator the opportunity to test the relationships among racial socialization, racial identity, racial attitudes, and trust in one data set, testing that otherwise cannot be done with the SCBS alone. Although a study that measures the influence of race on trust should include these measures, unfortunately, the SCBS does not. So, fourth, the NPSS offers a nuanced way to measure race and trust by including several split-sample embedded experiments on race and trust that provide unobtrusive measures of racial trust. Such measures are employed in a way that respondents are unaware that their responses will be analyzed for differences in trust across racial groups. Finally, the NPSS comprises a diverse, national sample with white (n = 252), Latino (n = 252), and black American (n = 517) respondents, a diversity that helps in the comparative analysis of racial attitudes among the groups in the sample.

The NPSS survey, unfortunately, does not include a representative sample of Americans. However, the respondents' gender and age characteristics are matched based on the percentages for these characteristics for each racial group in the 2004 and 2006 U.S. Census Current Population Survey. (See descriptive characteristics for Americans in appendix A. Additional information about the survey matching and the U.S. Census data can be found in appendix B.)

The respondents' household incomes, however, are not matched based on U.S. Census socioeconomic data, and socioeconomic characteristics for black Americans, for example, are not commensurate with those in the larger black population. The mean household income ($50,000–$74,000) in the NPSS sample is higher than the median income ($30,200) indicated for black households in the U.S. Census's 2004 American Community Survey Report on black Americans (issued in February 2007). The median household income in the Community Report reflects the median income of households in the twelve months prior to the respondents' being surveyed, and it includes a distribution based on the total number of households including those with no income.

Despite the NPSS's not being matched based on census "black alone" household income characteristics, the NPSS includes socioeconomic diversity among its respondents. According to data from a March 2004 report of 2003 "black alone" "family money income," for example, 16.3 percent of these families (N = 76,232) reported incomes between $50,000 and $74,999. This accounts for the second-highest categorical family-income group of "black alone" families. The leading total money family-income group for black families constitutes 17.4 percent of black families and a household income that is $75,000 and over.[7] Therefore, as noted in the descriptive characteristics in appendix A, the mean household income for this survey ($50,000 to $74,000) perhaps offers some similarity with the "family money income data" for black Americans. Nevertheless, the survey still offers *limited* representativeness of black Americans' general socioeconomic characteristics.

Socioeconomic diversity is a limitation of web-based surveys, and black and Latino households have lower home access to the Internet than do other groups (Couper 2000). However, there is evidence that, despite nonprobability sampling issues, Internet survey results mirror results in probability samples, and difficulties with Internet-mode surveying may not be as problematic as once believed (Alvarez, Sherman, and VanBeselaere 2003). Therefore, as a web-based survey, the NPSS still can offer important information about the experiences of black Americans in the sample, especially as it offers a glimpse of these experiences spanning several generations of black Americans.

Organization of the Book

The book, thus, includes empirical analyses from the two aforementioned data sets. It tests the theory about the way race is processed in blacks' social and political trusts. The book also helps us understand how black Americans process race in their social and political interactions. Chapter 2 provides a discussion about the theory of discriminative racial-psychological processing. The text examines black Americans' socialization experiences among younger generations of black Americans than those found in the 1979–1980 NSBA. It also scrutinizes to what extent these experiences influence how blacks internalize race and externalize it in their trust. The subsequent chapters in the book are organized into five empirical chapters that are divided into two parts: "Racial Internalization" and "Racial Externalization."

Part II on racial internalization includes chapters 3 through 5, which include empirical chapters on blacks' racial socialization (or learning about race, chapter 3), perceptions of racial discrimination and racial stereotypes (chapter 4), and perceptions of racialized trust (chapter 5). Using data analysis of the 2007 National Politics and Socialization Survey (NPSS), chapter 3 explores the sources of black Americans' learning about being black in America. The chapter examines ten measures of racial socialization and the level of emphasis at which black Americans learned about these racial socialization messages. NPSS data are analyzed with respect to the broader implications of black Americans' racial socialization experiences for their intraracial and interracial group relations. Consistent with the literature, socialization about racialized distrust, interestingly, is one of the least emphatically learned racial socialization messages among black Americans. Despite this low emphasis in blacks' parent-child socialization, chapter 4 elucidates how much these messages still affect blacks' racial perceptions.

Chapter 4 discusses the effect of racial discrimination on African Americans' lives. It also examines blacks' racial perceptions. I analyze data from the NPSS to discern blacks' racial attitudes. The chapter examines the perceived likelihood that blacks will be discriminated against by whites, Latinos, Asians, and even other blacks. It also determines the effect of blacks' knowledge about their groups' historical racial experiences on their contemporary relationships with other racial groups. To determine the influence of racial socialization on blacks' attitudes about various racial groups the chapter examines the relationship between racial socialization and subscription to racial stereotypes. Finally, the chapter investigates the explanatory factors for blacks' frequency of racial discrimination.

In the NPSS, I find that blacks' having received greater emphasis on social-ization messages about racial protectiveness increases their negative feelings and interactions with whites, Asians, and Latinos. More frequent racial dis-crimination experiences also enhance blacks' negative attitudes toward these groups. Blacks also racially homogenize racial groups in ways that ascribe certain groups to more favorable characteristics than others. Although blacks generally disagree with negative stereotypes about racial groups, blacks' ster-eotypes of Asian Americans and Latinos are often more positive than their stereotypes about whites. Furthermore, blacks exposed to socialization mes-sages emphasizing racial protectiveness messages subscribe less to positive stereotypes and more to negative stereotypes. Racial protectiveness messages also modestly increase blacks' perceived frequency of racial discrimination and perceived likelihood for discrimination in the future (racial uncertainty). Other factors such as greater connections to other blacks ("black linked fate"; Dawson 1994) and racial knowledge about black history also increase blacks' reported frequency of discrimination. Blacks also perceive that whites and Asians are the two groups that will most likely discriminate against them in their everyday life experiences.

Chapter 5 examines the way that blacks use race in their trust evaluations. It analyzes data from a split-sample embedded survey experiment in the NPSS that manipulates race in the trust measures. When commonly used general trust measures control for the race of the actor in the question, we see that blacks distinguish trust on the basis of race. Blacks trust whites least, and they trust Asian Americans and Latinos at levels that approximate their trust in others who are black. As for conceptions of trust predicting trust and comparing the effects of these predictors in models that control for the attitudes of black, white, and Latino racial groups, the results show that fair-ness and appearance matter more for blacks than for whites, and blacks and Latinos see fairness in similar ways. Whites view fairness as mattering less in their trust assessments.

Chapter 5 also examines the determinants of blacks' racialized trust by analyzing data in the SCBS and the NPSS. The chapter compares blacks' trust to whites', Latinos', and Asian Americans' to determine whether blacks are, in fact, more or less trusting than these groups. In many instances, as common evidence shows, blacks are less racially trusting than are other racial groups. However, in the comparisons of whom these racial groups trust more or less, we see that all racial groups trust certain groups more than others. Racialized trust, thus, is not a uniquely "black" phenomenon. Surprisingly, in the SCBS, blacks trust whites more than the other racial groups trust whites. The NPSS, however, indicates that blacks distrust whites more than they distrust other racial groups.

To test factors that influence blacks' trust in different racial groups, using NPSS data, I examine the effects of racial socialization and racial discrimination experiences on blacks' racialized trust in each racial group. Blacks who received greater emphasis on racialized distrust messages and who experienced more frequent racial discrimination are generally less trusting of both black and nonblack groups. Despite the expectation that racial uncertainty about the likelihood of being racially discriminated against in the future will reduce blacks' trust, this factor rarely influences blacks' trust at all. As an additional control for the effect of race on blacks' trust, black linked fate has the effect of either increasing or decreasing blacks' trust, depending on the race of the actor in question.

Part III on racial externalization includes chapters 6 and 7, which empirically explore black Americans' social trust and political trust, respectively. In chapter 6, I investigate how blacks trust in social contexts. I study the determinants of their social trust in the contexts of neighborhoods, workplaces, shopping places, and religious institutions. I analyze data from a race and social trust split-sample embedded survey experiment in the NPSS to determine how blacks trust differently in certain racial groups depending on the context. I also determine the extent to which racial socialization and discrimination experiences influence social trust. Using SCBS data, I compare blacks' social trust to other racial groups'.

I find that, as far as generalized social trust, blacks in the SCBS are more distrusting than are whites and Asian Americans only. They are equally as distrusting as Latinos. With respect to contextualized social trust, blacks are most distrusting of people in the context of the places in which they shop and in the context of their neighborhoods, with greater distrust in the context of shopping places. Despite the centrality of the black church in blacks' political development and religion, in general, in blacks' cultural experiences, they still are less trusting than are whites and Asians in this context. In fact, blacks are less trusting than are Asian and whites in the context of their neighborhoods, shopping places, and workplaces. They are only less trusting than Latinos are in the context of the workplace. Race and trust experiments in the NPSS show that race matters less in blacks' distinguishing trust in others in social contexts. Racial socialization messages that blacks have received that emphasized racial protectiveness, however, decrease blacks' social trust, and often with respect to Asian Americans, especially in neighborhoods, shopping places, workplaces, and religious institutions. Black linked fate mainly has the effect of reducing trust in whites in shopping places and religious institutions.

In chapter 7, I probe how black Americans think about race in political trust. The analysis in this chapter expands the literature on political trust and race and representation by examining how blacks think about trust as far as descriptive and substantive representations, by comparing blacks' trust in black political actors to their trust in white, Asian American, and Latino political actors. I examine NPSS split-sample survey experiment data to determine the extent to which race and partisanship influence blacks' political trust. I also test whether racial socialization and racial discrimination experiences affect political trust. The chapter also examines how blacks trust in federal versus local levels of government and, furthermore, determines the extent to which the race of a political actor influences trust in these actors to do what is right for blacks' interests. I also use SCBS data to determine the extent, if any, that blacks' political trust differs from whites', Asians', and Latinos'.

In the NPSS I find that blacks feel less politically close to whites and Asians and more politically close to Latinos. Interestingly, when controlling for black ethnicity, non–African Americans (as self-identified West Indians and Africans) feel less close to other blacks than do African Americans. Yet blacks' having received greater emphasis on racial consciousness messages during their racial socialization actually enhances their political connectedness to other blacks. Interestingly, racial protectiveness messages also have an adverse effect on insular ties to other blacks, as greater emphasis on these messages reduces feelings of political closeness to other blacks. Living in a predominantly black neighborhood also increases political detachment from whites. Age, interestingly, divides political closeness among blacks, as older blacks feel less close to Latinos than do younger blacks. Meanwhile, black linked fate enhances blacks' feelings of political closeness to Latinos.

As for race and representation, in the NPSS experiments, blacks trust whites least (as both Democrats and Republicans) in comparison to all racial groups. Yet, unlike the results suggesting blacks' apprehension about Asian Americans discriminating against them because of their race, Asian Americans and Latinos are trusted similarly to black representatives as Democrats and Republicans. Mean scores among blacks for black Republicans also reveal higher mean values than those for even white Democrats, thus presenting an interesting paradox as far as race, trust, and substantive representation. Results from the SCBS show us that blacks trust the federal government more than they trust local government, and whites trust federal government less than blacks do; yet whites trust local government more than blacks do. As for trusting political actors of a certain race to represent the interests of blacks in federal and local government, clearly whites and people in general are trusted least.

Chapter 8, the concluding chapter, analyzes the comprehensive effect of race on blacks' trust. Furthermore, it explores black racial attitudes, and hence distrust, as vestiges of racial construction and discrimination. Despite the general finding that blacks have had lower emphasis on racialized distrust in their parent-child racial socialization, their personalized experiences with racial discrimination and their racial attitudes structure their worldviews. Much of blacks' distrust depends on their historical relationship with whites and personal experiences with racial discrimination. Thus, the chapter argues that race and racial discrimination experiences normativize distrust among blacks and, more specifically, between blacks and whites. The vestiges of race continue to cue blacks about the quality of their lives and relationships with people in society and government. These phenomena illustrate the injurious nature of racial construction and racial discrimination.

The book concludes with a discussion about the prospects of trust among blacks in the postelection era of the United States' first African American president, President Barack H. Obama. It considers how his election will affect African Americans' political trust and influence black parents' racial and political socialization messages to their children. In a broader scheme, the conclusion considers the implications of President Obama's presidency for the future of trust and African American sociopolitical behavior, in general.

2

Explaining Blacks' (Dis)trust

A Theory of Discriminative
Racial-Psychological Processing

The Significance and Meaning of Trust

Trust is capital (Putnam 1993, 1995, 2000a). Anyone who is trusting, trustable, or trustworthy is empowered to fulfill actions on behalf of others, although fulfilling one's self-interest often involves trust also being reciprocated by others (Coleman 1988, 1990; Putnam 2000a; Hardin 2001; Hoffman 2006). As an evaluation of one person about another person, entity, or context, trust involves the *trustor* (the person making the evaluation) making normative judgments about how the behavior of others (the *trustees*) should be conducted in social, political, or economic contexts. This evaluation also involves the trustor considering what should be the effect of that behavior on him or her personally. The general expectation is that people trust when they feel as if the trustee will not cause a negative outcome, especially one that will harm the trustor.

Trust is not just an assessment. It is a belief about a person, institution, or context that stems from an assessment about who or what can deliver an outcome with the least harmful risk and with the greatest benefit to the trustor. There is a degree of uncertainty about outcomes being beneficial to the trustor, and whether trust can be garnered or sustained depends on the benefits outweighing the risks. In this sense, the trustor prefers avoiding harmful risks in order to incur from the trustee more beneficial outcomes such as cooperation, reciprocity, or tangible returns (Ostrom and Walker 2003; Hardin 2001; Heimer 2001; Warren 1999; Luhmann 1988). These trust calculations drive interpersonal, intergroup, and institutional relations, making trust invaluable for present and future relations.

Trust's worth depends on people's expectations for trustworthiness, and people discriminate trust accordingly (Barber 1983; Hardin 2001, 2004, 2006;

Heimer 2001; Messick and Kramer 2001). *Trust* is the action, but *trustworthiness* is the characteristic that is judged relative to the trustor's standards. To wit, people also have to trust the indicators that a person is trustworthy (Bacharach and Gambetta 2001). In my view, these trust indicators include the following: (1) *behavior*, (2) *context*, (3) perceived *outcomes*, and (4) perceived *risks*.

As for the assessment of others' *behavior*, people either consider others' reputation or make a prediction about their prospective behavior on the basis of the information available to them. If information is scarce, then stereotypes convey data about others. In addition to behavioral information, people use the *context* of trust to assess their previous experiences (or reputation) in dealing with people in certain spaces and at different points in time (or history). On the basis of the calculation about whether the resultant trust *outcome* will be positive or negative for the trustor's interests, the trustor evaluates how much (if at all) to trust others. Furthermore, the trustor weighs the perceived outcome with the probable risks that are associated with trusting the trustee. If the risks are higher for harming the trustor, then the trustor's potential to trust decreases, and vice versa: if the risks are lower for harming the trustor, then the trustor's potential to trust increases.

Because people's race affects how they are perceived to behave, *where* they are reputed to act in a given time period, *how* they are predicted to harm others or not, and *how much* they are predicted to harm others or not, race is a fundamental concept in understanding how and in whom people trust. Thus, race is integral to this book's conceptual framework and study of trust. First, however, we must understand how social scientists generally conceptualize trust and what this means for our knowledge of the effect of race on trust.

What We Know about Trust in America: Trust Trends and the Decline of Trust

Scholars are interested in the study of trust because of the concern about what *dis*trust can mean for sustaining democracy. For this reason, declining trust trends among all Americans have alarmed researchers (Hetherington 2005; Pew Research Center 2010b), and studies of trust have been attentive to political trust and social trust. Political science research, however, focuses more squarely on *political trust* (trust in political actors and institutions), with limited analysis of *social trust* (trust in people in general) and its greater implications for society.

As far as the trust that people have in government, political actors, and political institutions, or what is more commonly referred to as *political trust*, at the core of this concept is the constituent–political arena relationship, wherein the government (and various political apparatuses) is expected to respond to citizens' interests to promote justice, equality, and tranquility as a public good (Putnam 1993; Bianco 1994; Nye 1997; Hetherington 1998; Tilly 2005). Without citizens' political trust, political institutions lack legitimacy, lack faith in their existence, and lack credulity in their functioning (V. Braithwaite 1998), all of which can lead to disequilibrium in the political system.

Outside the political arena, the balance of social order rests on people's civility and quality of interpersonal relationships. *Social trust*, more commonly conceptualized as "generalized trust," thus connotes the extent to which one is able to trust others as strangers, perhaps without any specific prior knowledge or information about their character or with prior knowledge gained through limited interactions, context clues, or awareness of others' reputations (Fukuyama 1995; Blackburn 1998; Hardin 2001; Tyler 2001; Yamagishi 2001; Uslaner 2002). As Putnam (2000a) asserts, this trust can be embedded in rich, deeply rooted, and widely cast social networks that undergird "thick trust." Trust also can consist of casual, newly chartered, and temporary interactions of "thin trust" that, as Putnam states, "extends the radius of trust beyond the roster of people whom we can know personally" (2000a, 136). Social trust, hence, reinforces civil society.

Both trusts offer import as far as human relations and people's abilities to barter on behalf of their sociopolitical interests. They help people retain capital that they can expend in the future, what is often referred to as *social capital* (Brehm and Rahn 1997; Putnam 2000b). As far as the focus of research on trust, researchers have explored the social nature of political trust through assessing how social relations influence it through the multifaceted concept of *social capital*, or the "features of social organization, such as trust, norms, and networks that can improve the efficiency of society by facilitating coordinated actions" (Putnam 1993, 167). Social capital thus accounts for an economized value of social relations in various aspects of life—social and political. With more expansive, meaningful, and trusting connections, social relations carry greater value for coordinating prospective interactions, increasing political participation, and enhancing democracy (Coleman 1990; Putnam 1993; Brehm and Rahn 1997; Green and Brock 1998; Lin 2001a, 2001b; Keele 2007).

Scholars have been perplexed by the general decline in both social and political trusts among Americans, and they also fear that this decline indicates a downward trend in social capital. Why have they taken interest in these declines? For one, these declines may suggest a breakdown in social and political relations that have been theoretically presumed foundational for our nation and government. In fact, one of the largest puzzles facing trust research to date has been explaining the general decline in trust in the United States from the period of the 1960s through the 2000s (A. Miller 1974; Citrin 1974; Citrin and Green 1986; Orren 1997; Blendon et al. 1997; Brehm and Rahn 1997; Rahn and Transue 1998; Putnam 2000a; Bennett 2001; Citrin and Luks 2001; Chanley 2002; Hardin 2004; Hetherington 2005; Pew Research Center 2010b). Nevertheless, despite seminal social trust studies by Putnam (2000a) and Brehm and Rahn (1997), declining political trust has been more research attractive, with social trust mostly being studied as a component of political trust.

As for what we know about political trust, extant research also elucidates that Americans' political trust waxes and wanes during certain periods.[1] Over time, this political trust continues on a downward trend. Although consistent measures of political trust did not appear on national surveys until 1958, thus limiting trust comparisons predating that year, most of the longitudinal studies indicate political trust waning post-1964 (the Vietnam-conflict era) among most Americans. There appears to be a low point in political trust in the mid-1970s (post–Watergate scandal), with several upsurges during the first term of the Reagan administration, the first term of the Clinton administration, and immediately following the September 11th terrorist attacks. Within six months after 9/11, however, there was yet another downturn in Americans' political trust (Lawrence 1997; Damico, Conway, and Bowman Damico 2000; Alford 2001; Chanley, Rudolph, and Rahn 2000, 2001; Chanley 2002; Keele 2007). With the 2008 Great Recession, political trust has decreased with an even sharper decline, and more recently, only 22 percent of Americans say they trust the government to do what is right, compared to 73 percent who said so in 1958 (Pew Research Center 2010b).

Some of the top reasons that most Americans give for not trusting government, in order of their highest attribution, include perceptions that government expends money inefficiently and on the wrong things, that special interests overly influence government decision-making, and that politicians lack integrity (Blendon et al. 1997). Knowledge about political scandals also further reduces political trust (Bowler and Karp 2004).

Extant trust literature, in addition, abounds with empirical explanations for the general declining trend in political trust: people's *dissatisfaction with political regimes and governance* (Easton 1965; A. Miller 1974; V. Braithwaite and Levi 1998; Berstein 2001); *dissatisfaction with the performance of political incumbents* (Citrin 1974; Citrin and Green 1986; Feldman 1983; Parker and Parker 1993; Richardson, Houston, and Hadjiharalambous 2001; Citrin and Luks 2001) and *political institutions* (Blendon et al. 1997; Hibbing and Theiss-Morse 2001); *skepticism about political authorities' performance* (Cook and Gronke 2005) *or concern about their scandalous behavior* (Bowler and Karp 2004); *dissatisfaction with public policies* (Bok 1997; Hetherington 2005); *distinctions in trust in federal versus state governments* (Hetherington and Nugent 2001; Owen and Dennis 2001; Uslaner 2001); *negative media coverage of political institutions and political actors* (Orren 1997; Shah 1998); *ideological and partisan differences between constituents and incumbent political actors* (King 1997; Chanley, Rudolph, and Rahn 2000; Rudolph and Evans 2005; Keele 2005); *economic downturns and personal economic strains* (Lawrence 1997); *disparate socioeconomic and sociopolitical contexts* (Abramson 1977; Mansbridge 1997; Neustadt 1997; Nye 1997; Yamagishi 2001); and *political alienation* (Citrin et al. 1975; Abramson 1977; Nilson and Nilson 1980; Walton 1985).

Scholars also attribute dwindling political trust to declining social trust. With enfeebled social relations and social trust among citizens themselves, it is believed their political trust becomes vulnerable (Putnam 1995; Brehm and Rahn 1997; Rahn and Transue 1998; Putnam 2000a; Tilly 2005). Studies support this relationship, as well, as trust networks mutually reinforce political networks when they are stronger (Brehm and Rahn 1997; Keele 2005). Attention to trust in others in social contexts wherein people interact with one another in their everyday lives remains understudied in political science, however. (This critique and its importance is one that I elaborate on more in-depth later in my discussion.) Relatedly, how race affects the quality of these networks and social capital has garnered some scholarly consideration (Orr 1999; Hero 2007). Yet the effect of race on trust warrants closer examination and explanation especially, given evidence that Americans' trust differs by racial group membership.

Racial Differences in Americans' Trust: A View in Black and White

Many public-opinion studies substantiate that blacks' public opinion differs from whites. This difference also holds regarding trust. Notwithstanding general declines in social and political trust over time among all Americans, blacks have been generally more distrusting than whites have (Putnam 1995,

2000a; Brehm and Rahn 1997; Rahn and Transue 1998; Richardson, Houston, and Hadjiharalambous 2001; Tate 2003). Recently, however, blacks show greater trust in government than whites do (Pew Research Center 2010b),[2] and this trend supports other evidence indicating blacks and whites are more or less trusting in government during certain political eras. For example, studies show that blacks were more trusting during the Clinton administration, whereas whites were more trusting during the Reagan and Bush administrations (Citrin and Luks 2001).

More recently, 2010 Pew Research Center (2010b) data show that, during the current Obama administration, 60 percent of whites expressed that they were frustrated with government, compared to fewer blacks (48 percent) and Latinos (47 percent). In 2010, whites (55 percent) also reported more frequently than did blacks (44 percent) that government should be "very majorly reformed." Blacks (53 percent), however, reported more than whites did (47 percent) that a major problem they have with government is its interference in people's lives.

In addition to blacks and whites trusting differently depending on political eras, traditionally Americans trust differently depending on the level of government. Political trust studies indicate that many Americans trust state government more than they do federal government. The responsibilities of these levels of government, however, make a difference in how people trust them. For instance, Americans entrust the federal government more than they do the state government to be responsible for strengthening the economy and protecting civil rights (Blendon et al. 1997, 211). People who have more trust in federal government, in addition, have more "faith and confidence" in this level of government than they do in state and local governments (Hetherington and Nugent 2001).

For blacks, the centrality of civil rights in their group's political history resonates, as they display greater trust in the federal government over the state government (Uslaner 2001). Despite the federal government's complicity in blacks' oppression throughout much of American history, during the mid-twentieth century, it actively enforced black civil rights and liberties through presidents' enforcement powers, congressional legislation, and Supreme Court decisions. These actions contributed to blacks' seeing the federal government as more trustable than state governments that actively championed states' rights and segregation to the detriment of blacks' civil rights.[3]

In contrast, whites do not distinguish political trust between levels of government the same way that blacks do, and whites' perceptions of threat to their personal freedoms differ from those of blacks. For instance, in a 2010

Pew Research Center study on trust, almost half of whites (48 percent) said they feel that the federal government threatens their personal rights and freedoms, compared to 37 percent of blacks (2010b). Blacks (71 percent) were also more likely than whites were (53 percent) to report that they feel government does not do enough to help Americans. Such racial differences in political trust, however, are less evident with respect to branches of government (Richardson, Houston, and Hadjiharalambous 2001).

For most racial groups, political trust also rises and falls with the economy; however, there are racial differences in the effect of the health of the economy on peoples' political trust attitudes (Chanley, Rudolph, and Rahn 2000). Disproportionately among whites, political trust also varies with the perceived risk attached to public policies. Whites' political trust in government varies depending on whether they perceive that they are the beneficiaries of redistributive public policies compared to other racial groups (Hetherington 2005; Rudolph and Evans 2005). In addition, political trust influences whites' support of racial policies, whereas the reverse is the case for blacks. That is, when whites are less politically trusting, they are less supportive of racial policies, whereas blacks who are more supportive of racial policies are more politically trusting (Hetherington and Globetti 2002).

Blacks and whites also critique government differently. According to the 2010 Pew Research Center study, blacks are more likely to feel that government programs are run inefficiently (63 percent) than to believe that the government has wrong priorities (24 percent). Fewer whites, comparatively, feel that government is run inefficiently (47 percent); however, more whites than blacks feel that government has the wrong priorities (42 percent). This suggests that, in addition to distinctions in trust levels, perhaps blacks and whites conceptualize political trust differently as far as the government's programmatic prioritization.

As for the effect of intermediary institutions on political trust, evidence also shows that political trust declines when one's partisanship differs from the partisanship of the incumbent administration or a particular political actor (Citrin and Luks 2001; Bowler and Karp 2004). Because of the historically racialized segmentation of the American two-party system, wherein whites and blacks have supported political parties on the basis of whether the party platforms directly or indirectly address blacks' civil rights and socioeconomic conditions (Key 1949; Woodward 1974; Gurin, Hatchett, and Jackson 1989; Carmines and Stimson 1989; Frymer 1999; Morales 1999; Fauntroy 2007), it seems likely that race, partisanship, and trust are also intertwined (Gay 2002; Tate 2003).

Prior research on blacks' trust points to the importance of the effect of factors such as their social experiences and the racially imbalanced representation of their group's political interests on their decreased trust. Anecdotally, the trust literature claims that blacks' historical discrimination experiences should explain their distrust and distinctive trust compared to whites, in particular. But can we be sure? Providing a theory about the effect of race on blacks' trust, thus, is pertinent and constitutes the main objective of this chapter.

Prior Scholarship on Blacks' (Dis)trust

Most of the research on blacks' trust is found in the race and representation literature. The literature on blacks' trust questions how the race of political actors influences blacks' trust in their representatives and the political system (Aberbach and Walker 1970; Abramson 1972, 1977; Howell and Fagan 1988; Swain 1993; Mansbridge 1999; Gay 2002; Mangum 2003; Tate 2003; Avery 2006). Scholars of race and representation have explored blacks' political trust to uncover how blacks' relationships with the political system can be improved. For example, these studies have focused on the transformative effects of descriptive representation, substantive representation, and political efficacy.

Because of mirrored demographic qualities between blacks and their representatives—descriptive representation—it was believed that blacks would feel better represented by a politician who looked like them racially and who likely shared their historical experiences and sensitivities to race. Through policy responsiveness and, hence, substantive representation, politicians would be attuned to blacks' interests and work toward their incorporation into a political agenda. Through enhanced political efficacy, blacks would have a more positive outlook about their ability to influence the American political system (internal political efficacy) and about the fair operation of this system (external political efficacy). It was believed that, either through the representation of a black representative or a black political agenda, blacks would have more positive perceptions and relationships with government. Ultimately, as it was presumed, more "black representation" would enhance blacks' political trust.

Katherine Tate (2003), for example, finds that congruent race and partisanship of black representatives and their constituents increases blacks' reporting more favorable approval ratings for their representatives. Although partisanship has a greater effect on blacks' approval ratings, shared race with their representatives (descriptive representation) increases their feeling that their representative is more helpful in solving a problem, is better at keeping in touch with their constituents, works toward special returns for the district, and functions as a problem solver on behalf of constituents' interests. Positive views about the institution of Congress, nevertheless, do not improve once blacks have descriptive representation. Neither does descriptive representation improve blacks' political trust, per se; however, blacks who perceive that there is a larger number of blacks serving in Congress as representatives possess greater affinities for the institution. Thus, although there is scant evidence that descriptive representation enhances blacks' direct trust in government, it indirectly influences blacks developing more positive perceptions about aspects of their political representation. Other studies support similar effects of racial perceptions in blacks' political trust.

Claudine Gay (2002) finds that blacks' electoral participation increases when they are represented descriptively by black representatives. Conversely, she finds that whites who are represented by black representatives feel less connected to their representatives and are less inclined to be politically participatory. Thus, there is some evidence that race, representation, and trust affect blacks and other groups' political behavior.

Studies by James Avery (2006, 2009) illustrate the need for a closer examination of race and racial experiences as a means to understand blacks' political trust. Avery explores the factors and consequences of blacks' political distrust, considering the psychological effects that blacks' perceptions of race have on their trust in the political system. Blacks who have more of a feeling of linked fate with other blacks are more distrusting of government and more supportive of blacks, whites, and Latinos having their own representatives (descriptive representation) in government. Greater racial consciousness also reduces blacks' political trust in general, and blacks who believe there are socioeconomic disparities between blacks and whites are less trusting in government.

Avery, in addition, finds that beliefs about racial discrimination influence blacks' political trust in several ways. For one, those blacks who perceive that their group's socioeconomic circumstances are explained by racial discrimination as opposed to blacks' personal efforts are more politically distrusting. Second, blacks who believe that their group members persistently face racial discrimination are less trusting in government. Third, perceptions of discrimination reduce blacks' support of the political system in general. In fact, the perception of ongoing racial discrimination against blacks is the most consistent factor reducing group members' political trust. Interestingly, in Avery's study, the effect of discrimination decreasing political trust also is evident among whites: whites who feel they are discriminated against and underrepresented in Congress are also less supportive of the political system.

As for the scope of political institutions and policy outcomes and their relationship with blacks' trust perceptions, Avery also finds that perceiving that blacks are underrepresented in government positions decreases political trust. This even translates into blacks' level of trust in presidential administrations. Whereas negative perceptions of the Reagan administration in 1984 reduced blacks' trust in government, similar negative perceptions of the Clinton administration did not reduce blacks' political trust in 1996.

In Avery's study, satisfaction from policy outcomes does not influence blacks' political trust. Neither does political distrust increase blacks' support for majority-minority districts being formed to increase the representation and interests of blacks in the political system. As for the consequences of political distrust, blacks who are more distrusting of government are more participatory in certain forms of political participation, namely, picketing and contacting public officials. Political distrust among blacks also increases their likelihood of supporting the formation of third parties. These results suggest that political distrust influences the contours of black political behavior.

Past studies of blacks' trust focused on the influence of blacks' political socialization on their trust attitudes. Political trust studies gravitated toward this type of study during the 1960s and 1970s civil rights protest era, when blacks assumed unconventional forms of political participation (Sigel 1970; Dennis 1973; Renshon 1977; Ichilov 1990). While some blacks participated in peaceful protests, others participated in urban riots to object to blacks' exclusion from and discrimination in various aspects of life and abject poverty in the nation's cities. Studies also attempted to explain black political cynicism, which was believed to be associated with blacks' politics during the height of the Black Power Movement and after the assassination of Dr. Martin Luther King Jr. and other major civil rights players in the movement: President John F. Kennedy, Robert Kennedy, and Malcolm X, to name a few (Cross 1991; Abramson 1977).

Studies examining blacks' political socialization during this era also seemed to fit a tradition of explaining pathological behavior among blacks, behavior which, at the time, was perceived as deviating from the more conventional political participation modes associated with whites (Walton 1985; Cross 1991).[4] Because blacks were seen as dissatisfied, disruptive, politically alienated, and violent, these studies often attempted to explain their disposition. Unwittingly, many of these studies overlooked the extent of blacks' disparate sociopolitical realities compared to whites. For example, Abramson's (1977) review of early studies about blacks' trust reveals that theories about blacks' intelligence were associated with explaining their distrust. Blacks were believed to distrust the political system because they could not cognitively process the complexities of the system. Such theories were grounded in old-fashioned, scientific racism that relied on mythological explanations about blacks' inherent fallacies and that, ultimately, disparaged blacks' natural intelligence as a group.

Other researchers during this period, however, considered the influence of sociopolitical factors on blacks' distrust, by suggesting that their distrust was complicated by years of social and political mistreatment, some of which researchers felt was socialized by black parent-child transmission. Such early studies of black Americans' political trust, for instance, attributed childhood socialization experiences about an unfair political system as a seminal factor in reducing the group's trust (Abramson 1972, 1977; Aberbach and Walker 1970; Greenberg 1970). Aside from childhood socialization experiences, blacks' contextual references (including socioeconomic and racial disparities) were seen as major contributors to their distrust. Two theories dominated these contextual explanations: relative group deprivation and the political reality theses.

The theory of relative group deprivation argued that blacks' disparate resource acquisitions compared to whites forged their distrust, whereas the political reality thesis argued that restricted access to the political system and policy responsiveness caused their distrust (Abramson 1977). As a whole, these theories posited that blacks' distrust was learned from both parental and personal experiences with de jure and de facto discrimination. For example, one such study by Greenberg (1970) found that black children initially had positive views of the political system and political authorities that became more negative as they became older, perhaps due to developing a clearer consciousness of racial disparities. In the tradition of other political trust studies, blacks' behavior, however, was compared to whites', as if it were negatively deviant.

Studies of black political behavior should incorporate the group's social and political realities without negativizing blacks' behavior as if it is inherent to blacks' race. Rather, these studies should acknowledge racial construction and operation as a stimulus in blacks' (and others') behavior. By simply comparing blacks' behavior to that of whites and other nonwhite groups, we do gain insight about how race affects people similarly or differently. However, by valuating blacks' behavior compared to others as if it is negatively deviant, we, instead, contribute to racist epistemological canons that further marginalize blacks in the study of political science. Studying blacks' trust with a fuller integration of how race affects their lives presents several issues in the study of trust in political science in general. These several issues, which I identify in the next sections, illuminate the need for a theoretical approach in the study of blacks' trust that considers a comprehensive review of the extent to which race affects blacks' lives without essentializing black sociopolitical behavior.

The Analysis of Blacks' (Dis)trust: Critical Issues

As illustrated by the studies mentioned in the preceding section, race affects blacks' political behavior and trust in multifarious ways. Despite this significance, unfortunately, explanations for racial differences in trust remain scant, and extensive empirical investigations of blacks' distrust are even more remote. These epistemological practices point to several issues that I argue should be rectified in the approach to the general study of trust and trust among blacks in particular.

Issue 1: Trust Studies Mostly Examine Political Trust

Katherine Tate's (2003) book, *Black Faces in the Mirror: African Americans and Their Representatives in the U.S. Congress*, offers a rich and seminal analysis of black public opinion about race, representation, and trust. It ascertains some links between blacks' psychological desire for descriptive representation and trust. However, the book's analysis is limited to African Americans' *political* trust. Unfortunately, it does not examine African Americans' social trust.

Why should *social* trust matter to political scientists? For one, as I have recognized, social trust enhances political trust (Putnam 1995, 2000a; Brehm and Rahn 1997). Political trust differences among racial groups, age cohorts, education levels, and incomes attest to the social realities of trust (Brehm and Rahn 1997; Rahn and Transue 1998; Putnam 2000a). How blacks have perceived their interactions with nonblacks in social contexts and how they have protested ill-treatment in social spaces, furthermore, relates to their group politics, interests, and livelihoods (McAdam 1982; Morris 1984; Dawson 1994; Orr 1999; Pinar 2001). The quality of blacks' communal relationships has also defined the scope of politics and the range of possibilities for safe versus harmful living conditions.[5] Moreover, for blacks, historical mistreatment in both social and political spaces politicized them in a way that merged their social attitudes with their political attitudes.

Just as political science studies have recognized the importance of social trust for enhancing political trust and social capital writ large, similarly studying African Americans' social trust will assist us in understanding how blacks navigate their relationships with people and government. Political science studies, thus, should examine black Americans' social trust.

Even how we measure social trust should be expanded to move beyond standard measures of how much people trust in "people in general," as a generalized trust measure (Putnam 2000b). As a common measure of social trust, "trust in people in general" alone does not give us information about how blacks' trust may vary across social contexts such as neighborhoods, workplaces, shopping places, and religious institutions. Thus, following in the vein proposed by Putnam (2000b), who measures the contexts of social trust in the 2000 Social Capital Benchmark Survey, I suggest we also empirically study the aforementioned social contexts to glean whether blacks' social trust varies. With an emphasis on studying race and social trust, we also should investigate whether trust in these social contexts varies based on the race of the social actor.

Issue 2: Empirical Studies of Race and Trust Focus on Black-White Comparisons

The study of how race operates in trust is practically terra incognita in political science. Research that has been done has been limited to examinations of blacks' trust in whites versus blacks as political actors (Putnam 2000b; Avery 2006; Tate 2003; Gay 2002; Whitby 1997; Swain 1993). Interestingly, political science scholarship on trust disengages the work on race and representation that offers the comparison of blacks' trust in political actors on the basis of the actor's racial congruence (or lack thereof) with their own race. Despite the progressive engagement of race and representation literature, there has yet to be work that explores blacks' political trust in Latinos or Asian Americans as political actors. Furthermore, by not engaging race in social trust, we also lose sight of ascertaining whether blacks' trust varies in social contexts on the basis of the race of other nonwhites. By studying blacks' trust in whites, Latinos, and Asian Americans, we gain knowledge about blacks' interracial trust. Epistemologically, we also move beyond the limited analysis of the more traditional, black-white paradigmatic studies.

Furthermore, by studying blacks' trust in other blacks, we stand to learn more about intraracial attitudes among blacks. Although Allen, Dawson, and Brown (1989), for example, study African Americans' identity structure, political studies about blacks' perceptions of fellow racial group members are rare (Cohen 1999; Orey 2004). Harboring negative intraracial attitudes about intragroup members should lower trust in one's own racial group. Moving beyond the study of intergroup attitudes to incorporate a study of intragroup attitudes would prove beneficial for understanding intraracial relations. Therefore, it proves fruitful to analyze both *interracial* (whites, Asian Americans, and Latinos) and *intraracial* (fellow blacks) trust attitudes among blacks. Comparisons of blacks' trust to other racial groups should be used only to determine whether blacks trust distinctively from other racial groups in order to uncover nuances in their trust, such that they may, in fact, be more trusting than other racial groups.

Issue 3: Updating the Study of Political Socialization among African Americans

Political socialization inculcates society's members with information, normative values, attitudes, and practices about the functioning of the political system (Hyman 1959; Sigel 1970, 1989; Easton and Dennis 1970, 1973). Political socialization studies engaged how people learned specific messages about politics, sources of political socialization, generational transmission and differences in learning about the political system, and stability versus change in political learning over people's lifetime, including during historical periods (Hess and Torney 1967; Dennis 1973; Renshon 1977; Jennings and Niemi 1981; Sears 1990; Ichilov 1990).

Generational studies of political socialization tended to focus on the transmission of political information from one generation to another and differences in information acquired over the life process for various generations. "Political learning," as political socialization is sometimes called, was divided into preadulthood and adulthood learning stages. Scholars focused on four models of political socialization that described a lifelong process of learning: (1) the lifelong persistence model, (2) the lifelong openness model, (3) the life-cycle model, and (4) the generational model (Jennings and Niemi 1981).

The lifelong persistence model suggests that learned political messages in childhood persist over people's lifetimes, with people incorporating new information as it is introduced in their life experiences. The lifelong openness model emphasizes political learning subsequent to learning during the formative, preadult years. The life-cycle model recognizes the malleability of political orientations during specific life stages. Building on the seminal research of Karl Mannheim ([1928] 1952), the generational model proposes that political orientations persist throughout adult learning but are shaped based on salient influences of major political and social events.

Contemporary studies of political socialization among blacks are sparse. However, part of the reason why political socialization studies of black Americans have been limited may be attributed to the general decline in political socialization studies in political science (Sapiro 2004; Peng 1994). Scholars explain inattention to political socialization because of methodological concerns about measuring childhood learning and its stability over the life cycle, noting an oversimplification of child-to-adult attitudinal sustainability. They also question whether political socialization studies that focus on presaged attitudes lose sight of the importance of adult political learning (Niemi and Hepburn 1995; Merelman 1972). At the same time, scholars such as Niemi and Hepburn (1995) and Sapiro (2004) have been cognizant of the decline in political socialization research and have since promoted a return to political socialization studies so that such studies do not become moribund.

While there has been a resurgence of political socialization studies, especially in comparative politics studies, contemporary studies of black Americans' political socialization are still virtually nonexistent. One modern study of black political socialization is Simpson's (1998) study of black identity transmission and acquisition among black college students in the post–civil rights era.

In this study, political scientist Andrea Simpson interviews black college students at majority white and historically black colleges and universities. Through her research, she finds the continuing salience of race for post–civil rights, "integration generation" black young people. Race is the "tie that binds" young black people, whether it is through different meanings of blackness across the liberal-conservative ideological spectrum, gender, class, or even other generations of black peoples. In this sense, despite the integration efforts of civil rights protests and mobilization, whether it is through weak or strong ties to the black racial group, political perspectives on black people's progress, or vicarious or personal experiences with racial discrimination, young people have become knowledgeable about the significance of race in their lives, in postsegregation America. This work serves as a stepping stone for even more contemporary research on black political socialization and black identity formation. Contemporary longitudinal studies of black political socialization would be ideal and highly contributory to information about black identity development over time. Nevertheless, there is a dearth of empirical data to analyze such an inquiry.

More recent studies of black Americans' (racial) socialization mostly have employed data from the 1979–1980 National Survey of Black Americans (James E. Jackson, principal investigator), limiting current studies to data that are now over thirty years old and that exclude younger black Americans' socialization experiences. The literature suggests that acquisition of racial knowledge and racial consciousness influence blacks' trust assessments, making them distrusting socially and politically. While these are apropos propositions, unfortunately the evidence supporting the influence of political socialization on trust attitudes is quite outdated and untested among newer generations of black Americans, who did not have firsthand experiences of de jure racial discrimination.

Speculations about the role of socialization in learning about the political system and trust attitudes toward it invite a return to political socialization studies to determine the link between socialization and black Americans' trust attitudes. Updated research on black Americans' political socializations also would offer an important contribution to the political science literature because it would examine black Americans' socialization experiences in a post–civil rights political era.

Issue 4: Wedding Political Socialization with Racial Socialization Studies

Modern studies of African Americans' trust, in the same vein as earlier political socialization studies implicitly suggest that all blacks either (1) have firsthand experiences with historical racial discrimination, (2) have a knowledge set about this discrimination, (3) use either these experiences or this knowledge in their trust assessments, or (4) discriminate trust on the basis of assessments of racial groups in political (or social) contexts. This logic implies that this "knowledge" about racial discrimination is somehow lucid for all blacks, regardless of their circumstances and regardless of their disparate opinions about race. This reasoning likewise implies that blacks learn about race through an information-transfer process across generations of black Americans who had firsthand experiences with de jure and de facto discrimination.

Although political science scholars have pretty much accepted the significance of race in black Americans' identity formation, political consciousness, and group-based political interests (Miller et al. 1981; Shingles 1981; Allen,

Dawson, and Brown 1989; Tate 1993; Dawson 1994; Chong and Rogers 2005), these studies have not examined specific racial messages that are transmitted as a part of black Americans' political socialization experiences. In contrast, however, the social psychology and family studies literature examines black Americans' learning about race—the socialization process known as *racial socialization.*

Racial socialization is an important antecedent of black identity and psychological development (Peters 1985; Demo and Hughes 1990; McAdoo 2007). Yet it is less clear how and what messages about race and racial politics are transmitted across generations of black Americans. Certain messages about race, conceivably, are sustained over time, continually making race salient in black Americans' consciousness, and as the generational model of political socialization suggests, critical historical events or perhaps even knowledge of historical and contemporary racial group relations can influence the structure of this consciousness and, hence, trust.

Despite the importance of racial socialization, it is understudied in political science identity studies. By wedding the study of racial socialization to the study of African Americans' political socialization and attitudinal development, we gain leverage over a more comprehensive understanding of how race influences black public opinion and political behavior and gain an opportunity to study indicators of opinion continuity and stability among blacks. Further, studying racial socialization and its relation to trust allows us the opportunity to discern whether messages about race are transmitted generationally in tandem with messages about trust.

Issue 5: Literature That Oversimplifies Black Attitudes

Based on blacks' sociopolitical experiences, distrust seems inevitable. But what does this mean? Is distrust the end of society or democracy for blacks? Normatively, on the basis of expectations that trust sustains society and democracy, we might think so. Yet blacks have remained loyal citizens, fought wars during which they themselves have not had full citizenship, and continued to participate in formal political processes. Then, we might ask, is disproportionate distrust among blacks just a weird paradox resulting from racism in democracy? This leads to an even more important inquiry with respect to race: How do black Americans navigate race in their lives in order to overcome ill-fated racial determinism historically attributed to their racial group?

Despite the seemingly dismal implications of distrust for blacks' lives, in the trust literature, blacks' distrust has been approached as a seemingly uncomplicated phenomenon, one that nonetheless is a *given*, without much need for scholarly interest, empirical explanation, or contemporary understanding. Normatively, this is what I argue must change. Most important, we must consider a theory that explains blacks' distrust of, if not disillusionment with, social and political relations in the United States.

Although it is the case that African Americans have a group history with racial discrimination, the effect of this discrimination on their lives or public opinion is not monolithic (Cross 1991; Dawson 2001). Allen, Dawson, and Brown (1989), Cohen (1999), Price (2009), Dawson (2001), and Harris-Lacewell (2004), for example, move beyond a monolithic view of black public opinion, as they examine the psychological complexity of African Americans' identification with intra-racial-group members and their subscription to African American ideologies.

By accepting only anecdotal evidence for determining black Americans' trust, as much of the political trust literature does, we oversimplify the explanation of black distrust. Moreover, we appear to reduce black public opinion to a mere unique phenomenon that lacks value to be explained further. Studies also oversimplify African American public opinion by merely controlling for race in models that compare their attitudes to other racial groups (especially whites), without investigating separate models of blacks' trust to explain their specific behavior (if any). Black political and social distrusts are not the mere negation of white political and social trusts. As Harris-Lacewell (2003) suggests, part of recognizing the complexities of black public opinion rests in centering black people in the study of political inquiries that often focus on whites' political behavior. Therefore, black distrust deserves further examination to determine its explanatory factors and its complexities. Most important, it is through more explicit theorization and empirical examination that we can uncover the way *race* functions in blacks' distrust. It is with the charge to address these issues that I provide my theory of discriminative racial-psychological processing to describe the effect of race on blacks' trust.

A Theory of Discriminative Racial-Psychological Processing: Interpolating Race in Trust Studies

In my conceptualization of *trust*, I am interested in the way that racialized reputations and racial stereotypes influence trust perceptions. That is, I believe that people's knowledge about the reputations of certain racial groups in America influence how people trust others. People encode race and its related stereotypes, and they use information about race to formulate their attitudes. For one, they learn either a political consciousness or a racialized collective memory that also influences their support of race-related public policies (e.g., black collective memory; see Eyerman 2001; Lee 2002; Griffin and Bollen 2009). Second, people process information about race in the way they think about the historical relationships between racial groups and racial group members, and this affects how they perceive racial-group members will treat them in social and political interactions.[6]

As racial group members themselves, people acquire a reputation for racial behavior and discrimination on the basis of whether they are racial majority group members (whites) or racial minority group members (blacks, Asian Americans, and Latinos). Depending on whether people are majority or minority racial group members, their reputation in race relations and their perceived potential for racial discrimination differs.[7] This is to say that where people are situated in the American racial hierarchy influences the way they think and emote their sociopolitical attitudes. I suggest that blacks perceive whites as having the most potential for racially discriminating against them. This is because of whites' historical reputation as a racial group possessing the power to discriminate against blacks (and other racial groups) in de facto and de jure ways.

While Asian Americans and Latinos also have the potential to discriminate racially against blacks, I suggest that historical relationships between blacks and whites matter more in how blacks perceive the effect of race on their personal and racial group life chances. Blacks perceive Asian Americans and Latinos as racial minorities like themselves. They, however, perceive Asian Americans and Latinos differently than they perceive other blacks because they see them as being more likely to discriminate against them than blacks will, and matter-of-factly, Asian Americans and Latinos are not fellow group members.

To this extent, I argue that race and group-based *understandings* about other racial groups' reputations and statuses in the American racial order influence blacks' perceptions and socialized norms about trust. Whiteness studies scholar Dalton Conley summarizes my point about race as a part of reputation when he gives his definition of race: "In fact, race is nothing more than a language, a set of stories we tell ourselves to get through the world, to organize our reality" (2003, 196). I believe these "stories" that race tells inform people about others' reputation, prospectively and retrospectively. These "stories" and the cognitive and affective processes that are attached to them affect blacks' social and political outlooks and, ultimately, their trust.

What is critical for the understanding of trust through a racialized lens is the internalization of race through a group-centered consciousness of fellow black group members, what generally has been noted in the African American identity literature as a reference group orientation (RGO).

For example, Cross (1991) describes African American identity and effectual racial internalization through a five-stage process of psychological development: *Nigrescence*. Cross's initial model illuminates a self-deprecating black person developing a positive understanding of blackness. Stage 1 (the Pre-Encounter stage) is the raw, self-deprecating identity to be converted, wherein the black person has a myopic conception of how race affects one's life. Stage 2 (the Encounter stage) is the personal experience with race that evokes racial consciousness toward the black person's vulnerability to race. Stage 3 (the Immersion-Emersion stage) is the navigation of the black person's blackness with the intent to inculcate oneself with African-centered culture (immersion) and the expression of this culture in everyday life (emersion). Stage 4 (the Internalization stage) involves the black person's settling on a newfound black identity. Stage 5 (the Internalization-Commitment stage) is the actual resultant black identity that incorporates positive understandings of blackness, with less flagrant opposition to whites and racial discrimination of blacks. The black person evinces a more positive, enriched black self-concept, personal identity, and connection to one's racial group identity.

This transformation to a different reference group orientation prepares blacks further to navigate race in American society. As Cross notes, "Nigrescence is a *resocializing* experience; it seeks to transform a preexisting identity (a non-Afrocentric identity) into one that is Afrocentric" (1991, 190; emphasis in original). Thus, while Nigrescence is an important aspect of African American identity development, its focus is on Afrocentricity. While I acknowledge the import that Afrocentricity offers blacks in the realization of cultural value, my task here is to describe how blacks' understanding of race is multifaceted and foundational for their psychological processing of prospective relations with others in trusting relations. Therefore, in my conceptualization of racial internalization, I focus less on the transformation of black identity and focus more on racial influences on blacks' internalization of racial knowledge about American race relations and others' trustworthiness.

Trustors evaluate trustees' trustworthiness (Hardin 2002, 2004). But what does this mean for an assessment of race in trusting relationships? I submit that black Americans' disparate trust can be explained by *discriminative racial-psychological processing*. This psychological processing includes six effects of race on blacks' calculus of trust: (1) their racial socialization experiences, (2) their homogenization of racial group behavior in the form of racial stereotypes, (3) their perceptions of racial uncertainty about being racially discriminated against in the future, (4) their actual personal experiences with racial discrimination, (5) their racialized trust, and (6) their racial-contextual perceptions of racial groups. In effect, processes one through five are a part of blacks' racial internalization. Racial-contextual perceptions are parts of blacks' racial externalization. In the next few sections, I describe these processes as parts of my theory. I detail more specific hypotheses about the determinants of each of these effects in the respective empirical chapters.

Effect 1: Racial Socialization

Racial socialization is the process by which African Americans learn the meaning of their status as "low-status" racial group members (Peters 1985; Caughy, O'Campo, and Randolph 2002). This socialization serves as a preparation for black children to understand how race affects their social status, culture, and racial group history (Sanders Thompson 1994). Much of the research on racial socialization focuses on the messages that parents transmit to their children about race (McAdoo 2007; Martin and McAdoo 2007; McHale et al. 2006; Hughes and Chen 1997; Phinney and Chavira 1995; Demo and Hughes 1990; Sanders Thompson 1994). Extant studies of racial socialization also indicate that an overwhelming number of black Americans report having learned such messages from their parents (Hughes and Chen 1997; Thornton et al. 1990; Sanders Thompson 1994; Bowman and Howard 1985). Thus, racial socialization is a transgenerational process for black Americans.

Racial socialization messages focus on racial pride, cultural awareness, racism awareness, spiritual coping, familial caretaking, individual advancement, and egalitarianism (Martin and McAdoo 2007; Stevenson 1994; Boykin and Toms 1985). Still, these messages receive different emphases depending on parents' reasoning (Hughes and Chen 1997; Thornton et al. 1990) and even parents' own racial socialization experiences (Hughes and Chen 1997).

Aside from the racial socialization messages transmitted by black parents, several other socialization agents and institutions—familial ties and peer relations, black institutions (churches and educational environments), black media, and black social networks—provide contexts and networks that educate black Americans about race (Martin and McAdoo 2007; McAdoo 2007;

Dawson 1994). These agents also structure the heuristic link of black individual interests to black racial group interests (Dawson 1994).

In political science, the presumed connection between historical race relations and contemporary life experiences of black Americans often overlooks how younger black Americans who did not experience de jure racial discrimination come to know about historical discrimination. That is, at some point, younger generations of black Americans have to be socialized about these historical race relations. Even more, they have to have some knowledge about what this racial discrimination means for blacks' relationships with whites and even with other racial groups.

Blacks' and whites' opinions and lives remain divided by color (Schuman et al. 1997; Kinder and Sanders 1996). Researchers speculate that historical black-white racial experiences have a reductive effect on blacks' social and political trusts. It is interesting to note, however, that the racial socialization literature recognizes that socialization about what is called "cultural mistrust" (or mistrust of other racial groups) is one of the least conveyed messages in parent-child racial socialization. Nonetheless, the message is still transferred (Hughes et al. 2007) and potentially has meaning for trust perceptions. Given that political science scholars imply that racial knowledge and distrust is known and transferred across generations of black Americans, racial socialization becomes an important indicator for which to study its effect on blacks' trust. Although we may expect that civil rights legislation and improved equality in contemporary society would increase black Americans' trust, this has not been the case. Blacks' trust has declined even more over time, although there is a decline in whites' trust, as well (Tate 2003; Pew Research Center Study 2010b). While racial discrimination may not be as explicit or doggedly practiced by the state and civilians as it was in the pre-1960s, knowledge about these former experiences of the group can still influence contemporary intergroup interactions.

Despite the importance of racial socialization studies to political science inquiries, they have been mostly concentrated in psychology research. Studying racial socialization as a part of political science research, then, is important because (1) it considers the political implications of learning about race in different ways, (2) it considers the effect that the salience of race may have on black Americans' sociopolitical orientations, (3) it considers how different entities within black social and political spaces become sources of racial socialization, and (4) it considers how racial socialization experiences may vary across black Americans with different demographic backgrounds. Given the centrality of race in black Americans' psychological development

(Dawson 1994; Cross 1991), I borrow from the measures of racial socialization in the social psychology literature and build on them to test their effects on the racial attitudes and trust of African Americans.

Herein, I examine racial socialization as an experience that occurs in blacks' formative years and that affects blacks' racial perceptions over a lifetime. I distinguish blacks' perceptions and interactions with racial groups from the lifelong experiences that might also constitute a form of racial socialization in order to show the influence that early learned racial messages about race can have on navigating race in blacks' everyday lives. I offer that these racial socialization messages consist of the following information:

1. Who black group members are
2. How black group members behave
3. How black group members (should) get along with one another
4. The history of the black group in America (and abroad)
5. The relationship of blacks with whites
6. The relationship of blacks with other racial and ethnic minorities
7. How to interact with people, in general
8. The effect of race on black Americans' lives.

The extent to which these messages are emphasized in black Americans' socialization affect their knowledge about racial groups and how they attribute certain behaviors to racial groups. In other words, the intensity of socialization experiences (high, medium, or low) about racial group relations (intraracial or interracial) affects black Americans' views of these groups. Whether these messages are generally positive or negative also affects their racial attitudes and the extent of their trust in others in social or political contexts. I categorize racial socialization into ten messages:

1. Socialization about black group status
2. Socialization about black pride
3. Socialization about black discrimination
4. Socialization about black public behavior
5. Socialization about black intraracial relations
6. Socialization about black interracial relations
7. Socialization about racialized trust—intraracial
8. Socialization about racialized trust—interracial
9. Socialization about black politics
10. Socialization about less emphasis on race—race mattering less.

I elaborate on the specific messages associated with these general socialization categories in chapter 3. As we will learn, these messages are empirically tested and grouped further into *racial consciousness messages* that espouse blacks' cultural and historical knowledge and *racial protectiveness messages* that suggest that blacks be cautious in their human relations.

Effect 2: Racial Homogenization

Race remains an integral component of how black Americans learn about their social and political circumstances (Sanders Thompson 1992; Demo and Hughes 1990) and how they structure their identities (Dawson 1994; Allen, Dawson, and Brown 1989), their political preferences (Dawson 1994; Tate 1994), their worldviews (Harris-Lacewell 2004; Dawson 2001; J. White 1984), and their perceptions of other racial groups (McClain, Carter, et al. 2006; Bobo and Hutchings 1996). Race even influences how people attribute the causes of behavior, and it influences behavioral expectations (Ellison and Powers 1994). This is why it is within reason to expect that race is an important component in how people assess trust.

The uncertainty and risk associated with historical racial discrimination experiences of the black racial group, I argue, lead blacks to use race as a heuristic for trusting people differently. One way that we see race affect group attitudes is by way of stereotypes. As cognitive constructs, stereotypes are used psychologically to help people explain group behavior (McGarty, Yzerbyt, and Spears 2002). Whether positive or negative, these stereotypes categorize behavior on the basis of attributes that become identifiable with specific groups (Hewstone 1983) through their relationship to the perceiver as either an "in-group" member or an "out-group" member (Lippmann 1922; Allport 1954). These in- and out-group categorizations homogenize out-groups in ways that heighten differences between the perceiver's own group and the out-group (Judd and Park 1988, 1995; S. Taylor et al. 1978) and that lead to the distancing of out-group members from in-group members by associating out-group members with more negative group behavior (Brewer and Brown 1998). In-group members also see more individuation among their own group members and greater homogenization among out-group members (Tajfel and Turner 1986).

As far as psychologically processing in- and out-group membership and the related behavior of groups, in attribution theory, actors observe behavior and link it to causes that are either observable or unobservable (Heider 1944, 1958). Grounded in a social cognitive perspective, this theory posits that an "attribute," as a behavior or entity with a causal link, is ascribed a perceivable, social meaning. Simply put, how people perceive attributes as the consequences of a *cause* affects how they use this information in their affective judgments.[8]

Race is a heuristic that functions in people's perceptions of attributes and behavioral expectations. Psychologically, racial construction has ascribed behavioral expectations to skin color in American society. People, then, attribute race to behavior, and vice versa. Put in another way, *race is used to explain behavior*, and conversely, *behavior is used to explain race*. Using this logic, I contend that race and racial attributes assist people in making judgments about behavioral expectations and trust in certain social and political contexts.[9] Therefore, I hypothesize that the race of *Actor B* affects *Actor A*'s perception of whether *Actor B* is trustworthy to perform a *task X* in *context Y*.

As for racial stereotyping, we know that racial stereotypes can be both negative and positive, although negative stereotypes arguably have more detrimental effects on people's livelihoods and disparagement. Blacks subscribe to negative stereotypes about other racial groups (just as whites do) when they are in racially isolated environments. The extent of this negative stereotyping depends on whether blacks or whites constitute a majority in these contexts (Gay 2004; Oliver and Wong 2003; Oliver and Mendelberg 2000). Despite Latinos' possessing more negative stereotypes of blacks, blacks hold more positive stereotypes about Latinos (Mindiola, Niemann, and Rodriguez 2002). Black Americans also believe both positive and negative stereotypes about Asian Americans (Wong et al. 1998). Those blacks who possess more negative views about their own racial group also are more likely to possess negative attitudes about Asian Americans and Latinos (Cummings and Lambert 1997).

With regard to perceptions of discrimination, blacks perceive that Asian American men are more likely than Asian American women to discriminate against them (Timberlake and Estes 2007). With respect to whites, black Americans are more likely to stereotype them as possessing negative stereotypes of blacks (Sigelman and Tuch 1997), and these stereotypes about whites' attitudes about blacks are often confirmed, as blacks believe (Torres and Charles 2004). A study I conducted (2009) also found that black college students possess more negative stereotypes of whites than of blacks, Asian Americans, and Latinos. In the case of blacks' stereotypes about other blacks, they also stereotype themselves both positively and negatively (Allen, Dawson, and Brown 1989). Evidence also shows blacks stereotyping their own group's members as being more religious, viewing Latinos and Asian

Americans as more hardworking, and considering whites as more selfish and bossy than other racial groups (Nunnally 2009).

Given the way in which stereotypes homogenize racial attributes to specific racial groups, I argue that this racial homogenization influences how blacks trust others. These homogenizing attitudes also function as a part of their racial predispositions, which ultimately ascribe characteristics to racial groups in ways that can increase or decrease the potential for trust.

In order to discern how blacks subscribe to racial stereotypes, and thus racially homogenize groups, in chapter 4, I empirically test racial stereotypes among blacks and compare their attitudes to those of whites and Latinos in the NPSS. Furthermore, I examine how racial socialization messages influence their subscription to positive or negative stereotypes.

Effect 3: Racial Uncertainty

Another important racial predisposition is the perception of the *likelihood* that a racial group will discriminate against people. Therefore, additionally, I argue that trust in social or political contexts will differ based not only on contexts but also on the perceptions of uncertainty about whether racial groups are likely to discriminate against people in these contexts. The analysis of racial and political socializations in this study presupposes that blacks' personal, group, and vicarious experiences (transmitted via racial socialization) with racial groups influence the perceived likelihood that others will discriminate against them, or what I refer to as *racial uncertainty*. *Racial uncertainty* is the set of conditions under which actors of different races are uncertain about the discriminatory interests and behaviors of people who are members of racial groups other than their own and who may pose an adverse risk or harm to them as a member of a different racial group.

Studies of risk assessment and uncertainty in decision-making and interpersonal interactions (Alvarez and Franklin 1994; Cioffi-Revilla 1998) rarely investigate how race affects perceptions of uncertainty, especially as far as one's perceived risk of being racially discriminated against. Studies of racial perceptions that have been done focus on people's perceptions of different racial groups as threats to their socioeconomic well-being (Bobo and Hutchings 1996; Sigelman and Welch 1991) or on people's behaving against others in a racially discriminatory way that could be interpreted as either race-neutral or race-related, depending on the perspective of the perceiver (Combs et al. 2006; Sellers and Shelton 2003; Jefferson and Caldwell 2002). Current studies focus on people *perceiving* racial discrimination based on actions and do not account for the *likelihood* of people perceiving that they will be racially discriminated against. Studying racial uncertainty, therefore, contributes another aspect of how blacks process race in their intergroup interactions, lending more evidence to how race is perceived in trust assessments.

Examining the perceived *likelihood* that certain racial groups will racially discriminate offers important information about race, risk, and perceptions of uncertainty in human interactions. I posit that racial uncertainty should reduce blacks' trust. As I also test in chapter 4, blacks' racial uncertainty should be higher with respect to their assessment of nonblacks (especially whites) than with respect to their assessments of fellow group members. Blacks who received negative racial socialization messages emphasizing racial protectiveness, moreover, should be more racially uncertain.

Effect 4: Racial Discrimination Experiences

As a phenotypic characteristic, people's race cannot be easily shed or made inconspicuous,[10] and at any point, race can put people in jeopardy of being discriminated against or harmed by people who are prejudiced, resentful, or hateful of their racial group. In my previous discussion, I described how blacks' historical, political, and social experiences in America have been less than democratic and that as a group, they have been legally excluded, treated unfairly, treated unjustly, or terrorized merely because of their race. Moreover, I noted how, despite the passage of civil rights legislation, black Americans still experience racial discrimination in public places (Feagin 1991; Sigelman and Welch 1991; Broman, Mavaddat, and Hsu 2000). Physical violence committed against blacks because of their race also continues even today in America's post–Jim Crow society, with African Americans still ranking highest as the group with the most hate crimes committed against them (Federal Bureau of Investigation 2007).

Blacks, thus, face an uncertain probability that their race will increase their chances of being discriminated against by others, especially by nonblacks, as recognized by my conception of racial uncertainty. Actual personal experiences with racial discrimination should decrease one's trust in other racial groups. Therefore, blacks who have experienced racial discrimination more frequently should be more distrusting of nonblacks.

Blacks who received racial socialization messages that emphasized caution in their interactions with others also should report more frequent discrimination experiences. Chapter 4 tests the effect of racial socialization, racial uncertainty, and other determinants of the frequency with which blacks report having been racially discriminated against. It also tests the influence of racial knowledge on the perceived quality of relationships that blacks feel they have with other racial groups.

Effect 5: Racialized Trust

According to the racial calculus of trust, blacks will trust their own group members more than they trust nonblack group members. They will be least likely to trust white Americans, as they are members of the racial group that historically perpetrated racial discrimination against them the most. While blacks will trust Asian Americans and Latinos more than they will trust whites, those groups will still be trusted less than other blacks will.

In chapter 5, I examine how racial socialization, discrimination experiences, and racial uncertainty influence blacks' trust in blacks, whites, Asians, and Latinos. I interpret results from race and trust experiments to illustrate how blacks' trust varies depending on the race of the person in question. I also compare the extent to which blacks are more or less racially trusting than are other racial groups. This analysis will show that blacks are not the only people who trust distinctively on the basis of race. But, more important, the data analysis will show the patterns of racial distrust for blacks compared to other groups. These results also will indicate how these groups may be assessed differently by blacks depending on the context of their trust evaluation. The analysis in chapter 5 prepares us to understand how internalized knowledge about race affects how blacks externalize this knowledge in trust attitudes respective to social and political contexts.

Effect 6: Racial-Contextual Perception

The contexts of blacks' discrimination experiences have varied from their workplaces to their neighborhoods to their shopping places to their religious institutions. The sum of these exclusionary racial experiences have contributed to the formation of black institutions and a counterpolitical space that Dawson (2001) refers to as the "black counterpublic." Therefore, as I described previously, the spaces that political scientists might otherwise deem as social spaces, in fact, serve as dual political spaces for black Americans.

Context is important for studying trust because it influences people's expectations for behavior. I contend that several factors affect how racial actors are perceived in different contexts:

1. The perception of racial uncertainty in the interaction
2. The perception of racial attributes, which cue expectations for behavior in the context
3. The perception of contextual variation, wherein some contexts seem more harmful than others
4. The perception of racial actors being more or less harmful in these contexts

On the basis of the racial calculus of trust, wherein the perceived race of the actor, racial risk, and perceived probability of harm affect blacks' (dis)trust, I explore how blacks' trust varies in social and political contexts. Blacks should be more apprehensive and less trusting when they interact with non-blacks in contexts in which they have been discriminated the most or have experienced racial competition the most. Groups perceived as competition in certain social or political contexts also should be trusted less. Racial-contextual perception, thus, should influence which groups are trusted more than others in different contexts.

In chapter 6, I examine blacks' social trust specifically. I discern how they trust in others in general and in specific racial actors. Furthermore, I study blacks' trust in different social contexts such as neighborhoods, shopping places, workplaces, and religious institutions. I compare their social trust to whites', Asians', and Latinos' social trust to show whether blacks socially trust distinctively from other racial groups.

In my study of blacks' trust in political contexts, in chapter 7, I scrutinize how race operates in black Americans' feelings of political proximity to other racial groups. I also test whether the race and partisanship of political actors influences blacks' trust differently. Because blacks trust the federal government more than they do state and local governments, I determine whether their trust varies between the two levels of government when they are asked whether certain racial groups will be more trustable to represent black group interests in the political system.

Because political interests have been so intimately tied to racial group interests, I expect blacks to trust descriptively and substantively. That is, because blacks mostly identify with the Democratic Party, I expect them to be most trusting in Democratic, black political actors. And they should be most cautious and distrusting of Republican political actors of all races. Despite partisanship, blacks will distinctively distrust white political actors, in part, because of the historical, racially sensitive relations they have with whites. White Democrats will be trusted more than white Republicans, nonetheless. Asian Americans and Latinos (of either major political party), as groups sharing racial and ethnic minority status with blacks, however, will be trusted more than whites. In keeping with my theory about factors influencing blacks' discriminative trust, for both social and political trust, I examine how racial socialization, racial uncertainty, and racial discrimination experiences influence these trusts.

Summary of Theory

By studying blacks' racial experiences (transmitted from their families and experienced personally), we can trace how blacks internalize race and to what extent they externalize race through their social and political attitudes. To elaborate, as figure 2.1 indicates, blacks internalize race through the development of their racial predispositions: (1) learning different messages about race (racial socialization), (2) adopting racial stereotypes about groups (racial homogenization), (3) fearing prospective racial discrimination (racial uncertainty), (4) experiencing race through their daily interactions with racial groups (racial discrimination), and (5) trusting groups differently on the basis of race (racialized trust).

They also externalize race through their attitudes toward racial groups in different contexts (racial-contextual perception): (1) trusting in others differently on the basis of the race of the actor in either social or political contexts or (2) having more or less racialized trust, which affects their level of trust in these contexts. In sum, my theory of discriminative racial-psychological processing avers that race operates in blacks' trust by affecting how they perceive their own racial group members (intraracial trust) relative to other racial group members (interracial trust). Figure 2.1 also illustrates the relationships among the several manifestations of race in blacks' lives and their effect on the group's social and political trusts.[11]

As my theory suggests, differences in trust in these groups also will depend on blacks' internalized racial knowledge and racial attitudes and the externalization of these cognitive and affective components in certain contexts—neighborhoods, shopping places, religious institutions, workplaces, and political spaces. In essence, these spaces will serve as cues for how blacks interpret the way in which their race is read by others and how they perceive others' race as affecting their prospective treatment. Race, thus, affects how blacks interpret their risks, safety, and livelihood. Through this study of the effect of race on blacks' trust, we learn more about the transmission of racial knowledge across generations of blacks and the influence of personalized, lived experiences and perceptions of race on contemporary black social and political behavior.

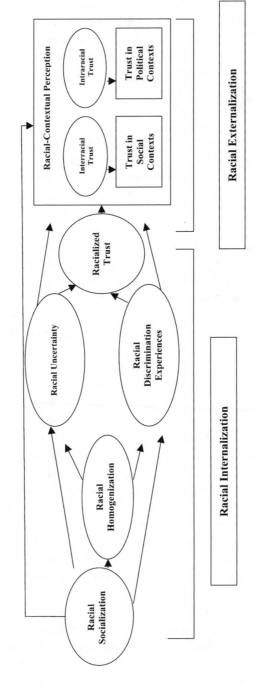

Fig. 2.1. Theory of discriminative racial-psychological processing

Part II

Racial Internalization

3

Being Black in America

Racial Socialization

Black Americans' Socialization about Race

As a young black person, I was always told by my grandmother to get a bag from the store clerk whenever I made a purchase (no matter how small or big the merchandise). She told me this because she was socializing me about race and preparing me to avoid experiencing racial discrimination. In her view, all it took was a black person leaving a store with an item in her hand and no bag as proof of purchase, and she would be reprimanded for stealing. My grandmother grew up in the South in the early 1900s, and this was a lesson among others that black people like her had to learn in order to avoid confrontation by whites (and possibly other racial groups) about things for which they may have had little responsibility or guilt. For my grandmother, it did not come down to having a bag or a receipt in one's hand as proof of purchase; it was your *race* and a *product* leaving the store that brought about a store clerk's alarm that a *black* person was stealing. To this day, I ask for a bag with my purchase (no matter how small or how big the merchandise), or I hedge the lesson a little by leaving the store with my purchase and a "visible" receipt in my hand.

As a matter of precaution, I learned from my grandmother that having black skin could carry a price in America—an albatross of guilt without trial or substantial evidence. This was one of my personal lessons in *racial socialization*, and it is experiences such as these that I have had personally and have heard about from other blacks that motivated me to study black Americans' racial socialization experiences and the influence of those experiences on their everyday social and political interactions. Regardless of blacks' class, gender, or sexuality, race either trumps other social identities or occurs intersectionally with them (Simien 2006; Cohen 1999; Hochschild

1995; Dawson 1994). Thus, whether a black American is a woman or a man, rich or poor, heterosexual or homosexual, race affects his or her life experiences. How black people learn about the effect of race on their lives and the meaning of being black in America, or the process of *racial socialization*, are the foci of this chapter.

Racial socialization is the process by which African Americans learn about and identify with the influence of race on their social status, culture, and group history in the United States (Caughy et al. 2002; Sanders Thompson 1994; Demo and Hughes 1990; Peters 1985). Although there are several sources from which black Americans learn about being black in America, including, for example, media, churches, schools, and social networks (Martin and McAdoo 2007; McAdoo 2007; Dawson 1994), children's parents and families are most integral to the transmission of racial socialization messages (McAdoo 2007; Martin and McAdoo 2007; McHale et al. 2006; S. Hill 1999; Hughes and Chen 1997; Phinney and Chavira 1995; Demo and Hughes 1990; Sanders Thompson 1994). An overwhelming number of black Americans report having learned such messages from their parents (Hughes and Chen 1997; Thornton et al. 1990; Sanders Thompson 1994; Bowman and Howard 1985). For example, in the National Survey of Black Americans, 63.6 percent of black American adults reported transmitting racial socialization messages to their children (Thornton et al. 1990), and in a study of black American adolescents, 68 percent reported having received racial socialization messages from their parents (Bowman and Howard 1985).

Messages about race comprise information that instills racial pride, cultural awareness, racism awareness, spiritual coping, familial caretaking, individual advancement, and egalitarianism (Martin and McAdoo 2007; Stevenson 1994; Boykin and Toms 1985). Still, these messages receive different emphases depending on parents' thoughts about race (Hughes and Chen 1997; Thornton et al. 1990) and even what parents learned about race themselves (Hughes and Chen 1997). Moreover, married parents, mothers, parents living in the Northeast, older parents, and more educated parents are more likely to relay racial socialization messages (Thornton et al. 1990).

Learning about race is important for understanding black Americans' political and social attitudes because it plays a salient role in African Americans' racial identity (Mutisya and Ross 2005; Sanders Thompson 1999; D. Miller 1999; Miller and MacIntosh 1999). Black identity includes several complex components that connect group members to the black American experience, including a reverence for distinct African American culture, or what is also known as black autonomy, feeling close to the black masses and to black leaders, and recognition of both positive and negative stereotypes about the group (Allen, Dawson, and Brown 1989). Socialization experiences, in turn, inform these racial identity constructs.

David Demo and Michael Hughes (1990), for example, examined and measured the effect of socialization experiences on racial identity among black adults. Their research includes data from the 1979–1980 National Survey of Black Americans (NSBA), which examines parents' socioeconomic status, the content of parental socialization, preadult interracial contact, quality of familial/friend relationships, adult interracial contact, religious involvement, and the respondent's socioeconomic status, age, and gender. They examined four components of racial socialization and their influence on black identity:

1. *Individualistic/universalistic.* Respondents had been socialized to deny race as important in their life circumstances.
2. *Integrative/assertive.* Respondents' parents told them to maintain a positive, group-orientation approach to life.
3. *Cautious/defensive.* Respondents' parents informed them about white prejudice and the importance of black empowerment to counter it.
4. *No socialization messages.* Respondents' parents gave them no socialization messages whatsoever about race.

Each message emphasizes the role that race plays in black Americans' life circumstances: recognizing a positive life outlook, knowing about white prejudice, developing black agency to counter racial injustice, and not learning about race at all. Some of these messages emphasize intergroup interactions and personal perspectives that relate to the ways that black Americans navigate interracial relations. Demo and Hughes, notably, found that there is a strong positive correlation between "integrative/assertive" parental socialization, or getting along with other racial groups, and feelings of group pride and interracial contact. Hence, racial socialization messages affect how black Americans perceive their own group and nonblack group members in interracial relations.

As for interracial relations, scholars find that younger black Americans report that their parents are more likely to stress racial socialization messages that emphasize not trusting whites and beliefs that whites are better and that blacks should "act white" to get ahead (Lesane-Brown et al. 2005). Black parents, however, less often stressed racial socialization messages concerning distrust of Asians. Messages focusing on blacks' racial advancement encouraged younger blacks to achieve anything, to be proud about being black, and to be aware of racial discrimination experiences. Moreover, adolescent black Americans report having been inculcated with more messages alluding to "race not mattering."

Racial socialization also plays an important role in informing black Americans about how to deal with race-related stressors and relations with other racial groups. Racial socialization messages transmitted from parents to children, for instance, assist African Americans with resiliency (Miller 1999; Miller and MacIntosh 1999) and strategies for coping with racial discrimination (Sellers et al. 2003; Scott 2003; Thompson, Anderson, and Bakeman 2000; Stevenson et al. 1997). Depending on emphases on different messages, racial socialization influences how African Americans identify with other groups and interact with these groups in different contexts (Harris 1995). Yet, there are mixed results related to the effect of racial socialization on reducing acculturative stress in interracial environments. Whereas Thompson, Anderson, and Bakeman (2000) find limited support for the effect of racial socialization messages on reducing acculturative stress, Demo and Hughes (1990) find evidence to suggest that certain racial socialization messages enhance cross-racial interactions, possibly leading to less stressful social interactions.

Socialization about race, thus, educates blacks about the social and political realities of race in America, lending to a race-centered consciousness, or what Joseph White (1984) refers to as an "African worldview." Despite race's having such an all-encompassing effect on African Americans' experiences, this worldview is not monolithic, and variant black ideological perspectives structure how blacks navigate and participate in their social and political contexts (Harris-Lacewell 2004; Dawson 2001). How race affected blacks' lives as a group influenced similar historical understandings about discrimination against the group. Messages about these understandings can be socialized from lessons about race that blacks learn through experiences or conversations about race. The latter socialization—including lessons transmitted by sources within black communities—is the focus of my examination. Some historical examples of racial socialization elucidate how blacks have had to think about their race with respect to their decision-making and actions.

For example, black-religion scholar C. Eric Lincoln describes his "first lesson" about being black in America and growing up in the Jim Crow South. As a boy, he went to the doctor's office to get an immunization, and as he stood in line, he noticed that none of the white children had to wait to be immunized. Noticing this injustice, Lincoln stepped forward and offered out his arm to be immunized without the nurse telling him to do so. Unbeknownst to him, he was about to violate a major principle of Jim Crow—deference to whites' being "first" and "superior" to blacks. In spite of his age, the white nurse made sure to let him know his "place" in Jim Crow society, and she reprimanded him with the reply, "Boy! Get back in line! *Get all the way back there! All you niggers have to wait*" (Lincoln 1996). As young as he was and as cruel as this message sounded, Lincoln's age did not comfort him from some of the harsh realities of Jim Crow: he was black in America during a time when being black meant waiting, being last, or "being without" because one was black.

One of the most infamous cases of a young black American violating racial etiquette is the brutal 1955 lynching of Emmett Till. Till was a fourteen-year-old black boy from Chicago, who upon visiting his relatives in Money, Mississippi, exchanged words with a white woman in a way that defied southern etiquette, because his utterance, "Bye, baby," implied sexual innuendo by a black boy toward a white woman, a violation of antimiscegenation practices in the South. Till, coming from Chicago, was unaware of his "place" in southern Jim Crow society and paid for it with his life. The white perpetrators of this crime also faced a trial with an all-white jury, and they were eventually acquitted. However, later, they disclosed in an interview with a journalist that they, in fact, killed Till. Till's death is thought to be one of the major catalysts of the modern civil rights movement.[1]

In my own family members' racial experiences, my father told me about growing up in Jim Crow. As a black male in the South, he had to "know his place" whenever he was around white people. That is, he had to know that whenever he was around white people, as a black person, he had to display a degree of deference to them, and if he chose to act otherwise, he had to understand the consequences for his "defiant" behavior. Or, if he were to exchange money with a white store clerk, he had to learn that some white store clerks would not allow a black person to place money directly in their hands because a hand-to-hand exchange of money indicated "racial equality." My father also had to know to carry a form of identification with him that identified who he was, because many criminal suspects in the South were described as black, and without any identification, he and other black men who fit that description were likely to become criminal suspects.

My mother, on the other hand, shared fewer stories about how she navigated her way through racial discrimination, but she recounted being among the first blacks to integrate schools in Norfolk, Virginia, and going to a high school where she was "allowed" to attend but not allowed to participate in many social activities that would have been fulfilling for her holistic educational experience. She even recounts how the only high school organization that willingly embraced black people as participants was the Teen Dems organization, a Democratic Party organization for students at her high school; maybe this embrace and other symbolic gestures by the Democrats in 1964 and beyond informed the overwhelmingly Democratic partisanship that black Americans have today. Her stories of Jim Crow center on her courage and triumph in fighting racial discrimination through her involvement as a teenager in the civil rights movement in sit-ins and, particularly, the March on Washington in 1963.

In addition, as a woman with a darker-skinned complexion, she confronted intraracial discrimination, also known as "colorism," which customarily disparaged darker-skinned blacks in favor of blacks with lighter-skinned complexions (Russell, Wilson, and Hall 1992; Hill 2000), although colorism is evident among various racial and ethnic groups, including Anglos, American Indians, Asians, and Latinos (Hochschild 2006). For darker-skinned blacks, notions of intelligence and beauty were tied to their complexions, deeming them as dullards and unattractive and thus further marginalizing them. This intraracial hierarchy, like class, further complicated how blacks related to one another, aside from hierarchical race relations they had with whites in larger American society.

These different experiences suggest how "race and place" are interwoven into the meaning, operation, experiences, and lessons of race. As for the stories shared with me by my parents, they relay two different foci and experiences with race: experiences with racial discrimination and political activism against racial discrimination. Other black parents, institutions, or peers similarly share their and others' stories and experiences in dealing with race and racism as black people in America—the transmission of black collective memory—in order to socialize other black Americans about the history, experiences, values, and politics of being black in America. These messages assume different approaches and emphases in order to assist and prepare black Americans for navigating race and interactions with others, black and nonblack. Collective memory about the civil rights movement, for instance, also affects the extent to which blacks and whites support racially liberal public policies (Griffin and Bollen 2009). This is why studying variant emphases on racial socialization messages carries with it the potential for understanding how black Americans perceive and interact with others in different contexts, especially examining how this influences their (dis)trust.

This chapter examines black Americans' racial socialization experiences using national survey data in the 2007 National Politics and Socialization Survey (NPSS). The chapter determines the sources of racial socialization messages, discerning whether familial, institutional, or peer sources of information are most relevant for relaying these messages. It also analyzes several racial socialization messages to determine the general level of emphasis that respondents recall was placed on these messages about being black in America. These messages relate more generally to knowing the history of black Americans' experiences with racial discrimination, relating to other black Americans and other racial groups, and advancing the black racial group politically, socially, and economically. I devise ten, additive racial socialization scales, which include the combination of several measures that form distinct messages about race. For each of these scales, I test ordered probit regression models in order to examine whether certain demographic characteristics affect differences in emphases—low, medium, or high—on these racial socialization messages. Using principal components analysis, I also test whether these measures cohere on a similar latent construct.

Analyzing Black Americans' Racial Socialization Experiences

In this chapter, I analyze black Americans' racial socialization experiences only, focusing specifically on those respondents who identified as black. Questions in the NPSS ask black respondents about their racial socialization and political socialization experiences, including where respondents learned the most information about being black in America. The racial socialization questions in the NPSS do not include an exhaustive list of messages that one may learn about being black in America, but many of the questions and measures in the survey draw on the measures used in the 1979–1980 National Survey of Black Americans (James Jackson 1991). Additional questions probe how trust in racial groups, or socialization about racialized distrust (intraracial and interracial), plays a part in one's racial socialization experiences. Respondents are asked, more specifically, to consider the extent to which messages about distrust were relayed in a manner that specifically stated race as a means by which to consider trust.

The ten scales of racial socialization that I analyze relay the following messages about race and black American life experiences:

1. *Socialization about black group status*: learning about racial discrimination and its effect on black Americans' social status

2. *Socialization about black pride*: learning to appreciate the cultural heritage and contributions of black people to American society
3. *Socialization about skin-color discrimination*: learning about how black Americans discriminate against one another based on skin color, or what is known as colorism
4. *Socialization about black public behavior*: learning about black stereotypes and how black public behavior affects the welfare of black group members
5. *Socialization about black intraracial relations*: learning about black ethnic differences among African Americans, West Indians, and Africans and emphases on positive intragroup relations
6. *Socialization about black interracial relations*: learning positive messages about getting along with whites, Asian Americans, and Latinos
7. *Socialization about racialized distrust—intraracial*: learning negative messages about relating to fellow racial group members and stressing distrust among African Americans, West Indians, and Africans
8. *Socialization about racialized distrust—interracial*: learning negative messages about relating to other racial groups and stressing distrust between blacks and whites, Asian Americans, or Latinos
9. *Socialization about black politics*: learning about how politics can be used to advance the status of black group members
10. *Socialization about less emphasis on race—race mattering less*: learning that race should not matter and that people should think less about racism

Respondents also were asked to tell the extent to which each of these racial socialization messages was "emphasized" in their learning about what it means to be black in America. Each item is coded to reflect the level of emphasis of the socialization message in the respondents' learning about what it means to be black—"0, no emphasis at all"; "1, not much emphasis"; "2, neither emphasized nor deemphasized"; "3, some emphasis"; and "4, much emphasis." Each of the ten additive scales varies according to the number of measure items in the respective scale. All additive scales are operationalized as a Likert scale of socialization emphasis—scaled from "0, no emphasis" to whatever is the highest numeric value on the additive scale per message, symbolizing "high emphasis." (See table 3.2 for the several racial socialization measures and the coefficients for scale reliability for each of the ten racial socialization scales.) The additive scales are divided further into three categories of emphasis placed on each racial socialization message: "low emphasis," "medium emphasis," or "high emphasis." Table 3.3 includes univariate statistics for these levels of emphasis on the racial socialization messages.

Additionally, I analyze models for each of the racial socialization scales, controlling for demographic variables. Namely, in being *non–African American* (where West Indian and African = 1, African American = 0), one's socialization experiences may differ from African Americans'. Although West Indians and Africans share historical experiences with racial oppression (Waters 1999; Assensoh 2000), because African Americans' political history includes race relations that are unique to the institution of Jim Crow, emphasis on certain racial socialization messages may vary. As for *gender* (female = 1, male = 0); *age* (eighteen and up), I anticipate that black women will have received more emphasis on racial socialization messages about skin-color discrimination than black men have. This is because skin-color discrimination has been a disproportionate concern for black women (and other women of color) as it relates to conceptions of beauty (Russell, Wilson, and Hall 1992; Turner 2005).

I also control for variables that contextualize the kinds of information that either parents or guardians or the respondents themselves likely would have received within the racialized contexts of the environments in which they grew up, such as growing up in the American South or outside the United States. For those respondents with *parents born outside the United States* (coded 1, else = 0), who also comprise black immigrants, their parents may have different understandings about U.S. race relations. As such, their racial socialization messages also may differ from parents born in the United States, who then also came of age in the context of U.S. race relations.

Respondents who have *parents that grew up in the South* (coded 1, else = 0) will have more likely received greater emphases on racial socialization messages imparting enhanced black cultural appreciation and awareness of relationships with members of nonblack groups, especially whites. This is because the southern context led to racial socialization in ways that involved black Americans' understanding their "place" in society relative to whites and being cognizant of racial etiquette in order to avoid the negative consequences of social and perhaps even legal sanctioning, depending on the era of racial socialization (Ritterhouse 2006). Such parents will more likely socialize their children in ways that are sensitive to their own experiences with race and formal segregation during Jim Crow.

Respondents who *grew up mostly outside the United States* (coded 1, else = 0) possibly learned different messages about U.S. race relations because they were not constricted by the racial norms operative in the direct, living context of the United States, and racial norms outside the United States also may have functioned differently. For example, someone living in the Caribbean may be aware of black-white dynamics stemming from centuries-old colonialism.

However, many Caribbean nations currently are predominantly black societies in which blacks also have autonomy in social, political, and economic spaces, unlike in many racial contexts in the United States (Waters 1999). Blacks raised outside the United States likely learn messages about blackness that are relevant for navigating their racial contexts. In Caribbean or African contexts, then, racial protective messages should be emphasized less because the power dynamics are not principled on a racial hierarchy, per se.

Respondents who *grew up in the American South* (coded 1, else = 0), on the other hand, likely learn greater emphasis on racial socialization because these messages would prepare them for navigating their blackness in the racial hierarchy, visible historically and, arguably, contemporarily in the South. Respondents who *grew up in a mostly black neighborhood* (coded 1, else = 0) also should receive more contextual cues about blackness—and thus have an enhanced awareness of being black in America—than those who grew up in neighborhoods that were not predominantly black.

Given the history of colorism, or skin-color discrimination, which heavily disparaged blacks (and other racial and ethnic minority groups) with darker skin tones, I include a control for the *respondent's skin color* (1 = very dark to 5 = very light). Respondents with a darker skin complexion should receive more socialization emphasizing the potential for skin-color discrimination. This variable appears only in the models of skin-color discrimination socialization and a composite measure of black protectiveness socialization. I conduct a principal components analysis to determine whether there are latent constructs evident among the ten racial socialization messages. As I discuss later, two constructs emerge, which I also examine separately to discern determinants of these latent construct messages.

In the next sections, I discuss the sources of NPSS black respondents' racial socialization messages, what they learned about being black in America, the level of emphasis these messages were given in their racial socialization, and the determinants of emphasis on the ten racial socialization messages and two latent racial socialization constructs (racial consciousness and racial protectiveness).

Learning about Being Black in America: Sources of Information and Message Content

Black respondents in the NPSS were asked to tell what they felt was the most important (least important) source for which they learned about being black in America. They could choose among the following socialization agents:

1. Parent(s), family, or guardians
2. Church or other religious institutions
3. Media, newspapers, Internet, or TV
4. Black media, black newspapers, websites
5. School or some other educational institution
6. Peers or friends
7. None of the above.

Table 3.1 illustrates that most respondents, or 55 percent, stated that they learned the most about being black from their "parent(s), family, or guardians." Conversely, they learned the least about being black from "schools or some other educational institution." The racial socialization literature focuses on the study of parent-child racial socialization experiences, in part, because parents and families, in general, continue to be the predominant agent of racial socialization about being black in America. On a personal note, I recall my father describing the reaction of one of my family members to his wearing an Afro hairstyle during the Black Power movement in the 1960s, when black Americans showed their embrace of African-centered culture by wearing Afros and African dashikis. Politely, my relative stated, "I don't know why all y'all young people are wearing all those Afros and dashikis to show how black you are. All you have to do is wake up in the morning, and everybody's gonna know you are black!"

TABLE 3.1

Importance of Sources for Learning about Being Black in America

Sources of learning	*Most important sources* % (n)	*Least important sources* % (n)
Parent(s), family, or guardians	55 (282)	7 (36)
Church or other religious institution	4 (21)	14 (70)
Media, newspapers, websites	9 (46)	20 (103)
Black media, black newspapers, websites	7 (38)	6 (29)
School or some other educational institution	10 (54)	30 (157)
Peers or friends	6 (29)	5 (26)
None of the above	7 (37)	12 (61)
N	517	517

Source: 2007 National Politics and Socialization Survey
Note: Percentages may not add up to 100 due to rounding.

This relative made his point clear that being black did not involve embracing African culture; skin color was *all* it took to be black in America. This racial socialization message shared by a family member to another family member imparted the notion that skin color trumps culture and behavior in describing one's black racial identity. Implicitly, this family member suggested that racial identity is something that is imposed on an individual and that does not necessarily have to be embraced by that individual in American society, especially for a black person to be viewed as black in America. Messages like these by family members tell other family members what it means to be black in America.

There also is a growing trend to study the influence of institutions in socializing black Americans about race (McAdoo 2007). Often in the study of racial socialization in the educational environment, the research questions focus on how racial socialization prepares students for obstacles within the educational environment. Less often do these studies analyze the reverse effect of educational institutions on black Americans' racial socialization. The premise that educational institutions can be a source of negative racial socialization is the focus of Carter G. Woodson's 1933 classic, *The Mis-education of the Negro*. In that text, Woodson suggests that educational institutions can socialize self-hatred and negative thinking about "blackness" by excluding from their curricula any history or positive contributions of blacks to society in America and around the world.

During the late 1960s, the push to include the study of African Americans as a part of the educational curriculum informed the development of many African American studies programs across the country. Research still indicates an underrepresentation of history about black Americans, especially during certain historical periods (Cha-Jua and Weems 1994). Then, it is no wonder that black Americans report similarly that they have had the least socialization about race in their educational institutions. The NPSS measure about racial socialization in an educational institution, however, does not probe respondents further to ask whether they attended a historically black college or university (HBCU), for perhaps respondents who attended these universities or even schools with Afrocentric curricula may report different and more informative learning experiences about being black in America.

Socialization about Black Group Status

Learning the history of racial discrimination perpetrated against African Americans is a very important aspect of racial socialization. Historical narratives about this racial discrimination are transmitted as a form of collective memory about blacks' collective experiences with race and racism or as a form of the personal experiences of African American parents, family members, or guardians. This information is transferred from generation to generation in a way that conveys the historical and contemporary group status of African Americans.

In the NPSS, as table 3.2 illustrates, 72 percent of respondents (n = 368) reported that in their learning about being black in America, they learned with "much emphasis" that "black people have dealt with racial discrimination throughout history." In addition, 52 percent (n = 267) reported that they learned "discrimination has affected black people's advancement in society" with "much emphasis," compared to 32 percent (n = 164) who learned this message with "some emphasis."

I constructed an additive scale of these two variables to form a scale of "socialization about blacks' status in America." Table 3.3 shows an overwhelming number of respondents (83 percent; n = 423) learned with "high emphasis" about blacks' historical discrimination status in the United States. In fact, this message is the most emphatic racial socialization message learned across all the racial socialization scales analyzed in the sample.

The Cronbach's alpha coefficient for this scale (Cronbach's α = .61) is lower than the conventionally accepted Cronbach's alpha coefficient.[2] Nonetheless, I examine predictors of racial socialization for this scale. According to table 3.4, black Americans with more education and with higher incomes received more emphasis on messages about black Americans' historical experiences with racial discrimination and its effect on black Americans' social status.

Socialization about Black Pride

When respondents were asked whether they were taught about the extent to which "black people contributed to society," 58 percent (n = 297) of black respondents in the NPSS reported that they learned about black societal contributions with "much emphasis"; 22 percent (n = 111) learned this message with "some emphasis." Of respondents who learned that "black culture and heritage are important," as much as 60 percent (n = 308) reported that they learned this message with "much emphasis." Over two-thirds of the black respondents stated that they learned "with much emphasis" that they "should be proud to be black."

In an additive scale of black pride, including the three aforementioned measures, table 3.3 shows, 67 percent of the respondents received

TABLE 3.2
Racial Socialization Messages Received among Black Americans

	Not emphasized at all % (n)	Not much emphasis % (n)	Neither emphasized nor deemphasized % (n)	Some emphasis % (n)	Much emphasis % (n)
Socialization about Black Group Status (Cronbach's α = .61)					
Black people have dealt with racial discrimination throughout history. (N = 513)	2 (12)	3 (13)	6 (30)	18 (90)	72 (368)
Discrimination has affected black people's advancement in society. (N = 511)	3 (15)	2 (11)	11 (54)	32 (164)	52 (267)
Socialization about Black Pride (Cronbach's α = .81)					
Black people have contributed to society. (N = 514)	3 (15)	8 (42)	10 (49)	22 (111)	58 (297)
Black heritage and culture are important. (N = 513)	3 (17)	7 (37)	10 (51)	19 (100)	60 (308)
One should be proud to be black. (N = 512)	3 (16)	3 (14)	9 (46)	17 (85)	69 (351)
Socialization about Black Skin-Color Discrimination					
Black people should treat one another differently based on whether or not they are light-skinned. (N = 511)	48 (246)	11 (55)	23 (118)	11 (55)	7 (37)
Socialization about Black Behavior in Public (Cronbach's α = .74)					
Black people should try to avoid behaviors that are characteristic of black stereotypes. (N = 510)	6 (30)	5 (26)	17 (87)	27 (140)	45 (227)
Black people should be sure to act properly when they are in public. (N = 510)	4 (20)	3 (14)	15 (76)	27 (136)	52 (264)

Socialization about Positive Black Intraracial Relations (Cronbach's α = .70)

Statement					
Black people have different ethnicities (American, African, and Caribbean), and they should work together. (N = 508)	14 (57)	13 (53)	25 (104)	21 (89)	28 (117)
Black people should get along with one another. (N = 513)	4 (19)	3 (16)	13 (68)	19 (100)	60 (310)
Black men and women should treat one another well. (N = 509)	4 (19)	3 (13)	13 (67)	18 (94)	62 (316)

Socialization about Positive Black Interracial Relations (Cronbach's α = .70)

Statement					
Black people should get along with white people. (N = 508)	5 (26)	9 (44)	24 (120)	31 (157)	32 (161)
Black people should get along with other racial minorities. (N = 507)	7 (35)	8 (38)	27 (136)	29 (145)	30 (153)
Blacks should build positive relationships with other minorities. (N = 509)	7 (35)	7 (35)	29 (150)	28 (140)	29 (149)

Socialization about Racialized Distrust—Intraracial (Cronbach's α = .64)

Statement					
Black people should not trust other blacks. (N = 509)	36 (181)	14 (72)	30 (152)	17 (85)	4 (19)
African Americans should be suspicious of working with Caribbeans and Africans. (N = 503)	42 (211)	14 (69)	28 (141)	12 (60)	4 (22)

Socialization about Racialized Distrust—Interracial (Cronbach's α = .75)

Statement					
Black people should not trust whites. (N = 507)	15 (77)	15 (74)	29 (149)	30 (150)	11 (57)
Black people should not trust Asian Americans. (N = 506)	40 (204)	14 (71)	33 (167)	9 (43)	4 (21)
Black people should not trust Latinos. (N = 509)	47 (241)	12 (62)	29 (149)	8 (43)	3 (14)
Black people should keep their guard up around whites. (N = 510)	9 (48)	8 (41)	26 (135)	34 (171)	23 (115)

(continued)

TABLE 3.2 (continued)

	Not emphasized at all % (n)	Not much emphasis % (n)	Neither emphasized nor deemphasized % (n)	Some emphasis % (n)	Much emphasis % (n)
Socialization about Black Politics (Cronbach's α = .80)					
Black people should fight against racial discrimination. (N = 512)	2 (11)	3 (16)	10 (49)	21 (109)	64 (327)
Black people should think about how politics affect black people as a group. (N = 506)	7 (33)	7 (34)	18 (89)	29 (147)	40 (203)
Blacks should consider ways to advance the black group in society. (N = 507)	4 (21)	4 (22)	19 (94)	30 (151)	43 (219)
Black people should start their own businesses to get ahead in life. (N = 510)	6 (32)	6 (30)	18 (93)	26 (133)	44 (222)
Socialization about Less Emphasis on Race (Cronbach's α = .46)					
Blacks should not care about what other racial groups think about them. (N = 505)	13 (68)	13 (64)	31 (158)	23 (114)	20 (101)
Blacks should think less about race and racism. (N = 508)	21 (105)	16 (83)	31 (158)	19 (97)	13 (65)
Black people should not think that all whites are racist. (N = 509)	9 (45)	7 (36)	19 (99)	36 (182)	29 (147)

Source: 2007 National Politics and Socialization Survey

Note: Percentages may not add up to 100 due to rounding.

TABLE 3.3
Categorical Emphases of Racial Socialization Messages

Emphasis of socialization	Black group status	Black pride	Skin-color discrimination	Black public behavior	Positive intraracial relations	Positive interracial relations	Intra-racialized distrust	Inter-racialized distrust	Black politics	Racelessness
Low										
%	2	3	59	5	4	6	49	28	3	12
Scale values	(0–2)	(0–3)	(0–1)	(0–2)	(0–3)	(0–3)	(0–2)	(0–4)	(0–4)	(0–3)
Medium										
%	15	30	23	24	44	61	42	57	23	73
Scale values	(3–5)	(4–9)	(2)	(3–5)	(4–9)	(4–9)	(3–5)	(5–10)	(5–10)	(4–9)
High										
%	83	67	18	71	52	33	9	15	74	15
Scale values	(6–8)	(10–12)	(3–4)	(6–8)	(10–12)	(10–12)	(6–8)	(11–16)	(11–16)	(10–12)
N	511	510	511	508	504	501	500	498	499	500

Source: 2007 National Political and Socialization Survey
Note: Percentages may not add up to 100 due to rounding.

TABLE 3.4

Ordered Probit Regression Models of Black Americans' Racial Socialization Messages

Covariates	Black status	Black pride	Skin-color discrimination (colorism)	Black public behavior	Positive intraracial relations	Positive interracial relations	Intra-racialized distrust	Inter-racialized distrust
Non–African American	.0785	-.1732	.2893	-.2720	-.1079	-.0768	.1535	-.1304
	(.2645)	(.2153)	(.2043)	(.2249)	(.2103)	(.2130)	(.2041)	(.2045)
Female	.1823	.1704	-.2226*	.0517	.0189	-.2513**	-.2691**	-.3318***
	(.1579)	(.1300)	(.1245)	(.1341)	(.1239)	(.1239)	(.1194)	(.1192)
Age	.0008	.0047	-.0062	.0115**	.0105**	.0081*	-.0018	.0022
	(.0058)	(.0048)	(.0046)	(.0049)	(.0046)	(.0046)	(.0045)	(.0044)
Income	.0844*	.0204	-.0017	.0206	.0237	.0318	.0133	.0364
	(.0448)	(.0360)	(.0345)	(.0366)	(.0340)	(.0344)	(.0330)	(.0332)
Education	.0979**	-.0022	.0330	.0245	-.0374	-.0275	.0281	.0272
	(.0428)	(.0339)	(.0320)	(.0348)	(.0320)	(.0322)	(.0309)	(.0307)
R's parent(s) born outside U.S.	-.3865	.1694	.0240	.0602	.5565	.2018	.3057	.5739*
	(.4028)	(.3399)	(.3309)	(.3450)	(.3421)	(.3586)	(.3255)	(.3306)
R's parent(s) grew up in South	.1797	.1950	.1415	.0387	.1297	.2810**	.1216	.1201
	(.1819)	(.1472)	(.1454)	(.1537)	(.1416)	(.1416)	(.1383)	(.1366)
R grew up mostly outside U.S.	-.3664	-.2785	.1758	.1636	-.8121**	-.1871	-.0126	-.4972
	(.4167)	(.3769)	(.3695)	(.3845)	(.3791)	(.3967)	(.3678)	(.3725)
R grew up in the South	-.0439	.1130	.2035	.0845	.0700	.0450	.0779	.0717
	(.1800)	(.1486)	(.1395)	(.1520)	(.1404)	(.1392)	(.1344)	(.1328)
R grew up in a mostly black neighborhood	.1741	.0443	.0461	.1966	.0668	-.1452	.0354	-.1180
	(.1574)	(.1289)	(.1229)	(.1319)	(.1224)	(.1220)	(.1186)	(.1170)
R's skin color (dark to light)	—	—	.1171	—	—	—	—	—
			(.0737)					
Cut 1	-.3954	-1.321	.7342	-.6902	-1.416	-1.392	.2218	-.1782
	(.5487)	(.4431)	(.4642)	(.4522)	(.4199)	(.4195)	(.4012)	(.4006)
Cut 2	.7270	.1119	1.402	.4942	.3276	.7025	1.619	1.521
	(.5428)	(.4363)	(.4666)	(.4488)	(.4137)	(.4162)	(.4065)	(.4054)
N	400	399	398	399	396	393	394	392
χ² probability	0.01	0.39	0.14	0.21	0.16	0.09	0.26	0.11
Pseudo R²	0.06	0.02	0.02	0.02	0.02	0.03	0.02	0.02

Covariates	Racialized distrust of whites	Racialized distrust of minorities	Overall racialized distrust	Black politics	Racelessness	Whites not racist	Factor 1: Black consciousness	Factor 2: Black protectiveness
Non–African American	-.1059 (.2044)	-.1431 (.2875)	.1316 (.2075)	.1305 (.2501)	.0825 (.2118)	-.0573 (.2239)	-.1387 (.2358)	-.1488 (.2095)
Female	-.2420** (.1176)	-.1586 (.1657)	-.2601** (.1198)	-.0342 (.1405)	.0821 (.1274)	.0521 (.1279)	.1579 (.1417)	-.3084** (.1228)
Age	.0004 (.0044)	-.0061 (.0061)	.0042 (.0045)	.0081 (.0052)	.0051 (.0047)	.0045 (.0049)	.0100* (.0053)	.0020 (.0046)
Income	.0171 (.0325)	.0115 (.0478)	.0305 (.0335)	.0464 (.0385)	.0016 (.0355)	.0977*** (.0366)	-.0128 (.0388)	.0100 (.0342)
Education	.0473 (.0305)	-.0265 (.0441)	.0435 (.0310)	.0169 (.0359)	-.0306 (.0327)	-.0674** (.0332)	-.0307 (.0372)	.0366 (.0316)
R's parent(s) born outside U.S.	.2432 (.3324)	.4753 (.4252)	.4232 (.3299)	.3650 (.3963)	.0679 (.3485)	.7054* (.3661)	.1539 (.3830)	.4477 (.3377)
R's parent(s) grew up in South	.1072 (.1352)	.0507 (.1942)	.0639 (.1378)	.1280 (.1572)	-.1812 (.1471)	.0015 (.1451)	.0334 (.1602)	.1021 (.1415)
R grew up mostly outside U.S.	-.2758 (.3652)	-.7703 (.5927)	-.3725 (.3772)	-.6996* (.4125)	.1618 (.3890)	-.1387 (.4232)	-.0252 (.4093)	-.2572 (.3798)
R grew up in the South	-.0720 (.1316)	.2291 (.1815)	.1977 (.1342)	.2179 (.1623)	.1248 (.1430)	.1752 (.1444)	.2628 (.1681)	.1927 (.1382)
R grew up in a mostly black neighborhood	-.0285 (.1159)	-.3613** (.1652)	.0001 (.1180)	.0373 (.1385)	-.1657 (.1253)	-.2336* (.1275)	.1786 (.1405)	-.0313 (.1212)
R's skin color (dark to light)	—	—	—	—	—	—	—	.1447** (.0738)
Cut 1	-.5183 (.3975)	.4725 (.5404)	.4075 (.4046)	-.8639 (.4742)	.1194 (.4270)	-.8738 (.4372)	-.9535 (.4813)	.7343 (.4642)
Cut 2	.7600 (.3985)	.7677 (.5413)	2.074 (.4130)	.2745 (.4696)	.4762 (.4273)	.3318 (.4357)	.2904 (.4756)	2.474 (.4752)
N	395	395	388	393	395	397	384	386
χ² probability	0.46	0.40	0.10	0.29	0.62	0.04	0.23	0.06
Pseudo R²	0.01	0.03	0.02	0.02	0.01	0.03	0.03	0.03

Source: 2007 National Politics and Socialization Survey

Note: Standard errors are indicated in parentheses.

* p ≤ .10; ** p ≤ .05; *** p ≤ .01; **** p ≤ .001

"high-emphasis" messages about black pride, with 30 percent having received "medium-level" emphasis on this message. Unfortunately, however, none of the variables modeled for the black-pride scale predict the scale.

Socialization about Skin-Color Discrimination

Another downside of racial construction and racial discrimination in the United States is the discrimination of black Americans against one another based on *colorism* (see M. Hill 2000; Russell, Wilson, and Hall 1992). Historically, not only were lighter-skinned blacks able to choose to reap the benefits of "passing for white"[3] if their skin color and their facial features were perceivably "white" and Eurocentric, but also white society and even many blacks themselves esteemed lighter-skinned blacks' value to be more than blacks with darker skin hues. For women, colorism remains an unsettling issue, especially as far as beauty norms that value Eurocentric beauty more than Afrocentric beauty (Russell, Wilson, and Hall 1992; M. Hill 2000; Turner 2005). Some scholars even note the disparate effect of skin color on blacks' socioeconomic status (Hochschild 2006; Hochschild and Weaver 2007). Thus, despite the historical nature of colorism, this concept is relevant for black Americans' contemporary understandings of what it means to be black in America. More specifically, the black discrimination/colorism measure comprises one question that asks respondents whether they learned, "Black people should treat one another differently based on whether or not they are light-skinned."

Forty-eight percent of the respondents reported that they did not receive "any emphasis at all" on this message about skin-color discrimination among black Americans. Moreover, a little over one-fifth of the respondents reported that this message was "neither emphasized nor deemphasized." Learning about skin-color discrimination's being a part of how black Americans should treat one another, in fact, is the least emphasized racial socialization message across all the messages examined, with 59 percent of respondents reporting that this message was conveyed to them with "low-level emphasis."

The model of colorism shows that women received less emphasis on messages about skin-color discrimination than men did, which disconfirms the hypothesis that women would receive greater emphasis on this message. Evidence about gender's being an important predictor of colorism seems to suggest that there are gender-distinctive emphases on messages that may even contribute to the "color complex" and intraracial color distinctions that appraise beauty and worth on the basis of skin complexion (Russell, Wilson, and Hall 1992), but perhaps this specific message is transmitted more to men. Although the measure did not ask the respondents about whether they were taught that skin-color discrimination is "wrong," the results beg the question of how socialization agents socialize women (girls) versus men (boys) about skin color and what this entails for self-esteem, intraracial interactions, and conceptions of beauty among black Americans.

Socialization about Black Behavior in Public

Historically, black people also have faced the challenge of controlling the imagery of blackness in order to counter society's negative racial stereotypes. To this end, black Americans have opted to display "appropriate" black behavior in public (Higginbotham 1993; Gaines 1996). "Appropriate" black behavior stresses refinement and good comportment, especially in the presence of whites, who historically would have characterized blacks as savage, hypersexual buffoons (Gaines 1996; Bogle 2001). Two measures in the NPSS ask respondents to consider the extent to which racial socialization messages emphasized displaying certain behavior in public as a black person: (1) "Black people should try to avoid behaviors that are characteristic of black stereotypes," and (2) "Black people should be sure to act properly when they are in public." These measures are combined into a scale (0–8) about socialization about black behavior in public, and the scale has an acceptable Cronbach's alpha coefficient ($\alpha = .74$).

According to the results shown in table 3.2, 45 percent (n = 227) of respondents received socialization about avoiding black stereotypical behavior with "much emphasis," compared to 27 percent (n = 140) with "some emphasis"; 17 percent (n = 87) reported, however, that this message was "neither emphasized nor deemphasized." A majority of black Americans (52 percent; n = 264) received messages with "much emphasis" about black people acting properly in public. In the categorized scale of socialization about black behavior in public (shown in table 3.3), 71 percent reported "high emphasis" on this message, compared to 24 percent who reported "medium emphasis."

The only statistically significant explanatory factor in the model is age, indicating that older blacks reported having received more emphasis on messages about blacks behaving well in public, in order to fight negative representations of the black racial group. Generational differences have been documented between blacks born before *Brown v. Board of Education* (pre-1954) and those born after *Brown* (post-1954), and studies confirm that there is a correlation between black Americans' current racial attitudes and the racial socialization messages that they received in childhood (Brown and Lesane-Brown 2006).

While the results of racial socialization about public behavior offer no clear-cut connection between these messages and racial attitudes, there is room to believe that such relationships exist between racial socialization and racial attitudes, as I discuss in the next chapter. That age also influences blacks' receiving more emphasis on intraracial relations also suggests that different age cohorts have potentially variant attitudes about race and trust. This seems likely given the progression of race relations in America.

Socialization about Positive Black Intraracial Relations

The black Diaspora comprises people with African descent from the continent of Africa, the Caribbean, and the United States. While many blacks in America have long ancestral heritage in the United States, approximately 7 percent of blacks are foreign born and come from countries in the Caribbean and Africa (U.S. Census Bureau 2004). Despite being considered black in the United States, these black ethnic groups have different cultural experiences than do native-born blacks and perhaps even have different histories with race in their former countries (Rogers 2000, 2006; Waters 1994, 1999). Moreover, some of the relationships between these black ethnic groups have been more competitive than friendly (Assensoh 2000; Rogers 2000, 2006). A racial socialization message that emphasizes that "blacks have different ethnicities, and they should work together" inculcates positive black intraracial relations, especially across ethnicity.

In the NPSS, a majority of black respondents received this message with "much" or "some" emphasis. Nonetheless, almost a quarter of respondents received messages that were "neither emphasized nor deemphasized." In the broader spirit of embracing all black people's building positive relationships with one another, most respondents reported that they received "much emphasis" (60 percent; n =310) or "some emphasis" (19 percent; n = 100) on messages that suggested that "black people should get along with one another." As far as messages about the extent to which "black men and women should treat one another well," most respondents also stated that they received "much" (62 percent; n = 316) or "some" (18 percent; n = 94) emphasis on this message. Once the messages are combined into the additive scale of black intraracial relations, we see in table 3.3 that most respondents received "high emphasis" on this aspect of racial socialization (52 percent;

n = 262), compared to 44 percent (n = 222) of respondents who reported "medium emphasis."

In the model for racial socialization about positive intraracial relations, shown in table 3.4, there are no ethnic differences in learning emphasis about this message. However, older blacks were more likely than younger blacks to have received more emphasis on building positive relations with fellow black group members. Older blacks may have learned these messages more than younger black Americans because they lived during an era when the collective social, political, and economic experiences of blacks as a racial group (irrespective of ethnicity) were salient in the fight against racial discrimination. Over time, despite the continuing significance of race, younger black Americans may have learned these messages with less emphasis, as their parents may have felt the world was changing in ways that did not necessitate specific messages about retaining a black community based on intraracial similarity. If these messages are not emphasized similarly over time, an important question is, what does this mean for learning about valuing relationships within the black community? Moreover, how will these age and generational differences in learning affect identity within the black community?[4]

What is interesting is that for those blacks who grew up mostly outside the United States, they received less emphasis on building positive, intraracial relations. Perhaps this speaks to the racial context in which they learned about being black. Intraracial unity outside the United States may be less of a sociopolitical resource because the political context dictates that people organize along other social cleavages. For instance, in a predominantly black society, focusing on intraracial relations would be seemingly moot because race is not a social group that defines social, economic, or political interests.

Socialization about Positive Interracial Relations

In addition to black people's learning about getting along with their own racial group members, learning about being black in America involves learning about the relationship of black Americans to other racial groups. Because of the historically strained relationships between blacks and whites, it is expected that blacks' learning about whites' roles in perpetrating de jure discrimination should be accentuated. For southern blacks, learning about relating to whites included learning about racial etiquette, or how to act properly in the presence of whites, making sure to exemplify their deference to whites (Ritterhouse 2006; Brown and Lesane-Brown 2006). But, despite learning about historical etiquette and denigrating aspects of black-white discrimination throughout much of American history, black Americans also can learn messages that blacks should try to get along with whites. Whites who were friendly to blacks and who participated in the civil rights movements, for example, we would expect would not be viewed negatively in ways that whites who were wedded to blacks' subjugation would be.

As for messages learned about other nonwhite racial groups—Asian Americans and Latinos—these groups also experienced discrimination in ways similar to black Americans (McClain and Stewart 2006). These experiences can be perceived by blacks as integral for learning about nonwhite racial groups and a shared minority-group status. More important, these experiences can support messages of getting along with minority groups.

Messages about positive interracial relations include the following three messages: (1) "Black people should get along with whites," (2) "Black people should get along with other racial minorities," and (3) "Blacks should build positive relationships with other minorities." As noted in table 3.2, the highest percentage of respondents, 32 percent (n = 161), reported that they received "much emphasis" on "getting along with whites," and another 31 percent (n = 157) received this message with "some emphasis"; 24 percent of respondents (n = 120), however, reported that "getting along with whites" was "neither emphasized nor deemphasized" as a racial socialization message. Thus, while black Americans learn about historical discrimination against blacks and perhaps even the role that whites played in this discrimination, positive emphatic messages about getting along with whites also are relayed to black Americans.

As for the message about "getting along with other racial minorities," the highest percentage of respondents, 30 percent (n = 153), reported that they received this message with "much emphasis," with 29 percent (n = 145) reporting this message was delivered with "some emphasis." Yet 27 percent (n = 136) claimed that getting along with racial minorities was a message that was "neither emphasized nor deemphasized." When asked if they were taught that "blacks should build positive relationships with other minorities," an equal percentage of respondents responded that they had with "much emphasis" (29 percent; n = 149) as responded that the message was "neither emphasized nor deemphasized" (29 percent; n = 150).

When the measures for getting along with whites and racial minorities and building positive relations are measured as an additive scale, as table 3.3 indicates, 61 percent (n = 306) received "medium emphasis" on messages about intergroup relations, with only 33 percent (n = 165) receiving "high emphasis" on this racial socialization message. According to the results in table 3.4, being older and having parents that grew up in the South increases the likelihood that one received emphasis on messages about positive interracial relations.

The results seem to suggest that parents who grew up in the South (especially older parents) made a concerted effort to stress to their children the importance of building positive relations across races, and this message transmission seems to occur notwithstanding the southern history of blacks and whites, especially. Black women, however, had less emphasis than did black men did on building positive interracial relations, perhaps indicating the protective nature of how parents navigate race on the basis on gender. Emphasizing positive racial relations for boys more than for girls may suggest parents' attempts to safeguard their male children from racial confrontation and fatal violence that black men face disproportionately compared to black women, although black women disproportionately face sexual violation compared to black men (Pinar 2001).

Socialization about Intraracial Distrust

As displayed in table 3.2, the highest percentage of respondents, 36 percent (n = 181), reported that they received "no emphasis at all" on racial socialization messages that conveyed "not trusting other blacks." Another 30 percent (n = 152) of respondents report this message was "neither emphasized nor de-emphasized." Yet, 17 percent (n = 85) of respondents state that they, in fact, received "some emphasis" on this message. The same is the case as far as what black respondents learned about "relating to black Americans with different ethnicities." For messages that black respondents learned about "being suspicious [of] working with Caribbeans and Africans," most respondents (42 percent; n = 211) report that intraracial, ethnic suspicion was "not emphasized at all." At the same time, however, this message may not have been a salient part of many respondents' racial socialization messages, as 28 percent (n = 141) report that this message was "neither emphasized nor de-emphasized."

When we examine table 3.3 for the percentage of respondents receiving low- (0–2), medium- (3–5), or high- (6–8) emphasis about intraracial distrust, we see that 49 percent (n = 245) learned "low-emphasis" on intraracial distrust messages, followed by 42 percent (n = 210) who learned this message with "medium-level" emphasis, and only 9 percent (n = 45) who learned "high-emphasis." When we turn to the model of socialization about intra-racialized distrust featured in table 3.4, we see that the only statistically discernible factor is gender. Black women learned less emphasis than black men about distrusting other blacks.

Socialization about Interracial Distrust

In comparison to messages about distrust in other blacks, as we see in table 3.2, respondents were generally not told messages that emphasized distrust in Asian Americans (40 percent; n = 204) and Latinos (47 percent; n = 241). However, when we turn to the percentage of black respondents who received messages emphasizing distrust in whites, or "keep(ing) their guard up when they are among whites," 56 percent of respondents received emphasis on this message. Still, a little over a quarter of respondents reported that this message was "neither emphasized nor deemphasized." Comparatively, roughly two-fifths of blacks reported having received messages that emphasized distrust in whites. Meanwhile, almost 30 percent indicated that distrust in whites was "neither emphasized nor deemphasized."

The additive scale of all interracial distrust measures in table 3.3 indicates that most respondents (57 percent; n = 283) received "medium-level" emphasis on interracial distrust. Only 15 percent of the respondents (n = 75) reported "high emphasis" on interracial distrust. In this case, black women were less likely than black men to have received emphasis on interracial distrust. Yet, unexpectedly, there is modest evidence that people with parents born outside the United States received higher emphasis on interracial distrust.

When we examine separate models of racial socialization messages about distrust of whites and distrust of Asian Americans and Latinos, black women were socialized less emphatically than were black men about distrust of whites but also about overall distrust in nonblack groups; however, there were no gender differences in socialization about distrust of nonwhites. The only factor statistically discernible in this model is growing up in a predominantly black neighborhood, which reduced the likelihood that blacks learned messages emphasizing distrust of other racial minorities.

Socialization about Black Politics

Dawson (1994) argues that black linked fate, or the linkage of the political interests of individual black Americans to the political interests of the larger black racial group, is learned by way of socialization messages. The racial socialization messages that emphasize black politics should include messages about group-centered political and economic interests and group-based political strategies. Accordingly, I investigate four messages related to socialization about black politics: (1) fighting discrimination, (2) thinking about how politics affects black people as a group, (3) considering ways to advance blacks in society, and (4) starting black businesses to advance black people's socioeconomic standing.

As evident in table 3.2, with 64 percent of respondents having received "much emphasis" on fighting racial discrimination, this was the most highly emphasized message about black politics. While socialization about black consciousness, or thinking about how politics affects blacks as a group, and black group advancement were not emphasized as much as fighting racial discrimination, black respondents mostly reported having had emphasis on messages stressing group-centered thinking. This also includes political thinking about building a black economy in order to promote socioeconomic advancement.

Table 3.3 shows that 74 percent of respondents reported having received "high emphasis" on messages about sustaining black group politics. In the model of socialization about black politics scale, a very modest relationship exists regarding one's having grown up mostly outside the United States: blacks who grew up outside the United States received less emphasis on messages advocating politics that advance the black racial group.

Socialization about Racelessness

While racial socialization implies that one learns specifically about the ways that race affects one's livelihood, racial socialization can also take the form of emphasizing the extent to which race should *not* be central in one's life. That is, black Americans also can be socialized that (1) they should not care about what other racial groups think about them, (2) they should think less about race and racism, and (3) they should not think that all whites are racist —what I term here as socialization that emphasizes *racelessness*.

For one, learning that "blacks should not care about what other racial groups think about them" suggests that in not thinking about what other racial groups think, one is able to live comfortably without considering the effect that race, racial distinction, or racial disparagement may have on one's life. Second, one may learn, specifically, "Blacks should think less about race and racism," which implies that perhaps blacks focus too much on race. In addition, it can imply that by not thinking about race, blacks may stand to achieve some better, common good, because in thinking that race is an impediment to one's progress blacks hold themselves back. Finally, given the historically segregated relationship between blacks and whites, whites as a group may be perceived as culpable in blacks' racial discrimination. This is to say that one may think that *all* whites are racist. Thus, a socialization message that deemphasizes race and racism among whites would suggest that "all whites are not racist."

When respondents were asked how emphatic were messages about racelessness in their learning about being black, about "not caring about what other racial groups think about them" and "thinking less about race and racism," as shown in table 3.2, the highest percentage of respondents reported that these messages were "neither emphasized nor deemphasized" (31 percent). Nonetheless, combining respondents who received either "some emphasis" or "much emphasis" on messages about not caring what other races think, over 43 percent of respondents received emphasis on this message.

As far as the message about "thinking less about race and racism," in comparison, just over one-fifth of respondents stated that this message was "not emphasized at all." However, with respect to "not thinking that all whites are racist," the highest percentage of respondents, 36 percent (n = 182), received this message with "some emphasis," with just under 30 percent having received this message with "much emphasis." Thus, despite blacks' having learned about racial discrimination against them and most likely having learned about how whites played a role in this discrimination, negative messages about whites were counterbalanced with those that emphasized not characterizing all whites as being racist.

In all, when we analyze the results of the additive scale to check for the percentage of respondents who had different emphases in messages about "racelessness," we see that in a scale from 0 to 12 (0–3, low; 4–9, medium; 10–12, high), as shown in table 3.3, most respondents, or 73 percent (n = 365), reported "medium emphasis" on messages about racelessness, although there is almost an even split between those who received either "low emphasis" (12 percent; n = 58) or "high emphasis" (15 percent; n = 77) on messages about racelessness. The Cronbach's alpha coefficient for the "racelessness" scale, however, is very low and does not meet conventional standards, and the ordered probit model offers no statistically significant predictive relationships.

However, when we turn to a model that specifically analyzes determinants for messages about "not all whites being racist," several factors influence blacks' having received emphasis on this message. Blacks with higher incomes and, interestingly, parents who grew up in the South received greater emphasis on all whites' not being racist. On the other hand, having higher levels of education and growing up in a predominantly black neighborhood reduced emphasis on messages that all whites are not racist. With more education, blacks possibly learn more about historical relationships between blacks and whites that provide broader references to the racism of whites. Living in a mostly black neighborhood also may enhance the feelings of racial isolation, often attributed to segregation in housing in the United States (Massey and Denton 1993).

Underlying Factors of Racial Socialization

To determine underlying constructs for the ten scales of racial socialization, first I test the reliability coefficient for the combined racial socialization measures. The racelessness measure (excluding the "whites are not mostly racist" measure) decreases the reliability of the socialization scale. Therefore, I exclude it from a principal components analysis, which identifies latent constructs in the measures. Subsequently, two factors emerge in the data: (1) *black consciousness* (factor 1: including the scales of black status [Eigenvalue 0.75], black pride [Eigenvalue 0.83], black public behavior [Eigenvalue 0.67], intraracial relations [Eigenvalue 0.86], interracial relations [Eigenvalue .72], and black politics [Eigenvalue 0.87]) and (2) *black protectiveness* (factor 2: including the scales of skin-color discrimination [Eigenvalue 0.79], intraracial distrust [Eigenvalue 0.87], and interracial distrust [Eigenvalue 0.84]).[5]

Table 3.4 shows that for the black consciousness factor, there is a modest effect of age, such that older black Americans received greater emphasis on measures emphasizing black solidarity and building positive relationships among nonblack group members. Of the two factors emerging in the data, the black protectiveness measure also has the better fit.

As for the black protectiveness factor, black women received less emphasis than black men did on racial socialization messages that impart caution in navigating race relations. The gender difference in socialization emphasis on protective messages, once again, seems to reflect possible distinctions in messages that parents feel disproportionately affect black men more than black women, as an artifact perhaps of historical experiences of black men versus black women in the American racial structure. Contrary to the expectation that darker-skinned blacks receive greater emphasis on protective messages to prepare them for colorism based on bias against darker-skinned blacks, here, lighter-skinned blacks received more emphasis on messages warning about the vagaries of racial mistreatment. Maybe this is because lighter-skinned blacks are aware of their historically favored treatment, and they are cautious of being treated differently or poorly because of this history.

Summary and Conclusion: The Implications of Racial Socialization for Trust

Results from the 2007 NPSS elucidate the crucial role that black parents play in socializing their children about what it means to be black in America. In the racial socialization of black Americans, the most emphatic message that black Americans learn about being black in America concerns the group's historical experiences with racial discrimination, suggesting the willingness of black Americans to retain black collective memory about their racial status in U.S. history. But in addition to learning about the historically negative effects of black group exclusion and discrimination on blacks' status in America, black Americans in the survey learned messages about black pride that conveyed the positive value of black culture, heritage, and contributions to society, all of which seem to undergird a larger message about resiliency of the black racial group amid a history of racial oppression.

The second-most-emphasized racial socialization message conveyed to black Americans is black politics, or becoming engaged politically on behalf of black group interests. This message relays a concern about overcoming racial discrimination and promoting socioeconomic advancement for black Americans' social mobility. Moreover, learning proper display of black public behavior instills the value of countering negative black stereotypes. This politicizing message implicitly supports black Americans' retaining control over black imagery and black cultural production, which historically have been used by whites to negatively stereotype "blackness" (see Bogle 2001).

Racial socialization messages stressing positive intraracial relations among black group members support instilling a sense of community across black ethnic variation. Messages emphasizing racial solidarity can prove meaningful for mobilization efforts and what Marion Orr (1999) describes as black social capital, and a large percentage of blacks received emphasis on building positive intraracial relationships. In contrast, black discrimination based on colorism—historically used to create complexion hierarchies and divisiveness in the black community—would detract from blacks' racial solidarity. Despite the historical significance of this intraracial discrimination, colorism, or messages that people should discriminate based on skin color, is the least emphasized racial socialization message. Thus, black American parents, by not stressing colorism, seem to recognize its potential for sustaining chasms in the black community. Regardless of the low emphasis on this racial socialization message, as the results from the NPSS indicate, men received these messages with greater emphasis than did black women, suggesting that black men are taught more disparaging messages about colorism. This supports evidence that many black men prefer dating women with lighter skin hues, consequently affecting partnership opportunities for black women who are subjected to these preferences (Hunter 2002; Hill 2000).

With respect to building positive interracial relations with whites, Asian Americans, and Latinos, black Americans mostly received medium-level emphasis on this message. Thus, despite awareness of blacks' historical racial discrimination experiences interracially, not many blacks received high emphasis on messages inculcating interracial distrust. More blacks received low-level emphasis on intraracial distrust than they received on interracial distrust. Nevertheless, for interracial distrust, most blacks received medium-level emphasis on this message. More specifically, respondents received different emphasis on messages about trust of Asian Americans and Latinos than they did about whites. Blacks were more likely to report that they received messages suggesting some *dis*trust of whites, whereas they reported having received "no emphasis at all" on messages about distrusting Asian Americans and Latinos. Generally, interracialized distrust messages concentrate more on blacks' distrust of whites. Historically hierarchical relationships between blacks and whites, logically, lead to messages focusing on perceptions of whites in blacks' interracial relationships in the United States.

Notwithstanding these historical relationships, black families as major agents of racial socialization are not overly fixated on inculcating messages about whites. Rather, racial socialization messages that black families convey seem to focus on imparting knowledge about U.S. racial history, protecting their children against prospective racial discrimination, and promoting concepts integral to the social, political, and economic advancement of the black racial group. Emphasizing messages about interracial relationships also appears to be secondary to black parents' concerns about positive characterizations and mobility of the black racial group. As the two resultant factors of the several racial socialization scales suggest, black racial consciousness and black protectiveness messages are prevalent in black families' transmission of racial knowledge.

Despite the foci of these factors and their intent to prepare blacks for racial discrimination, the probability that a black person is discriminated against remains uncertain. This *racial uncertainty* influences how black

Americans interact in their social and political environments. It is thus pertinent to determine what effect black consciousness and black protectiveness messages have on ways that blacks perceive other racial groups and navigate racial uncertainty. For, how blacks perceive racial groups and how they perceive their likelihood for racial discrimination are important indicators of trustworthiness. On the one hand, greater emphasis on racial socialization about positive black racial consciousness should enhance intraracial and interracial trust. On the other hand, greater emphasis on racial protectiveness should reduce intraracial and interracial trust. Both factors of racial socialization still center on the significance of race in blacks' lives. Despite the fact that racial socialization about caring less about race did not load well as a factor of racial socialization, it is important to gauge what influence, if any, such messages have on racial and trust attitudes. Receiving higher emphasis on this message should not affect how one perceives other racial groups, but controlling for this message will empirically indicate whether it is consequential. The message emphasizing that "whites are not racist," however, should take on a different flavor. Those who were taught this message should perceive whites more positively.

Aside from the transmission of racial socialization messages in blacks' formative years of development, scholars recognize that socialization is an ongoing process. For example, as I mentioned previously, William Cross (1991) explicates a theory of Nigrescence that involves several stages of racial awareness, learning, and navigation of race in blacks' interpersonal relationships. Similarly, I recognize the incremental development of racial knowledge over blacks' lifetimes. Differently, however, I focus on the influence of formative racial socialization experiences on blacks' perceptions of race and its effect on them as group members, in order to illustrate how blacks use internalized racial knowledge as a reference to inform their quotidian experiences. While personal experiences continue to update blacks' racial awareness, I suggest that their identities are structured early in life, remain relatively stable, and adapt to racial experiences to avoid the harm of distrustful and poor, cross-racial relations.

In the next chapter, I explore how black Americans' racial socialization experiences influence their perceptions of discrimination, their perceptions of intergroup relations, their perceptions of racial group stereotypes, and their perceptions of the frequency of personal discrimination experiences. It is only through the analyses of intraracial and interracial attitudes that we can learn how racial socialization messages affect black racial predispositions and, ultimately, influence black Americans' trust. Given several gender differences in learning about racialized distrust, we should expect that with less emphasis on messages about racialized distrust, black women should be less likely than black men to subscribe to discriminating beliefs about other racial groups. Older black Americans also should display more affinities for in-group, intraracial contacts. As we learn in the next chapters, however, the black gender differences do not parcel out as stated here. Additionally, older black Americans actually express more affinities than younger people toward intergroup, interracial contacts. Further analysis of blacks' attitudes speaks to the complexities of these factors and their effects on racial perceptions.

4

Trust No One

Navigating Race and Racism

Black Americans' Contemporary Racial Discrimination Experiences

It would be ahistorical not to acknowledge that much of the fret about racial discrimination rests among nonwhites, who in the American racial hierarchy have been historically and socially constructed as the negation of whites and deemed inferior to them (Bonilla-Silva 2001; Pickering 2001). Therefore, it comes as no surprise that, generally, nonwhites perceive more racial discrimination than whites do (Sigelman and Welch 1991; Weitzer and Tuch 2004).

Despite the abolition of Jim Crow, the arrival of an era of supposed equality before the law, and declining trends in whites' animosity toward blacks (Schuman et al. 1997; Tuch, Sigelman, and MacDonald 1999), black Americans living in the post–Jim Crow United States continue to experience and perceive racial discrimination (Sigelman and Welch 1991; Laudrine and Klonoff 1996; Sanders Thompson 1992, 1996; Jefferson and Caldwell 2002; Sellers and Shelton 2003; Combs et al. 2006). More nuanced, however, are blacks' perceptions that blacks' disproportionate indigence is increasingly being attributed more to group members' personal commitment to group advancement rather than being attributed to systemic discrimination (Hunt 2007). Black Americans, nevertheless, continue to perceive that their race leads others to threaten the quality of their everyday lives, as they continue to experience racial discrimination in public places (Feagin 1991; Sigelman and Welch 1991; Broman, Mavaddat, and Hsu 2000; Rodriguez 2008). To illustrate, higher-income blacks report more experiences with racial discrimination in their work, education, and living environments than do lower-income blacks (Hochschild 1995). Still, evidence suggests that people with lower incomes perceive more employment discrimination than do people with higher incomes (Rodriguez 2008).

Despite the fact that both black men and black women mostly attribute their discrimination experiences to their race (Rodriguez 2008), evidence suggests that black men and black women perceive discrimination differently and more frequently in certain contexts (Broman, Mavaddat, and Hsu 2000). For example, black men report more discrimination experiences than black women do in their relations with police, especially via racial profiling and police harassment (Weitzer and Tuch 2004, 2006; Brunson and Miller 2006), and in the context of employment and housing (Rodriguez 2008). Notwithstanding some evidence that both black men and women perceive that they are discriminated against in the workplace and in shopping places (Broman, Mavaddat, and Hsu 2000), black men generally perceive discrimination in those places more than black women do (Rodriguez 2008). Black men's perceptions of systemic discrimination also are heightened with higher levels of racial identity, whereas black women's perceptions of systemic discrimination increase with perceptions of blacks' power imbalances in American society (Reese and Brown 1995). More generally, a greater number of black men and black women than white men and white women report being perceived as mistrusted, perhaps as a consequence of their race (Rodriguez 2008). Thus, it seems the uncertain probabilities attached to discrimination and race would enhance blacks' concern about the likelihood of being mistreated due to their race wherever they go, and such uncertainty seems to promulgate a groundswell of distrusting attitudes in people in contexts where blacks have been discriminated against the most.

Furthermore, as much as 60 percent of African Americans experience or encounter racial discrimination throughout their lifetime (Kessler, Mickelson, and Williams 1999), and these experiences are evident even among young black adults, a generation that did not experience de jure and de facto segregation. For example, 41 percent of African American college students report that they have heard racial epithets, 41 percent report that they have heard them frequently, and 59 percent report that they have been the targets of such remarks (Kessler, Mickelson, and Williams 1999). In an era of supposed equality, moreover, younger blacks perceive more discrimination in ambiguous social relations than older blacks do (Broman, Mavaddat, and Hsu 2000; Rodriguez 2008). It is even more unsettling that physical violence committed against blacks because of their race continues even today in America's post–Jim Crow society.[1]

Considering black Americans' perpetual experiences with racial discrimination, it is highly likely that they are concerned about being racially discriminated against in their future social interactions with other racial groups.

Just as racial socialization messages influence black identity, they also should influence how people process racial information such as racial stereotypes, the frequency of racial discrimination experiences, and the perceived risk for prospective racial discrimination, all of which can influence how blacks interact with others, especially nonblack group members.

For example, it seems likely that black Americans who received emphasis on protectiveness racial socialization messages (factor 2) should have a higher likelihood of perceiving the risk of racial discrimination in their intergroup interactions. Socialization messages emphasizing racial consciousness (factor 1) should only increase positive attitudes toward black and nonblack groups, excluding perhaps whites, who have historically been associated with disparaging blacks. Although, as noted in the previous chapter, socialization about whites' not being racist did not load well as a part of the two racial socialization factors, such a message may have import for reducing negative attributions about whites, in particular. Likewise, racial socialization messages emphasizing race's mattering less, which also proved to be a poor fit with the two racial socialization factors, should reduce the subscription to racial stereotypes, the perception of the likelihood of prospective racial discrimination, and the reported frequency of racial discrimination experiences.

In order to understand factors that influence how blacks perceive the risk of racial discrimination, or what I call *racial uncertainty*, in this chapter I examine how racial socialization experiences influence the ways that blacks process racial information. This chapter investigates the determinants and the processing of race for blacks with respect to their racial homogenization, racial uncertainty, and personal racial discrimination experiences. In particular, I am interested in determining how racial socialization influences blacks' perceptions about their interracial interactions, their subscription to racial stereotypes (as a part of racially homogenizing various groups, or Effect 2), and their perceived discrimination experiences both prospectively and retrospectively (Effect 3: Racial Uncertainty and Effect 4: Racial Discrimination).

Race, Risk, and Black Americans' Interracial Attitudes and Interactions

Race has structured differential power and resources between whites and nonwhites, including African Americans, American Indians, Asian Americans, and Latinos (Omi and Winant 1994). Differences in power between groups increase perceptions of risk in their social interactions (Lupton

1999), and as noted previously, perceived power imbalances between blacks and others increase blacks' belief in the discriminatory practices of societal institutions. Blacks' uncertainty about how race will affect their being discriminated against suggests that they may be concerned about the risk of being racially discriminated against in future interracial interactions, or what I have referred to previously as *racial uncertainty*. To reiterate, racial uncertainty is the set of conditions under which actors of different races are uncertain about the discriminatory interests and behaviors of people who are members of racial groups other than their own who may pose an adverse risk of harm to them as a member of a different racial group.

Risk can be defined in numerous ways, and knowledge about risk is culturally defined (Rayner 1992; Rohrmann and Renn 2000). Here, I conceptualize risk to account for outcomes that are adverse to blacks as black racial group members—principally, the risks and harm experienced from racial discrimination. Risk, in this circumstance, is heightened in interracial relations, as race functions as a heuristic for processing information about the person with whom people interact. Therefore, the perceived heightened risks in interracial relations should increase racial uncertainty more between people with different racial group memberships (in- and out-group members) than between those with shared racial group membership (in-group members). Put in these terms, more simply, when blacks interact with nonblack group members, they assume an uncertain, probabilistic risk of racial discrimination. Historical references, or racial knowledge, inform blacks about the potential for racial discrimination. Borrowing from cultural theories of risk, which emphasize that risk is defined based on perceptions and principles inherent to the social organization of society (Rayner 1992), I suggest that blacks perceive risk in intergroup interactions based on how they process racial information.

Scholars recognize that people can be risk averse or risk acceptant, depending on whether they perceive that the benefits outweigh the costs of a risk (Kahneman and Tversky 2000). If we were to apply this same logic of risk to social interactions and racial discrimination, then some people may be more inclined to engage in interracial interactions than others because they perceive the risks of these interactions differently. This presents an interesting question: how do blacks come to understand the perceived risks of interacting interracially? The literature on interracial attitudes and interracial contact offers several possible influences on race and risk, but more important, it implicates the relationship that racial identity and racial context may have on racial knowledge, aside from racial socialization experiences.

For one, the literature on blacks' perceptions of racial discrimination suggests that racial consciousness is an important predictor of perceived racial bias. Black Americans with higher levels of black consciousness are more likely to attribute racial discrimination to whites than they are to blacks (Caldwell and Jefferson 2002). Those who view race as central to their identity also are more likely to perceive racial discrimination in ambiguously discriminatory events. Moreover, black Americans who subscribe to a nationalist racial ideology are more likely to report discrimination experiences (Sellers and Shelton 2003). Therefore, having a closer identity to other blacks and feeling an interconnection to their fates, or what is referred to as "black linked fate" (Dawson 1994), should enhance perceptions of racial discrimination and racial uncertainty.

Interracial attitudes also affect how blacks interact with racial groups, and vice versa. For example, blacks who have close social interactions with whites have more positive interracial attitudes about them as a group (Ellison and Powers 1994; Powers and Ellison 1995). In addition, black women, younger blacks, and higher-income blacks are more likely than black men, older blacks, and lower-income blacks to believe that whites think about blacks in negative, stereotypical ways, and they also are less likely to believe that whites have positive attitudes about blacks (Ellison and Powers 1994; Powers and Ellison 1995). A large number of blacks (well over a majority) believe that whites harbor negative stereotypes about blacks as a racial group (Sigelman and Tuch 1997). Blacks and whites also are more likely to misinterpret nonverbal interracial communication than they are to misinterpret nonverbal intraracial communication (Weathers, Frank, and Spell 2002). These interracial attitudes and perceptions suggest that blacks will more likely perceive their interactions with whites in suspicious ways.

Scholars also find that racial groups perceive one another in zero-sum terms, based on the threat that racial groups pose to them in social or economic contexts (Sigelman and Welch 1991; Bobo and Hutchings 1996). Aside from the suspicion that blacks may have about whites, blacks' perceptions of tangible group threat are higher for Asian Americans and Latinos than they are for whites in the economic context. Blacks who possess more negative perceptions about their own group also are more likely to report negative attitudes about Asian Americans and Latinos (Cummings and Lambert 1997).

Despite the inclination to believe that heightened black racial identity increases social distance between blacks and nonblacks, research suggests otherwise (Reese and Brown 1995). Greater social distance, however, is more likely when blacks live in racially isolated environments, wherein blacks or

whites constitute a majority, leading them to become more likely to subscribe to negative racial stereotypes about other racial groups (Gay 2004;
Oliver and Wong 2003; Oliver and Mendelberg 2000). A greater extent of
interracial contact between black Americans and other racial groups also can
induce more positive attitudes about other racial groups (D. Harris 1995).
What is implied from this research is that the racial composition of one's living context and interracial contact can influence positive or negative attitudes
about members of other racial groups. Racial isolation, or living in areas that
are predominantly composed of one's own racial group, thus, seems likely
to increase blacks' negative perceptions of members of other racial groups.
With this expectation, blacks living in predominantly black neighborhoods
would be expected to think of nonblacks more negatively.

As a general trend, by the 1990s, African American youth expressed less
positive views about interracial interactions than they had in the 1970s and
1980s (Tuch, Sigelman, and MacDonald 1999). Thus, increasingly, race relations appear more complex and oblique than can easily be predicted. What is
clearer, however, is that blacks' perceptions of other racial and ethnic minorities tend to be somewhat more positive than their perceptions about whites
are. For instance, blacks feel a greater affinity or closeness with Latinos than
they do with whites (McClain, Carter, et al. 2006; D. Harris 1995). Nevertheless, Latinos' attitudes about blacks are not necessarily as positively recipro-
cal, as Latinos feel closer to whites than they do to blacks, while whites feel a
greater closeness to blacks, and blacks feel the least close to whites (McClain,
Carter, et al. 2006). Evidence also suggests that Latinos subscribe to more
negative stereotypes about blacks than blacks subscribe to about Latinos
(Mindiola, Niemann, and Rodriguez 2002). As far as Asian Americans, African Americans view Asian Americans in similarly negative, stereotypical
ways as they do whites (Cummings and Lambert 1997; Guthrie and Hutchison 1995). Conversely, Asian Americans who endorse identification with
whites and subscribe more to cultural resistance of culture outside their own
ethnic practices perceive African Americans more negatively and stereo-
typically than those who do not; U.S.-born Asian Americans, however, view
blacks more positively (Kohatsu et al. 2000).

Thus, race is an attribute that influences people's information processing
and assists them in qualifying intergroup interactions. How blacks perceive
other racial groups feel about them, thus, can influence their perceptions
of racial uncertainty about interacting with these groups, leading to more
favorable perceptions of groups that they perceive view them favorably and
to more unfavorable perceptions of groups that they perceive view them

negatively. For one, blacks must reference their racial group membership (the in-group) in comparison to others' racial group membership (the out-group). Second, depending on whether blacks share or differ in their experiences of racial discrimination with members of other racial groups, perceptions of risk and uncertainty about future racial discrimination will vary.

Examining how blacks process racial information also should include how racial socialization influences positive and negative attributions about groups. To examine the influences of racial socialization on blacks' perceptions of racial groups, I submit that the emphasis that blacks received on racial socialization messages about racial consciousness (factor 1), racial protectiveness (factor 2), race's mattering less for blacks' circumstances, and whites' not being racist should influence the following racial perceptions: (1) perception of the effect of their knowledge on their interracial interactions, (2) subscription to racial stereotypes, (3) personal racial discrimination experiences, and (4) perceptions of future racial discrimination, or what I refer to as *racial uncertainty*.

Racial consciousness messages should enhance blacks' positive attributions about Asians and Latinos, supposing that these groups share in similar histories of racial discrimination. Conversely, racial consciousness and protectiveness socialization messages should negativize perceptions of whites. Protectiveness socialization messages should increase perceived risks in interacting with all nonblack groups. Racial socialization messages emphasizing racelessness in society (or emphasis on racism's mattering less in blacks' lives) and whites' not being racist should reduce blacks' perceptions that other racial groups and whites, respectively, pose a risk to them. In sum, these relationships suppose that racial socialization transmits information about racial risks in human interactions.

Blacks' linkages to their racial group, or black linked fate (Dawson 1994), and the composition of their current living environments, in addition, offer explanations for assessing racial risks. Controlling for these factors in multivariate models of racial stereotypes, racial discrimination, and racial uncertainty assists in determining whether they mitigate the effects of racial socialization. In the next few sections, I examine the results from the NPSS that test the hypotheses regarding the effects of racial socialization, racial identity, and racial contexts on blacks' perceived racial risks. I also discern blacks' racial stereotypes and which intergroup interactions are perceived as riskier than others.

Personal Knowledge about Blacks' Racial Discrimination and Effects on Interracial Interactions

In the NPSS, 76 percent of black respondents (N = 499) acknowledged that their parents taught them about racial segregation experiences of blacks in the Jim Crow South, and as noted in chapter 3 on blacks' racial socialization, almost 80 percent of blacks expressed that they received high emphasis on blacks' history of racial discrimination. Black Americans' knowledge about historical racial discrimination against blacks also should affect their feelings toward whites, Asians, and Latinos. More disproportionately, however, this knowledge should affect how blacks interact with whites, as much of blacks' racial discrimination history contextualizes relations between them and whites.

Although blacks learn about racial discrimination toward their group through their racial socialization experiences, asking them simply whether they have learned about blacks' racial discrimination experiences will not gauge how much they feel this knowledge has affected their relations with other racial groups. While parents and other family members emphasize racial socialization messages about racial groups, we still do not know the extent to which blacks feel that their interracial relations are affected by this knowledge unless we ask them directly. Blacks who are more familiar with the historical racial discrimination experiences of their group should perceive greater risks in their interactions with whites (as historical perpetrators of group-based racial discrimination) and should perceive fewer risks associated with their interactions with Asians and Latinos (as they are racial and ethnic minorities who also experienced historical racial discrimination).

In the NPSS, black respondents were asked, "If you were to describe how your knowledge of racial discrimination against black people in the United States has affected the way you interact with people of different racial groups, how would you describe the extent to which this knowledge has *negatively* affected your feelings and relations with (whites, Asians/Asian Americans, Latinos)?"[2] As shown in figure 4.1, most blacks said they feel that their knowledge about racial discrimination against blacks "somewhat" influences their feelings and interactions with whites. In contrast, they mostly said they feel that their racial discrimination knowledge does "not at all affect" their feelings and relations with Asians and Latinos.

Turning to the multivariate model of the effect of racial knowledge on interracial interactions in table 4.1, we see that demographic variables are influential in only two models: the model of interactions with whites and

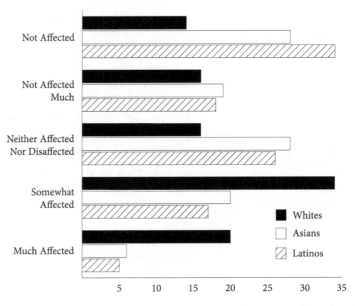

Fig. 4.1. Effect of racial knowledge on feelings and interactions with racial groups

with Latinos. Counterintuitively, older blacks are less likely than younger blacks to feel that their racial knowledge influences their interactions with whites. Perhaps this indicates how younger people have learned more about racial discrimination experiences through absorption of information relayed to them about these historical experiences, as opposed to learning through lived, personal experiences with de jure segregation, as older blacks are more likely to have experienced. (As we see later in the discussion, older blacks do report more frequent experiences with racial discrimination than younger blacks do.) Having a higher level of education reduces the feeling that one's knowledge about blacks' racial discrimination experiences negatively affects one's interactions with Latinos. With higher education, one is likely to learn more about the racial discrimination experiences of blacks with specific racial groups, and this can translate into a keener consciousness of other groups' racial discrimination experiences, which can reduce animosity toward groups that have shared discrimination experiences, as is the case with Latinos.

Sensitivity to blacks' contextual circumstances in black neighborhoods also may heighten blacks' awareness of Latinos' racial circumstances, thus decreasing negative feelings toward this group. Increasingly, in environments where blacks and Latinos share spaces and compete for resources, the potential for perceived discrimination is likely to increase over time and to contribute to a knowledge base of such negative interactions. For now, however, Latinos also may be a group that lacks a historical reference affecting blacks' cross-racial interactions.

TABLE 4.1

Model of Effect of Racial Discrimination Knowledge on Interracial Feelings and Interactions

Covariates	Whites	Asians	Latinos
Non–African American	.0837	−.0047	−.1320
	(.1937)	(.1845)	(.1908)
Female	.0704	.1655	.1960
	(.1338)	(.1269)	(.1324)
Age	−.0677*	.0097	.0008
	(.0410)	(.0386)	(.0403)
Income	.0180	.0085	.0193
	(.0370)	(.0349)	(.0364)
Education	.0182	−.0215	−.0682**
	(.0338)	(.0321)	(.0336)
South	−.1275	.0912	−.0084
	(.1407)	(.1332)	(.1390)
R lives in a mostly black neighborhood	−.0634	−.2196	−.2806*
	(.1756)	(.1682)	(.1753)
Racial consciousness socialization (factor 1)	.0065	.0046	−.0043
	(.0059)	(.0052)	(.0055)
Protectiveness socialization (factor 2)	.0322***	.0582****	.0505****
	(.0111)	(.0105)	(.0109)
Whites not racist socialization	−.0954*	—	—
	(.0553)		
Frequency of racial discrimination experiences	.3176****	.2036***	.2261***
	(.0733)	(.0696)	(.0726)
Black linked fate	.2515****	.1528**	.0916
	(.0630)	(.0596)	(.0624)
Constant	.3747	−.2737	.8483
	(.5265)	(.4985)	(.5203)
N	359	356	355
R^2	0.19	0.18	0.13

Source: 2007 National Politics and Socialization Survey
Note: Standard errors are indicated in parentheses.

Of the three racial socialization messages tested in the model about each racial group—racial consciousness, protectiveness, and whites' not being racist—receiving greater emphasis on protectiveness racial socialization messages increases blacks' negative feelings and interactions with whites, Asians, and Latinos. Greater emphasis on the message that all whites are not racist modestly reduces blacks' belief that their racial discrimination knowledge influences their having negative feelings and interactions with whites. Having more frequent experiences with racial discrimination also increases blacks' negative perceptions about their interactions with all the groups. Black linked fate matters only in the models for whites and Asians, suggesting that blacks with a greater linkage to other black racial group members also feel to a greater extent that their racial discrimination knowledge negatively affects their interracial interactions with these groups.

Beyond determining the effects of racial discrimination knowledge on blacks' interracial interactions, racial stereotypes also have influence on how people think about groups and attribute behaviors to them. Subscriptions to certain stereotypes suggest whether people perceive that others have questionable character or trustworthiness. If it is the case that blacks think more negatively than positively about racial groups, then it also seems logical that they will limit their interactions and, ultimately, their trust in these groups. In the next section, I examine blacks' subscription to positive and negative stereotypes about racial groups to determine the degree to which they homogenize these groups.

Racial Stereotypes and Homogenization of Groups

As cognitive constructs, stereotypes assist people in processing information (Lippmann 1922; Allport 1954). They provide information about group members, groups' attributes, and groups' relationships to other groups (McGarty, Yzerbyt, and Spears 2002). These cognitive categorizations further differentiate groups into in- and out-groups as far as their behavior and relationship to the perceiver. As noted previously, in-group members see more individuation among their own group members and greater homogenization among out-group members (Tajfel and Turner 1986). Cognitively, groups become associated with specific behavioral attributes (Hewstone 1983). In-group perceivers generally homogenize out-groups in ways that heighten differences between their own group and the out-group (Judd and Park 1988, 1995; S. Taylor et al. 1978), which contributes to more negative behavioral attributions about out-group members (Brewer and Brown 1998).

When people subscribe to racial stereotypes, they homogenize group members based on group-specific character attributes (S. Nunnally 2009), and these stereotypes can take the flavor of bipolar, positive, or negative characterizations (Levine, Carmines, and Sniderman 1999). While scholars debate whether perceived risk that relies on cultural (racial) knowledge amounts to mere stereotyping (Rayner 1992), it is here that I recognize the significance of racial stereotypes in people's assessments of others, especially those who they do not know and who, through a social interaction, will have to prove their trustworthiness. With respect to the political realm, candidates and political parties have reputations and accessible political information on the basis of which people can make informed decisions (Bianco 1994), although time costs may reduce the likelihood that one seeks such information or may reduce the amount of political information one attempts to process (Rosenstone and Hansen 2003). Nevertheless, in politics, political actors' social group memberships still function as heuristics, especially in low-information elections (McDermott 1998). A person's race is the medium through which I argue behavioral attributions are encoded and facilitate cognitive and affective information processing for trust assessments in both social and political contexts.

There is a large body of literature on racial stereotypes, in particular. This research, however, generally focuses on whites' subscription to racial stereotypes. Although stereotypes can be either positive or negative, these studies tend to adopt a special interest in negative racial stereotypes, which historically have disparaged nonwhites (Schuman et al. 1997; Bobo and Kluegel 1993). Negative racial stereotypes adversely characterize nonwhite groups in ways that ascribe negative attributes to them—being lazy, unintelligent, violent, and hypersexual—akin to what is referred to as "old-fashioned racism" (Kinder and Sears 1981). Determining how blacks subscribe to racial stereotypes, in general, offers a glimpse of this group's racial orientations. More important, regressing racial stereotypes on the two main racial socialization factors (racial consciousness and protectiveness) offers import for determining whether these socialization messages increase or decrease subscription to negative or positive racial stereotypes.

To determine how black Americans subscribe to racial stereotypes, I analyze data from a split-sample experiment on race and stereotypes in the NPSS. The experiment asks respondents to evaluate the extent to which either people in general or whites, blacks, Asians, or Latinos in particular are likely to display each of the following positive or negative stereotypes: being competent, trustworthy, hardworking, honest, or religious (positive

TABLE 4.2

Arithmetic Means for Blacks' Positive and Negative Stereotypes

Stereotypes	Control/People	Blacks	Whites	Asians	Latinos
Positive					
Competent	2.5	3.0	2.3	2.8	2.5
Trustworthy	2.3	2.8	1.9	2.3	2.3
Hardworking	2.6	3.1	2.3	3.1	3.0
Honest	2.4	2.8	1.9	2.3	2.4
Religious	2.4	3.0	2.1	2.5	2.9
Negative					
Lazy	1.7	.99	1.7	.94	1.0
Neglect their families	1.5	1.2	1.4	1.0	1.0
Lie	2.5	1.3	2.1	1.8	1.6
Give up easily	2.0	1.2	1.5	1.1	1.2
Selfish	2.5	1.3	2.3	1.9	1.5
Bossy	2.1	1.7	2.5	2.1	1.7

Source: 2007 National Politics and Socialization Survey
Note: Variables are scaled from 0 = strongly disagree to 4 = strongly agree. Higher arithmetic means indicate greater subscription to the stereotype.

stereotypes) and being lazy, neglectful of their families, likely to lie, likely to give up easily, selfish, or bossy (negative stereotypes). Responses for each stereotype are scaled from 0 = strongly disagree to 4 = strongly agree, with higher numbers indicating more agreement with the stereotype.

Respondents were randomly selected with equal probability to receive a survey that asked questions specifically about one of five targets in the survey: (1) the control group, people in general, (2) whites, (3) blacks, (4) Asians, and (5) Latinos. The randomization of the survey experiment increases the internal validity of the survey results. Comparing the means of blacks' responses to stereotypes about each racial group provides an unobtrusive account of how blacks attribute characteristics more to one group than to another. Table 4.2 shows the arithmetic means for blacks' positive and negative stereotypes for each of the targets in the experiment.

Table 4.3 illustrates blacks' subscription to positive stereotypes about racial groups. Blacks largely view their own group members as more competent than other racial groups, with the exception of Asians. Similarly, blacks are viewed as the most trustworthy of all the groups, and Asians and Latinos are believed to be more trustworthy than whites, who overall are trusted

TABLE 4.3

Statistically Significant Comparisons of
Arithmetic Means for Positive Stereotypes

Positive stereotypes	Target 1	Target 2	p-value
Competent	People [2.5]	Blacks (+) [3.0]	0.000****
	Whites [2.3]	Blacks (+) [3.0]	0.000****
	Whites [2.3]	Asians (+) [2.8]	0.000****
	Latinos [2.5]	Blacks (+) [3.0]	0.001****
Trustworthy	People [2.3]	Blacks (+) [2.8]	0.000****
	People (+) [2.3]	Whites [1.9]	0.002***
	Whites [1.9]	Blacks (+) [2.8]	0.000****
	Whites [1.9]	Asians (+) [2.3]	0.001****
	Whites [1.9]	Latinos (+) [2.3]	0.004***
	Asians [2.3]	Blacks (+) [2.8]	0.000****
	Latinos [2.3]	Blacks (+) [2.8]	0.000****
Hardworking	People [2.6]	Blacks (+) [3.1]	0.000****
	People [2.6]	Whites (+) [2.3]	0.001****
	People [2.6]	Asians (+) [3.1]	0.000****
	People [2.6]	Latinos (+) [3.0]	0.001****
	Whites [2.3]	Blacks (+) [3.1]	0.000****
	Whites [2.3]	Asians (+) [3.1]	0.000****
	Whites [2.3]	Latinos (+) [3.0]	0.000****
Honest	People [2.4]	Blacks (+) [2.8]	0.001****
	People (+) [2.4]	Whites [1.9]	0.000****

(*continued*)

TABLE 4.3 (*continued*)

Positive stereotypes	Target 1	Target 2	p-value
	Whites	Blacks (+)	0.000****
	[1.9]	[2.8]	
	Whites	Asians (+)	0.001****
	[1.9]	[2.3]	
	Whites	Latinos (+)	0.000****
	[1.9]	[2.4]	
	Asians	Blacks (+)	0.000****
	[2.3]	[2.8]	
	Latinos	Blacks (+)	0.000****
	[2.4]	[2.8]	
Religious	People	Blacks (+)	0.000****
	[2.4]	[3.0]	
	People	Latinos (+)	0.000****
	[2.4]	[2.9]	
	Whites	Blacks (+)	0.000****
	[2.1]	[3.0]	
	Whites	Asians (+)	0.000****
	[2.1]	[2.5]	
	Whites	Latinos (+)	0.000****
	[2.1]	[2.9]	
	Asians	Blacks (+)	0.000****
	[2.5]	[3.0]	
	Asians	Latinos (+)	0.001****
	[2.5]	[2.9]	

Source: 2007 National Politics and Socialization Survey
Note: Arithmetic means are indicated in brackets. All statistically significant comparisons indicate comparisons that are significant accounting for the Bonferroni adjustment method, or $p \leq .005$, where *** $p \leq .01$; **** $p \leq .001$. Variables are scaled from 0 = strongly disagree to 4 = strongly agree, where higher values indicate more subscription to the stereotype. (+) indicates the group that exemplifies the stereotype more than the comparative group.

even less than the control group (people in general). As far as stereotypes about people's work habits, blacks mostly perceive their own group members, Asians, and Latinos as more hardworking than whites. Blacks and Latinos also are perceived to be more religious than are whites, Asians, and people in general.

Generally, blacks in the NPSS disagree with negative stereotypes about groups. For one, they reject the stereotype that various racial groups are lazy and neglectful of their families. Although blacks do not subscribe to perceptions that these groups are lazy and neglectful, as table 4.4 indicates, blacks view whites and people in general more negatively than they do fellow blacks, Asians, and Latinos. In particular, whites and people in general are also perceived as being more likely to lie than other racial groups. Despite respondents' perceiving Asians as being more likely to lie than blacks are, the substantive differences are minimal. Likewise, differences in the stereotype about racial groups' "giving up easily" offer minimal substantive meaning. Clearly, however, blacks perceive whites and people in general to be more selfish and bossier than are blacks, Asians, and Latinos. Yet Asians are stereotyped as more selfish than blacks are and bossier than Latinos are. Interestingly, there are no negative stereotypes that are statistically distinguishable between blacks and Latinos.

In sum, black respondents in the NPSS were less likely to subscribe to negative racial stereotypes and were more likely to subscribe to positive stereotypes. While there is obvious support for blacks' in-group favoritism toward their own racial group, their stereotypes about Asians and Latinos more closely resemble their stereotypes about blacks. When blacks in the survey subscribe to negative racial stereotypes, they perceive whites as being likely to lie, exemplifying selfish behavior, and being bossy. Black respondents have more similar perceptions and sensitivities between racial and ethnic minorities and their own racial group and perceive their own group more positively, in general. Stereotypes about "people in general" compared to other racial and ethnic minorities, moreover, suggest that blacks have less faith in the positive attributes of "people" than in racial and ethnic minorities, and they also attribute more negative attributes to "people" than to racial and ethnic minorities. "People" and whites are perceived as more alike.

Do certain racial socialization messages enhance or diminish subscription to racial stereotypes? In order to discern the effects of racial socialization messages on NPSS respondents' subscription to positive and negative stereotypes about racial groups, I examine ordered probit models of separate scales of positive and negative stereotypes.[3] The scales are additive scales calculated for respondents based on the target they received in the survey experiment. Put simply, each model represents attitudes of respondents who were asked specifically about stereotypes for one of the five survey targets in the race and stereotypes experiment. The scales of positive and negative stereotypes are further divided into low, medium, and high levels of subscription to the stereotypes, hence the reasoning behind modeling the stereotype attitudes using an ordered probit model.

Table 4.5 shows the results of ordered probit models predicting blacks' subscription to positive and negative stereotypes of the targets in the race

TABLE 4.4
*Statistically Significant Comparisons of
Arithmetic Means for Negative Stereotypes*

Negative stereotypes	Target 1	Target 2	p-value
Lazy	People (+) [1.7]	Blacks [.99]	0.000****
	People (+) [1.7]	Asians [.94]	0.000****
	People (+) [1.7]	Latinos [1.0]	0.000****
	Whites (+) [1.7]	Blacks [.99]	0.000****
	Whites (+) [1.7]	Asians [.94]	0.000****
	Whites (+) [1.7]	Latinos [1.0]	0.000****
Neglect	People (+) [1.5]	Asians [1.0]	0.001****
	People (+) [1.5]	Latinos [1.0]	0.000****
	Whites (+) [1.4]	Asians [1.0]	0.002***
	Whites (+) [1.4]	Latinos [1.0]	0.002***
Lie	People (+) [2.5]	Blacks [1.3]	0.000****
	People (+) [2.5]	Whites [2.1]	0.004***
	People (+) [2.5]	Asians [1.8]	0.000****
	People (+) [2.5]	Latinos [1.6]	0.000****
	Whites (+) [2.1]	Blacks [1.3]	0.000****
	Whites (+) [2.1]	Asians [1.8]	0.004***
	Whites (+) [2.1]	Latinos [1.6]	0.000****
	Asians (+) [1.8]	Blacks [1.3]	0.001****
Give up easily	People (+) [2.0]	Blacks [1.2]	0.000****
	People (+) [2.0]	Whites [1.5]	0.000****

TABLE 4.4 (*continued*)

Negative stereotypes	Target 1	Target 2	p-value
	People (+) [2.0]	Asians [1.1]	0.000****
	People (+) [2.0]	Latinos [1.2]	0.000****
	Whites (+) [1.5]	Asians [1.1]	0.003****
	Whites (+) [1.5]	Latinos [1.2]	0.005***
Selfish	People (+) [2.5]	Blacks [1.3]	0.000****
	People (+) [2.5]	Asians [1.9]	0.000****
	People (+) [2.5]	Latinos [1.5]	0.000****
	Whites (+) [2.3]	Blacks [1.3]	0.000****
	Whites (+) [2.3]	Asians [1.9]	0.003***
	Whites (+) [2.3]	Latinos [1.5]	0.000****
	Asians [1.9]	Blacks [1.3]	0.000****
Bossy	People [2.1]	Blacks (+) [1.7]	0.003****
	People (+) [2.1]	Whites [2.5]	0.001****
	People (+) [2.1]	Latinos [1.7]	0.003***
	Whites (+) [2.5]	Blacks [1.7]	0.000****
	Whites (+) [2.5]	Asians [2.1]	0.005***
	Whites (+) [2.5]	Latinos [1.7]	0.000****
	Asians (+) [2.1]	Latinos [1.7]	0.005***

Source: 2007 National Politics and Socialization Survey
Note: Arithmetic means are indicated in brackets. All statistically significant comparisons indicate comparisons that are significant accounting for the Bonferroni adjustment method, or p ≤ .005, where *** p ≤ .01; **** p ≤ .001. Variables are scaled from 0 = strongly disagree to 4 = strongly agree, where higher values indicate more subscription to the stereotype. (+) indicates the group that exemplifies the stereotype more than the comparative group.

TABLE 4.5

Ordered Probit Models of Blacks' Subscription to Racial Stereotypes

Covariates	Positive stereotypes of people	Negative stereotypes of people	Positive stereotypes of blacks	Negative stereotypes of blacks	Positive stereotypes of whites	Negative stereotypes of whites
Non–African	.2661	.2362	−.1549	.3642	−.5367	−.2777
Americans	(.5137)	(.4724)	(.4873)	(.5377)	(.5766)	(.4924)
Female	.3629	−.0913	.2078	−.1330	−.7491*	−.0848
	(.3820)	(.3440)	(.3059)	(.3451)	(.4008)	(.3115)
Age	.0516	−.0074	.0230	−.1745	.1540	.0228
	(.1072)	(.0948)	(.0984)	(.1181)	(.1229)	(.0976)
Income	−.0012	−.0139	.0391	−.1328	.1035	−.1912**
	(.0993)	(.0896)	(.0789)	(.0919)	(.1152)	(.0925)
Education	−.0172	−.0350	.0048	.0131	.0291	.0877
	(.0920)	(.0817)	(.0733)	(.0772)	(.0901)	(.0774)
South	.3349	−.2262	−.0433	−.1198	−.3478	.4066
	(.3814)	(.3364)	(.3311)	(.3780)	(.3896)	(.3329)
R lives in a	.0599	.2793	−.1361	.3219	−.2201	−.2551
predominantly	(.5659)	(.4955)	(.3955)	(.4305)	(.3919)	(.3290)
black						
neighborhood						
Racial	−.0153	−.0191	.0212	.0018	.0105	.0061
consciousness	(.0139)	(.0134)	(.0131)	(.0142)	(.0166)	(.0134)
socialization						
(factor 1)						
Protectiveness	−.0463*	.0209	.0195	.0795***	−.0056	.0229
socialization	(.0278)	(.0248)	(.0258)	(.0296)	(.0320)	(.0272)
(factor 2)						
Whites not racist	—	—	—	—	.0001	.0564
					(.1782)	(.1551)
Frequency of	.2582	.1536	−.2219	.1386	−.2928	.1110
discrimination	(.2243)	(.2156)	(.1625)	(.1843)	(.2026)	(.1727)
experiences						
Black linked fate	.3674**	−.0913	.2684**	−.3420**	−.2046	.1242
	(.2243)	(.1440)	(.1356)	(.1532)	(.1981)	(.1620)
Cut 1	−.0773	−2.273	.4478	−1.012	−.7454	.4917
	(1.482)	(1.363)	(1.099)	(1.248)	(1.584)	(1.339)
Cut 2	2.581	−.6137	2.375	−.1482	2.805	2.422
	(1.522)	(1.341)	(1.124)	(1.246)	(1.655)	(1.357)
χ^2 probability	0.28	0.86	0.28	0.10	0.28	0.31
Pseudo R2	0.14	0.06	0.09	0.13	0.16	0.10
N	65	64	80	78	74	71

TABLE 4.5 (*continued*)

Covariates	Positive stereotypes of Asians	Negative stereotypes of Asians	Positive stereotypes of Latinos	Negative stereotypes of Latinos
Non–African Americans	.3118	.2176	−.0743	1.018
	(.4557)	(.4619)	(.6376)	(.6700)
Female	−.5220	−.0907	.0105	−.2308
	(.3230)	(.3287)	(.4130)	(.4634)
Age	.0146	.1129	−.0445	−.2275
	(.1047)	(.1084)	(.1130)	(.1488)
Income	.0525	−.1364	.3255**	−.1894
	(.0888)	(.0960)	(.1412)	(.1436)
Education	.0663	.1023	.1540	.1821
	(.0805)	(.0890)	(.1204)	(.1490)
South	.0306	−.1309	−.0292	.1290
	(.3225)	(.3434)	(.4218)	(.4829)
R lives in a predominantly black neighborhood	−.1831	−.0126	1.435	−8.497
	(.4484)	(.4340)	(.9839)	(1.55e+07)
Racial consciousness socialization (factor 1)	−.0023	.0004	.0106	.0197
	(.0164)	(.0205)	(.0182)	(.0238)
Protectiveness socialization (factor 2)	−.0412	.0737***	−.0426	.0677
	(.0256)	(.0284)	(.0364)	(.0423)
Whites not racist	—	—	—	—
Frequency of discrimination experiences	−.0528	.0772	−.1239	−.4838
	(.1878)	(.1894)	(.2567)	(.3249)
Black linked fate	.2183	−.0631	.4982**	.1453
	(.1810)	(.1972)	(.2159)	(.2634)
Cut 1	−.7789	1.639	2.788	1.819
	(1.471)	(1.732)	(1.787)	(2.090)
Cut 2	1.727	4.105	5.886	3.455
	(1.489)	(1.825)	(2.009)	(2.104)
χ^2 probability	0.62	0.31	0.08	0.06
Pseudo R^2	0.09	0.12	0.23	0.27
N	70	69	54	53

Source: 2007 National Politics and Socialization Survey
Note: Standard errors are indicated in parentheses.
* $p \leq .10$; ** $p \leq .05$; *** $p \leq .01$; **** $p \leq .001$

and stereotypes experiment. Several models do not predict blacks' subscription to stereotypes well and should be interpreted cautiously. In the model for positive stereotypes of people, racial protectiveness messages modestly reduce subscription to positive stereotypes, whereas higher black linked fate increases positive stereotypes about people. None of the predictors for negative stereotypes about people is statistically distinguishable. As for positive stereotypes about blacks, feeling more linkage to other blacks increases subscription to positive stereotypes about blacks and reduces subscription to negative stereotypes about the group. Receiving more emphasis on racial protectiveness messages, however, increases subscription to negative stereotypes about fellow group members. With respect to whites, on the one hand, being a black female modestly reduces the likelihood that she subscribes to positive stereotypes about whites. On the other hand, having a higher income reduces blacks' subscription to negative stereotypes about whites.

Turning to the model for positive stereotypes about Asian Americans, we see that none of the covariates is statistically predictive. In the model of negative stereotypes about Asian Americans, however, having received greater emphasis on racial protectiveness socialization increases blacks' subscription to negative stereotyping about this group. As for stereotypes about Latinos, we see that higher-income blacks think more positively about Latinos than do lower-income blacks, and having more linked fate with other blacks increases the likelihood that blacks subscribe to positive stereotypes about Latinos. In the model of negative stereotypes of Latinos, there are no statistically significant variables predicting blacks' subscription to negative stereotypes about Latinos.

Personal Racial Discrimination Experiences

Already we have seen how racial socialization experiences influence blacks' interactions and stereotypes of racial groups. But how might racial socialization experiences also influence how frequently blacks feel they have been racially discriminated against? It is important to model the influence of racial consciousness, racial protectiveness, and socialization about race's mattering less on discrimination experiences. Blacks who received greater emphasis on protectiveness messages should report more frequent experiences with racial discrimination. Because racial consciousness messages emphasize blacks' racial history of discrimination, presumably making blacks more aware of different forms of racial discrimination, those who received more emphasis on these messages also should be more likely to report frequent racial discrimination experiences. Unlike consciousness and protectiveness racial socialization messages, socialization about race's mattering less should reduce perceived frequency of racial discrimination experiences.

The highest percentage of NPSS black respondents (39 percent, N = 510) reported that they "rarely" experience racial discrimination. Yet this number is followed by one-third of black respondents who reported that they experience racial discrimination "sometimes." Approximately another 15 percent claimed that they experience racial discrimination either "very often" or "often," which is a similar number to the 13 percent of black respondents who claimed that they "never" experience racial discrimination. In today's society blacks have multifarious experiences with racial discrimination, and being black does not deterministically will one to racial discrimination as it may have historically. To determine factors influencing the frequency of perceived personal racial discrimination experiences, I examine a multivariate model that controls for demographic characteristics and the three racial socialization factors.

According to table 4.6, in Model 1 of perceived personal racial discrimination experiences, black women in the survey reported having experienced racial discrimination less frequently than black men did, following evidence in prior research. As we might expect, older blacks reported having experienced racial discrimination more frequently than younger blacks did. Furthermore, the racial history of the South as a bastion of institutionalized racism prevails, as blacks living in the South reported more than blacks elsewhere that they have been racially discriminated against. There also is a modest relationship of greater emphasis on protectiveness socialization messages increasing the frequency of blacks' perceived racial discrimination experiences. Thus, the frequency of blacks' perceived racial discrimination experiences is influenced by messages conveyed to them about race and contextual influences such as where they currently live. Feeling a linkage with other blacks, or black linked fate, also increases perceived personal discrimination experiences.

Model 2 of frequency of perceived racial discrimination experiences includes the same variables as Model 1, with the addition of controls for the effects of previous knowledge about blacks' racial discrimination experiences and their influence on blacks' developing negative feelings and relations with specific racial groups. Similar measures are statistically distinguishable in this model as are in Model 1. Of the added measures, only the measure for the effect of racial discrimination knowledge on interactions with whites affects the frequency of blacks' perceived discrimination experiences, in

TABLE 4.6

Multivariate Models of Blacks' Racial Discrimination Perceptions:
Experienced Racial Discrimination and Racial Uncertainty

Covariates	Frequency of perceived racial discrimination experiences (Model 1)	Frequency of perceived racial discrimination experiences (Model 2)	Expectation for future racial discrimination/ racial uncertainty (Model 1)	Expectation for future racial discrimination/ racial uncertainty (Model 2)
Non–African American	−.0232	−.0099	−.1247	−.1337
	(.1409)	(.1395)	(.1669)	(.1673)
Female	−.3764****	−.3837****	−.1426	−.1301
	(.0952)	(.0940)	(.1121)	(.1120)
Age	.1014****	.1057****	−.0042	.0062
	(.0289)	(.0288)	(.0342)	(.0344)
Income	−.0148	−.0130	−.0133	−.0069
	(.0268)	(.0264)	(.0315)	(.0314)
Education	.0167	.0163	.0747***	.0620**
	(.0246)	(.0245)	(.0290)	(.0293)
R lives in the South	.2150**	.2052**	.0284	.0125
	(.1014)	(.1003)	(.1191)	(.1193)
R lives in a predominantly black neighborhood	.0782	.0807	−.1856	−.2356
	(.1268)	(.1274)	(.1489)	(.1517)
Racial consciousness socialization (factor 1)	.0014	−.0013	.0031	.0027
	(.0040)	(.0040)	(.0047)	(.0047)
Protectiveness socialization (factor 2)	.0174**	.0086	.0119	.0122
	(.0079)	(.0083)	(.0093)	(.0099)
Knowledge about race and effect on interactions with whites	—	.1278***	—	.1503***
		(.0410)		(.0488)
Knowledge about race and effect on interactions with Asian Americans	—	.0302	—	−.0211
		(.0512)		(.0612)
Knowledge about race and effect on interactions with Latinos	—	.0598	—	−.0703
		(.0479)		(.0571)
Black linked fate	.2817****	.2282****	.3058****	.2763****
	(.0433)	(.0446)	(.0508)	(.0530)
Constant	.4401	.2713	1.090**	1.039**
	(.3804)	(.3797)	(.4490)	(.4532)
N	361	354	358	352
R²	0.22	0.28	0.15	0.18

Source: 2007 National Politics and Socialization Survey
Note: Standard errors are indicated in parentheses.
* p ≤ .10; ** p ≤ .05; *** p ≤ .01; **** p ≤ .001

effect, increasing the frequency of blacks' reported racial discrimination and attesting to the significance of historicized relationships between blacks and whites and their effects on blacks' perpetual experiences with discrimination. While measuring frequency of racial discrimination experiences offers import, this measure only gauges retrospective experiences. Understanding how blacks perceive the likelihood for being discriminated against in the future, or prospective discrimination, additionally helps us ascertain factors that lead to racial uncertainty.

Perceptions of Racial Uncertainty

As I have mentioned previously, because of blacks' uncertainty about whether they will be racially discriminated against and the negative consequences of this discrimination, they should be more risk averse to interracial interactions. Racial uncertainty among blacks should be greater in their interactions with whites than in their interactions with Asian Americans and Latinos. However, because people perceive and experience racial discrimination differently (Sellers and Shelton 2003; Feldman Barrett and Swim 1998), we cannot assume that black Americans possess a monolithic perception of racial uncertainty toward whites or any other racial group. Blacks' racial socialization experiences, their perception of the effect of their racial discrimination knowledge on their interracial interactions, and their personal discrimination experiences should determine their racial uncertainty in interacting with other racial groups.

Racial uncertainty can be measured in two ways: (1) the expectation for future racial discrimination and (2) the perception of the likelihood that specific racial actors (whites, Asian Americans, Latinos, or blacks) will discriminate against them racially. First, I examine a multivariate model of *future racial discrimination*, which asked respondents, "Do you expect you may be discriminated against based on your race someday in the future?" Second, I also examine a measure of *the likelihood for racial discrimination by a specific racial actor*, which asked respondents, "How *likely* do you think it would be that a [person, black person, white person, Asian person, or Latino person] would discriminate against *you* based on your race?" This variable is tested as both a dependent variable in a multivariate model and as a part of a split-sample, unobtrusive survey experiment to determine differences in racial uncertainty among the five targets.

As I previously noted in the race and stereotypes experiment, mean responses for each of the five targets are calculated and compared, using unpaired t-tests in order to determine any statistically significant differences in the means that can be attributed to the mention of the target in the question. Statistically significant differences in the means indicate that the respondents view this person (target) as more likely to discriminate against them racially, again, as an indicator of racial uncertainty. Responses for both measures of racial uncertainty are scaled from 0 to 4, or from "very unlikely" to "very likely," that blacks (1) would be discriminated against based on their race in the future and (2) would be racially discriminated against by the target mentioned in the respondent's survey.[4]

In the multivariate models, those blacks who received more emphasis on racial socialization messages about protectiveness in racial relations should be more likely to report the risk of future racial discrimination, in general. Greater emphasis on this racial socialization message also, more specifically, should lead blacks to perceive more racial uncertainty in their interactions with whites, Asian Americans, and Latinos. Perceived riskiness of future racial discrimination should be lessened by receiving socialization messages that suggest race should matter less to blacks' lives. As well, those who feel that their knowledge of historical racial discrimination against blacks affects their interactions with whites, Asian Americans, and Latinos should perceive a greater likelihood for racial discrimination against them.[5] Receiving the racial socialization message that "not all whites are racist" should reduce racial uncertainty about whites.

Just as in the model for the perceptions of personal racial discrimination, black females should be less likely than black men to be racially uncertain about their interracial interactions. This is especially the case considering that the literature on racial discrimination suggests that black men are more likely to report racial discrimination experiences than black women are (Sigelman and Welch 1991). Living in the South should elevate racial uncertainty about whites, in particular, because of the region's racial history. Living in a predominantly black neighborhood likely contributes to negative attitudes about people who are not in-group members and who may be perceived as choosing not to live in black neighborhoods, as prior research also indicates that racial isolation increases black Americans' negative attitudes about nonblacks (Gay 2004; Oliver and Wong 2003). Such attitudes, in turn, likely become linked to associating nonblack group members with supporting social segregation in housing, a form of racial discrimination. Therefore, blacks who live in predominantly black neighborhoods should be more racially uncertain than those who do not.

Finally, knowledge about racial discrimination against blacks and its negative effects on interactions with whites should predict racial uncertainty, in general, and about whites, in particular, whereas knowledge about racial discrimination and its effects on relations with Asians and Latinos should be inconsequential to racial uncertainty, in general, but more predictive in respective relations with each group. Just as the literature finds that racial identity and consciousness fortify perceptions of racial bias, here, the expectation is that greater linkages to other blacks will increase the expectation for future racial discrimination and, hence, racial uncertainty.

In the model of racial uncertainty, measured as the likely expectation for future racial discrimination, as shown in table 4.6, in Models 1 and 2, we see that blacks with higher education levels are more likely to exemplify racial uncertainty and to be concerned about prospective racial discrimination. Unlike the models of personal discrimination experiences, living in the South does not increase blacks' racial uncertainty. Living in a predominantly black neighborhood also does not increase this uncertainty. While both models test influences of racial consciousness socialization and protectiveness socialization, neither of these socialization messages is statistically significant. Although these specific socialization messages are not influential in predicting blacks' expectations for future racial discrimination, in Model 2, as historical racial discrimination experiences with whites might suggest, when blacks feel that their knowledge about race negatively affects their interracial interactions with whites, they become more uncertain about future racial discrimination. Higher levels of black linked fate, furthermore, increase concerns for future racial discrimination in both Models 1 and 2.

When we turn to the results of the racial uncertainty survey experiment, which compare blacks' perceptions of the likelihood for specific racial groups to discriminate against them because of their race, as illustrated in table 4.7, we find additional support for heightened apprehension in blacks' interactions with whites. Results indicate that blacks believe all groups, including their own racial group members, are "somewhat" likely to discriminate against them on the basis of race. With respect to the prospect of other blacks being racially discriminatory, this may attest to some of the racially constructed discrimination practices that disparage in-group members, such as colorism.

The most lucid differences among the various groups are in the "very likely" category. Among all the groups in the experiment, "people" and "whites" have the highest percentages of respondents indicating racial uncertainty about them. One-third of blacks in the sample said they feel that whites are "very likely" to discriminate against them. Table 4.8, furthermore,

TABLE 4.7

Univariate Results for Black Attitudes in the
Racial Uncertainty Survey Experiment

Expectation for future racial discrimination	People (%)	Blacks (%)	Whites (%)	Asian Americans (%)	Latinos (%)
Not very likely	1	26	2	4	15
Barely likely	16	25	13	22	28
Somewhat likely	28	31	36	33	31
Likely	28	14	17	23	16
Very likely	28	4	33	18	10
N	101	96	104	91	89

Source: 2007 National Politics and Socialization Survey
Note: Percentages may not add up to 100 percent due to rounding.

TABLE 4.8

Comparisons of Means in the Racial Uncertainty Survey Experiment

Target 1	Target 2	p-value
People (+) [2.7]	Blacks [1.4]	.000****
People [2.7]	Whites [2.7]	.948
People [2.7]	Asians [2.3]	.019
People (+) [2.7]	Latinos [1.8]	.000****
Whites (+) [2.7]	Blacks [1.4]	.000***
Whites [2.7]	Asians [2.3]	.017
Whites (+) [2.7]	Latinos [1.8]	.000****
Asians [2.3]	Blacks [1.4]	.000****
Asians (+) [2.3]	Latinos [1.8]	.000****
Latinos [1.8]	Blacks [1.4]	.049

Source: 2004 Black American Socialization and Trust Survey
Note: Arithmetic means are in brackets. (+) indicates the group that is expected to racially discriminate against the black respondents more than the comparison group. The Bonferroni adjustment method for comparison of means requires that the statistical significance of ten comparisons must be adjusted by dividing a .05 statistical significance level by the number of comparisons made. Therefore, the level of statistical significance for this analysis is p ≤ .005.

elucidates in the survey experiment on racial uncertainty that, comparatively, "people" and "whites" are perceived as more likely to discriminate against blacks than blacks and Latinos are. Interestingly, in comparing the means of Asians and Latinos, Asians are perceived in more racially uncertain terms than Latinos are. Differences between blacks and Latinos, however, are statistically indistinguishable, as previously noted even in the race and stereotypes experiment.

To determine factors that predict the increased likelihood for racial uncertainty for each target in the racial uncertainty experiment, as I mentioned before, I test multivariate models for each racial target. Results are displayed in table 4.9. Models of racial uncertainty about blacks and Latinos should be interpreted cautiously, given the poorer fits of some of the models. In the model for racial uncertainty about people in general, only gender and black linked fate are statistically significant, indicating that black women are moderately less racially uncertain about people than black men are and that blacks with greater linkages to other blacks are more racially uncertain than are those with less linkages.

Racial socialization emphasis on racial consciousness moderately reduces the perception of racial uncertainty about other blacks. Socialization emphasis on protectiveness messages, however, increases racial uncertainty about other blacks. As for racial uncertainty about whites, southern blacks are moderately more racially uncertain about this group than are blacks elsewhere. Stronger black linked fate also increases uncertainty about whites. Interestingly, non–African Americans (or self-identified West Indians and Africans) are more apprehensive about their relations with Asian Americans. Furthermore, having received emphasis on racial protectiveness socialization messages enhances blacks' racial uncertainty about Asian Americans. None of the variables is statistically discernible in the model for racial uncertainty about Latinos, and this model also has the poorest fit.

Summary and Conclusion: Blacks' Racial Knowledge and Predispositions

Although blacks in the NPSS did not report overwhelmingly that they feel that their knowledge about racial discrimination greatly affects their interracial relations, most respondents perceive that their relations with whites have been affected, whereas their relations with Asians and Latinos have been barely affected at all. Furthermore, blacks who received emphasis on racial protectiveness socialization messages were more likely to express a

TABLE 4.9

Multivariate Models of Black Americans' Racial Uncertainty

Covariates	People	Blacks	Whites	Asian Americans	Latinos
Non–African Americans	.4990	.3122	−.2647	.8572**	.0428
	(.3686)	(.4853)	(.3954)	(.3716)	(.4587)
Female	−.4014*	−.3788	.0342	.3285	.5042
	(.2301)	(.2873)	(.2451)	(.2744)	(.3174)
Age	.1092	.0623	−.0187	.1029	.1138
	(.0702)	(.0948)	(.0752)	(.0881)	(.0855)
Income	.0382	−.0240	−.1087	−.0074	−.1438
	(.0657)	(.0787)	(.0752)	(.0752)	(.0918)
Education	−.0592	.0342	.0863	−.0065	.0761
	(.0610)	(.0695)	(.0619)	(.0655)	(.0927)
South	.0320	.2987	.5295*	.0490	−.0353
	(.2490)	(.3236)	(.2737)	(.2742)	(.3284)
R lives in a predominantly black neighborhood	.0843	−.0230	−.0498	−.1463	−.4873
	(.4044)	(.3594)	(.2652)	(.3683)	(.5702)
Socialization about racial consciousness	.0047	−.0249*	.0018	−.0095	.0104
	(.0093)	(.0137)	(.0097)	(.0134)	(.0122)
Socialization about racial protectiveness	.0105	.0655**	.0234	.0556**	.0168
	(.0192)	(.0248)	(.0218)	(.0222)	(.0278)
Whites not racist socialization	—	—	−.0078	—	—
			(.1122)		
Black linked fate	.3885***	−.1344	.3996***	.0423	.0510
	(.1087)	(.1313)	(.1156)	(.1408)	(.1363)
Constant	.8859	2.115*	.7650	1.235	−.0393
	(.9731)	(1.137)	(1.000)	(1.194)	(1.128)
N	64	76	75	72	55
F probability	0.01	0.14	0.01	0.07	0.55
R²	0.34	0.19	0.31	0.24	0.17

Source: 2007 National Politics and Socialization Survey
Note: Standard errors are indicated in parentheses.
* $p \leq .10$; ** $p \leq .05$; *** $p \leq .01$; **** $p \leq .001$

nexus between their racial knowledge and their current negative attitudes and relations with all nonblacks. Personal experiences with racial discrimination also enhance this relation between messages taught and those personally felt by black respondents toward nonblacks. Black linked fate increases the link between racial knowledge and negative attitudes toward only whites and Asians.

As for racial stereotyping, blacks in the NPSS generally perceive their own racial group more positively than other groups. They also perceive Asians and Latinos more positively than they do whites and people in general. Although black respondents do not generally perceive any of the racial groups negatively, evidence suggests that they perceive whites and people in general more negatively as far as ascribing to them less admirable traits such as being likely to lie, being selfish, and being bossy. Statistical models predicting blacks' subscription to positive and negative stereotypes about people in general, blacks, whites, Asian Americans, and Latinos do not perform well. However, there is evidence to suggest that blacks' having received more emphasis on racial protectiveness socialization messages reduces their subscription to positive stereotypes about people in general and increases their subscription to negative stereotypes about other blacks and Asian Americans, in particular. There also is evidence that black linked fate increases blacks' subscription to positive stereotypes about people in general, blacks, and Latinos and reduces negative stereotyping about blacks.

In post–Jim Crow America, black Americans still experience racial discrimination. In the NPSS, the greatest number of black respondents reported having experienced racial discrimination "rarely," with the second-greatest number reporting that they have "sometimes" experienced racial discrimination. Racial socialization messages about racial protectiveness moderately influence respondents' perceived racial discrimination. This effect, however, is mitigated by the addition of the variable measuring the effect of blacks' knowledge about racial discrimination on their interactions with whites, in particular. Consequently, blacks in the NPSS who feel that their knowledge about racial discrimination against black people influences their interactions with whites reported more frequent racial discrimination experiences. Even in the model for racial uncertainty, or prospective racial discrimination, again, the effects of racial socialization messages are mitigated by racial knowledge about whites specifically, which increases blacks' racial uncertainty.

The results from the split-sample survey experiment on racial uncertainty indicate that black Americans believe that people in general and whites are the most likely to be perpetrators of racial discrimination, whereas blacks, Asians, and Latinos are the least likely to be perpetrators. Of all the targets in the split-sample experiment, whites are perceived most apprehensively. Comparing Asians and Latinos, blacks are more racially uncertain about the potential for Asian Americans to discriminate against them. As expected, blacks are perceived to be least likely to racially discriminate against fellow blacks, suggesting that the lowest perceived risk of racial discrimination rests among in-group members. Having a greater linkage to other blacks also increases racial uncertainty about people in general, whites, and Asian Americans. In particular, as we may expect with the racial history of the South, living there moderately increases racial uncertainty about whites. Receiving more emphasis on racial protectiveness messages, in addition, increases racial uncertainty about other blacks and Asians. Specifically, West Indians and Africans are more racially uncertain about their interactions with Asians than African Americans are. Research on Asian American and black American relationships, moreover, points to some of the strained relationships that these two groups have had in urban environments, especially in relationships between black consumers and Asian American merchants (Kim 2000). These studies, however, do not indicate black ethnic distinctions in black-Asian relations.

Overall, black NPSS respondents' racial protectiveness socialization messages have greater import than racial consciousness socialization messages in increasing negative attitudes toward nonblack groups. Perceptions of whites, however, appear to be mitigated by how much black respondents feel their racial knowledge influences their racial attitudes and relations with this group, especially as far as prospective and retrospective discrimination experiences. The most consistent factors that influence blacks' racial perceptions are having received emphasis on racial protectiveness messages and the extent of their black linked fate. Having received racial protectiveness messages induces more negative attitudes toward both black and nonblack racial groups. Most notably, this linkage to other blacks increases negative attitudes about whites and Asians and increases the likelihood of reporting retrospective racial discrimination experiences and perceived risks of racial uncertainty.

To the extent that black Americans feel that their knowledge about racial discrimination affects their feelings about certain racial groups and to the extent that race affects who black Americans perceive will be most likely to discriminate against them because of their race suggests that how black Americans process race in their lives influences their intergroup interactions. Further, when black Americans have little information other than a person's race to act as a heuristic for determining the risk of racial discrimination, intergroup differences promote more racial uncertainty. In order to establish the effect these attitudes have on blacks' trust in specific racial groups, in the next chapter, I examine how racial socialization, black linked fate, and racial uncertainty influence racial trust.

5

Trusting Bodies, Racing Trust

In the previous chapters I examined how blacks' perceptions develop based on racial knowledge networks that inform their cognitive and affective judgments about people. In particular, racial socialization, racial identity, racial discrimination (retrospective and prospective), and racial stereotyping all influence how blacks perceive others as far as their behavior and characterizations of these groups' intergroup relations. For trust assessments, such knowledge networks have the potential for increasing or decreasing trust in others, based on blacks' interpretations of whether the trustees share similar or dissimilar racial group membership with them. From chapter 4, we learned that blacks perceive nonwhites such as Asian Americans and Latinos more similarly to the way that they perceive their own group members than the way they perceive whites. Blacks perceive racial uncertainty more in their relations with whites.

Despite the influence of race on cognition and affection often documented in public-opinion literature, studies that examine trustworthiness often focus on people's perceived behavior and character, absent of their linkage to race. For example, such studies often account for perceptions of trustworthiness based on whether people are perceived as being likely to fulfill an act either competently, honestly, credibly, fairly, or reliably—all considered characteristics of trust (Hardin 2002); yet these studies lack examinations of how people ascribe these characteristics differently based on race. Studying race and perceptions of trustworthiness offers import because the construction of race has entailed ascribing behavior to racial groups, and this behavior and stereotypes associated with it affect assessments of others. Evidence in chapter 4 attests to these group-based character distinctions. So, we may even ask, is it that blacks conceptualize trustworthiness differently from other racial groups? Do we see that certain trust characteristics weigh more heavily in blacks' assessments of people than they do in other groups' assessments? Moreover, do blacks trust differently depending on the race of the trustee? If so, is their racialized trust distinct from other racial groups'? This chapter addresses these several inquiries in order to determine the extent of blacks' racialized trust and the factors explaining it.

To develop my analysis, first, I explore how different racial groups conceive trust. Next, I discuss how race influences social capital and what this means for a racial calculus of trust and, hence, the functioning of racialized trust. Then, I discuss evidence in the literature that describes how blacks might trust various racial groups on the basis of their cultural experiences and attitudes about these groups. I segue into an empirical analysis of both intraracial trust (blacks' trust in other blacks) and interracial trust (blacks' trust in nonblacks). I also examine how blacks' prior racial experiences and attitudes about racial groups influence their trust in other groups. In considering how conceptions of trust may influence racialized trust, I test the effect of trustworthiness characteristics on trust in each racial group. To culminate my analysis, I examine how blacks trust in each racial group and compare whether blacks trust these groups more or less than other racial groups trust them.

Race in Absentia: Perceiving Trustworthiness without Cognizance of Skin Color

To begin our analysis of blacks' trust, one might ask whether there is a distinctive way that blacks think about trust compared to other racial groups. To tackle this inquiry about whether blacks conceptualize trustworthiness differently from other racial groups, several questions in the NPSS asked black, white, and Latino respondents how much they feel characteristics such as someone's *appearance* (how someone looks), being *honest* (whether someone tells the truth), being *competent* (whether someone has the ability to get things done right), being *credible* (whether someone is a good source of information), being *fair* (whether someone has been known to act fairly), and being *reliable* (whether someone can be depended on to do things in the future) matter in assessing a person's trustworthiness. Responses were scaled from 1 = not very much to 5 = very much.

Table 5.1 shows results from regression analyses of the NPSS data that suggest, in some ways, that blacks do perceive and conceptualize trustworthiness differently from whites and Latinos. Using blacks as the comparative group and, hence, the omitted category in the table, we see that one's race as a trustor does in fact influence how blacks, whites, and Latinos in the NPSS perceive trustworthiness. It is interesting to note that, as less likely targets of

TABLE 5.1

Determinants of Aspects of Trustworthiness

Covariates	Honesty	Fairness	Appearance	Credibility	Competence	Reliability
White	−.0341	−.1316**	−.2041**	−.0226	−.0495	−.0705
	(.0613)	(.0665)	(.0985)	(.0908)	(.0833)	(.0701)
Latino	−.0675	−.0105	.1869*	−.0529	−.1750**	−.1355*
	(.0628)	(.0678)	(.1006)	(.0930)	(.0852)	(.0720)
Female	.1540***	.0795	−.0858	.0720	.0466	.1709***
	(.0488)	(.0528)	(.0783)	(.0722)	(.0662)	(.0558)
Age	.0055	.0563****	−.0163	−.0536**	.0285	.0163
	(.0142)	(.0154)	(.0228)	(.0211)	(.0193)	(.0163)
Education	.0270**	.0351**	−.0122	.0235	.0028	.0389
	(.0125)	(.0136)	(.0201)	(.0186)	(.0170)	(.0144)
Income	.0190	.0048	−.0042	−.0423**	.0037	.0121
	(.0139)	(.0150)	(.0223)	(.0207)	(.0188)	(.0159)
South	.0307	.0890	−.0521	.0779	.1801***	.1570***
	(.0509)	(.0551)	(.0817)	(.0754)	(.0691)	(.0583)
Constant	.0307****	3.798****	2.587****	3.947****	3.943****	3.794****
	(.0509)	(.1700)	(.2520)	(.2326)	(.2132)	(.1800)
N	777	773	775	772	774	773
R^2	0.03	0.04	0.02	0.02	0.02	0.04

Source: 2007 National Politics and Socialization Survey
Note: Standard errors are indicated in parentheses.
* $p \leq .10$; ** $p \leq .05$; *** $p \leq .01$; **** $p \leq .001$

racial discrimination, whites in the NPSS also are less likely than blacks to perceive that fairness and appearance matter in perceptions of trustworthiness. It lends credence to the asymmetrical effect of racial discrimination on disparaged groups' interactions with others, wherein disparaged groups continually receive information about the effects of appearance (perhaps racial) and fairness on their quality of life.

For instance, historically, addressing stereotypes about black behavior even entailed dressing and acting with moral comportment in ways that would certify a black person's dignity and deservedness of equality, citizenship, and humanity (Gaines 1996; Higginbotham 1993). Subsequently, appearance became critical not only for blacks' navigation of race throughout much of their de jure and de facto racial discrimination experiences but even for their trials with modern discrimination, as some blacks attempt to avoid racial discrimination by "wearing class" and appearing worthy of receiving respect, as historically privileged classes did (J. Lee 2000). Historical traditions and thoughts protecting blacks' presentations as a racial group in American culture remain in contemporary black society, as blacks continue to challenge the repercussions of negative racial stereotyping that affect their group's everyday life experiences.

In short, appearance not only matters for blacks' attempts to overcome the potential for racial discrimination but also matters perhaps for assessing others (via their race) to determine their likelihood for racial discrimination. This supports the finding in the previous chapter about how blacks process racial uncertainty. The possibility that this conceptualization of fairness might matter for other groups that have been historically discriminated against seems to hold true for Latinos, who in the NPSS perceive appearance mattering only moderately more than blacks do.

As for fairness, the perceived relevance of this factor in trustworthiness is statistically indistinguishable between Latinos and blacks, suggesting that the two groups perceive the relevance of this trustworthiness concept in similar fashion. Whereas whites perceive fairness and appearance as mattering less in trustworthiness than blacks do, Latinos perceive competence and reliability as mattering less than blacks do. This latter finding suggests that a person's reputation and previous deeds matter more in blacks' trust assessments.

Considering the effects of other demographic characteristics on aspects of trustworthiness, table 5.1 also shows that older people perceive fairness as mattering more in trustworthiness than younger people do. Conversely, older people perceive credibility as mattering less than young people do. In a world with technological advancements that have made information more readily and abundantly accessible, perhaps younger people are more interested in credibility because their formative years have been inundated with information networks (especially the Internet) in which they must assess the accuracy of information. As for fairness, clearly with outright egregious violations of civil rights among racial and ethnic minorities and women, older Americans have experienced living conditions defined by the popular thinking of the historical period in which they lived. In seeing disparate treatment among these groups and being able to compare modern advances in civil rights by way of their longer existence than younger people, it seems likely that older people may appreciate fairness more.

Gender differences emerge only with respect to honesty and reliability, with women valuing these characterizations more than men do. This effect seems consistent with many societal roles that women undertake that commonly rely on their judgment of honesty and reliability as a matter of their personal safety and safeguarding others. In the results, higher levels of education also increase the appreciation for honesty and fairness. This seems consistent with characteristics that assist such persons in navigating professional work environments that require decision-making and, hence, honest assessments for optimal decision-making and that rely on decision-making regarding professional advancements and, hence, fairness for optimal outcomes. As for regional effects, compared to nonsoutherners, southerners value competence and reliability more, seemingly suggesting an appreciation for networks that can verify a person's reputation and perhaps productivity.

In sum and with specific focus on blacks' characterizations of trustworthiness, it seems that blacks in the NPSS have greater concerns about people who present themselves in ways that signify the potential for disparate treatment. Both appearance and fairness can circumscribe the potential for disparagement, and this supports the previous finding in chapter 4 that skin color can evoke greater uncertainty about racial discrimination. The relevance of fairness for blacks further supports data in a Pew Research Center report (2010c) that indicate that blacks still fret about racial unfairness. The concern about racial unfairness relates to a larger empirical inquiry about race and human relations, in general.

Racialized Social Capital: The Effect of Race on Human Relations

Social capital conceptually emphasizes the value that social relations bring to people's social, political, or economic productivity. People with broader social networks have more capital in interpersonal bargaining and are able to use their networks to facilitate a variety of actions (Coleman 1988, 1990; Putnam 1993; Lin 2001a, 2001b). For Putnam (1993), trust is the resource that binds social networks. On the basis of this reasoning, we would expect that people who are more trusting should also enjoy greater benefits of social interactions.

Nevertheless, the quality of social relations also depends on societal structures, as vertical (hierarchical) societal structures are less conducive for cooperation than are horizontal (equally distributed) ones (Hero 1992; Putnam 1993; Fukuyama 1995). According to Putnam (1993), whenever there is poorer quality of cooperation among citizens and between citizens and their government,[1] then there should be less trust and a breakdown of democracy. As I have mentioned previously, this assertion, however, lacks accounting for racialized networks in parallel societies, which can function independently of one another without interrupting democracy for privileged racial groups, a system that operates to the disparagement of nonprivileged groups (Hero 1992, 2007).

Hierarchical relationships between whites (as a racial majority group) and nonwhites in the United States lessened the quality of democracy. From the nation's inception through well into the mid-twentieth century, vertical and horizontal social structures operated dually to accommodate a racial hierarchy. Social, economic, and political structures functioned to institutionalize racism and to benefit white group interests over racial and ethnic minorities' interests (Omi and Winant 1994). Public opinion about racial groups and race relations, furthermore, has sustained divisive racial group interests (Kinder and Sanders 1996; Schuman et al. 1997). In turn, we may expect that such racial attitudes were important for sustaining separate social and political networks for whites and for racial and ethnic minorities. Race, as a social construct, divides social networks, institutions, and arguably trust in such a way that separate, racialized horizontal relationships function within a society of hierarchical relations (see Schneider, Teske, Marschall, et al. 1997; Schneider, Teske, Rosch, et al. 1997).

For black Americans, the stringent institutionalization of de facto and de jure racial discrimination marginalized black social networks into a "counterpublic," wherein blacks' needs were addressed by black resources and institutions (Dawson 1994, 2001; Harris-Lacewell 2004). Racialized public and private spaces, thus, led to separate racialized networks that also promoted the interests of specific racial groups. *Black social capital* facilitated enhanced horizontal relationships among blacks, specifically, whereas *intergroup social capital* facilitated cooperation between blacks and whites (Orr 1999). By the same token, if trust is important to social capital, as Putnam (1993) suggests, then in order for black social capital and intergroup social capital to be most efficient, racial group members likely trust along racial lines, as well, in response to racialized societal structures. Scholars even find that individuals' interpersonal trust can create "bridges" that connect networks for community organizing. Nevertheless, such individuals assume personal risks that may either facilitate or disincentivize cross-racial relations (Rusch 2009).

Increased intergroup social capital reportedly enhances blacks' sociopolitical advancement, and building noninsular communities expands blacks' opportunity structures in various aspects of society (Orr 1999). But what does this mean for the function of trust, which supposedly undergirds these cross-racial networks? To what extent is trust also racialized? How does race operate in trust?

How Race Is Calculated in Trust

Partha Dasgupta states, "Trust is based on reputation, and reputation is acquired on the basis of observed behavior over time" (2000, 333). A person's reputation connects him or her to a social group that, relatedly, has historical experiences with race in the U.S. social structure. One's social standing in this U.S. racial structure affects not only how one experiences race individually but also how one experiences race in intergroup relations. For Nan Lin (2001a, 2001b), the social reputation attached to one's group affects his or her *group capital*. The nexus between racial reputation and people's racial group membership is at the core of how bodies are interpreted in the racial calculus of trust.

Collective memory aggregates African American experiences by linking group members to one another (Dawson 1994, 2001). Historical, racially dichotomous relationships between blacks and whites should structure how blacks perceive the actions of whites as actors in social and political contexts. Blacks' should trust nonwhite racial groups (i.e., Latinos and Asian Americans) more because the historical relationships between these groups are less divisive. However, the contemporary realities of relations between blacks and other nonwhites should be mitigated by personal racial discrimination experiences and attitudes toward these groups.

As I discussed in chapter 3, blacks learn the "reputation of races" by way of their racial socialization experiences. In chapter 4, we examined the extent to which racial socialization influences racial perceptions. Likewise, experiences with racial discrimination diminish positive perceptions about interracial relations. Black-white relationships are perceived by blacks to be most affected by prior knowledge of blacks' American racial experiences. Whites, furthermore, are perceived by blacks as less trustworthy and more likely to discriminate against them, thus indicating more racial uncertainty in blacks' interracial relations with whites than in their relations with Asian Americans and Latinos.

The results presented in the previous chapters of this text lend credence to Claus Offe's (1999) contention that group membership can increase (or decrease) the likelihood of trust in other group members on the basis of the stereotypes that are associated with these groups, or what he refers to as "stereotypes of trustworthiness." Although blacks in the NPSS were less likely to subscribe to negative stereotypes than to positive stereotypes about each of the racial groups, they nonetheless attributed more negative behavioral characterizations to people in general and to whites. In short, the cognitive-affective perceptions associated with specific racial groups suggest that perceived trust in these groups also may be racialized.

Racialized trust, whether it is *intraracial* (trust in one's own racial group) or *interracial* (trust in members of other racial groups), is trust based on the perceptions associated with the trustee's racial group. With racial phenotypic characteristics acting as heuristics for trust, racial trust thus involves cognitive processing of individuals as racial group members, conjoined with recollection of information about these racial groups that is either transmitted through racial socialization and personalized racial experiences or assumed because of expectations for racial behavior or racial discrimination.

Depending on the aforementioned factors, people will be more or less trusting of their own racial group or members of other racial groups. I expect intraracial trust to outweigh interracial trust. Put more simply with respect to the present study, blacks should trust their fellow racial group members more than they do members of other racial groups. However, racial protectiveness messages, negative personalized racial experiences, and racial uncertainty about prospective racial discrimination should reduce blacks' generalized trust and their trust in various racial groups (including fellow black group members). Racial consciousness messages should reduce blacks' trust in whites and enhance their trust in nonwhites.

Racialized trust, thus, is a consequence of historical racial construction and its continuing effects on society. Racialized trust (or the lack thereof) does not have to indicate normatively negative behavior, nor does it have to indicate a deprivation of resources or a deficiency in social capital, as traditional scholarship in social capital may suggest. Instead, racialized trust for groups that have been historically discriminated against can serve several meaningful functions:

1. To enhance racial networks among one's own racial group (intraracial trust)
2. To serve as a protective mechanism against prospective racial discrimination (interracial trust)
3. To reconnect historically segregated racial groups with institutions from which they had been previously excluded
4. To reconnect these segregated racial groups to a larger society with other racial groups, with which they previously did not have equal social or economic status.

The fact that these functions of racialized trust seemingly operate in a fashion respective of nonwhites' racial experiences is, quite frankly, also an artifact of racial construction in America, in which many nonwhite groups were racially disparaged and many whites were not. When trustors use racial trust to discriminate further against and marginalize trustees, however, this functioning of trust proves to be problematic because it reifies historical racial discrimination patterns based on gender, class, and skin color.

Without interracial trust, most importantly, the prospects for cross-racial networks and interracial cooperation are limited. Nevertheless, African American ideological perspectives have engaged the debate about what this means for blacks' progress, interrogating, specifically, the extent to which blacks should cooperate and coalesce with whites, especially, and with other nonblack groups (Dawson 2001; Harris-Lacewell 2004). How democracy deals with racial construction and its effect on social relations is a larger concern about the broader implications of interracial cooperation. This concern, however, is beyond the scope of this book. Clearly, however, the complexities of the benefits (or the lack thereof) of racialized trust suggest even more how different racial calculi of trust may prove more or less beneficial to black group members' individual life experiences and group-oriented political interests.

What is important to recognize is that race continues to affect interpersonal perceptions and intergroup relations. Race also continues to affect memory, mores about interracial group relations, and perceptions of trust in social and political institutions (Williams 1998). Therefore, in studying how race affects trust among blacks, we can learn more about the boundaries of black group relations and their larger meaning for social capital inquiries. The literature on blacks' cultural mistrust offers some import for how blacks trust whites, in particular, and later, I turn to literature on interracial attitudes to illuminate how blacks may trust Asian Americans and Latinos.

Black Cultural Mistrust

When we examine race-specific assessments of trust, extant studies of blacks' trust in specific racial groups are more heavily concentrated in health-related disciplines such as psychology and medicine, and these studies often contextualize blacks' trust vis-à-vis whites. There is no wonder that such studies have emerged in these disciplines, as blacks have historically faced egregious mistreatment in the medical context, becoming the subjects of unjust and inhumane medical experimentation and public policies targeting their reproductivity (Roberts 1997; Washington 2006). Most infamously, black men infected with syphilis were discriminately targeted as unknowing subjects in a forty-year, government-sponsored research project on the progression of syphilis, "The Tuskegee Syphilis Study." This "study" denied the men treatment under false pretenses and, inadvertently, led to ill-health and death among many of the study's subjects. This ordeal seemingly further institutionalized disdain for the value of black life. It illustrated how medicine could be used in ways that have either intended or unintended genocidal effects. For example, even more recently, evidence suggests that blacks subscribe to conspiratorial thinking about diseases such as AIDS being created in laboratories in a concerted effort either to control the growth of the black population or to destroy the black population entirely (Sniderman and Piazza 2002). With this conspiratorial thinking, perceivers harbor suspicion and, ultimately, distrust regarding others' general concern for, regard for, and interests in protecting the lives of black people.

As similarly noted in political science literature, cultural mistrust literature finds that blacks tend to be less trusting than are whites and other racial groups (Boulware et al. 2003; Schnittker 2004). These studies, just as those in political science, also focus on the extent to which blacks trust whites, concentrating specifically on the dyadic relationships between blacks as patients and whites as therapists or physicians. Additional research focuses on constructs of cultural mistrust that encompass different aspects of blacks' lives —education and training experiences, interpersonal relations, business and work environments, and politics and law (Terrell and Terrell 1981).

Two areas in which blacks are most culturally mistrusting are in their interpersonal relations (Terrell and Terrell 1981) and in politics and law (Whaley 1998). These contexts, consequently, are those in which blacks have high levels of distrust and likely many negative attitudes toward whites. This distrust, thus, conceivably encapsulates power-imbalanced relationships between blacks and whites, more generally. Overall, cultural mistrust studies point to resultant alienation or psychological health that mistrusting blacks feel when they are unable to sustain qualitatively substantive relationships with others (especially whites) in contexts that can be beneficial for enhancing their quality of life.

At debate in this literature is whether blacks' mistrust is indicative of cultural paranoia (Grier and Cobbs 1968), contributive to a clinically distinct condition such as depression (Whaley 1998), or promotional for better psychological health, self-protection, and social adaptation (Bell and Tracey 2006; Whaley 2001). The assessment of blacks' psychological conditions, then, becomes controversial not only because it can mischaracterize blacks' behavior but also because it can potentially lead to misdiagnoses of blacks' psychological conditions and imprecise treatments for these misdiagnoses (Whaley 1998, 2001). Such assessments have even broader implications for how blacks are treated as a group and how their mental health is assessed, more specifically.

For one, the severity of paranoia is identified along a continuum of symptoms that "range from relatively mild symptoms including mistrust, self-consciousness, and suspiciousness to severe types of delusions, often involving hallucinatory experiences found in psychotic disorders" (Whaley 1998, 326–327). Although victimization is conceptualized in this framework as a mild form of paranoia, blacks' perceptions of discrimination and mistrust, thus, become professionally deemed misguided, delusional, illegitimate, psychotic, and psychologically pathological. Second, this pathologization of blacks' perceptions may lead to more endogenous attitudes, or "metastereotypes," about how blacks perceive the way that whites perceive blacks (Sigelman and Tuch 1997). Consequently, black group members perceive that their white health providers racially stereotype them and do so inaccurately. This results in yet another example of blacks' experiences with racial discrimination and their perception of others' cultural insensitivity toward blacks (Schnittker 2004; Whaley 2001). Third, cultural paranoia characterizes black behavior devoid of blacks' sociohistorical realities. This is to say that this diagnosis ignores the fact that blacks actually have reason to fear prospective racial discrimination or to be suspicious of others because of their historical experiences as a racial group with state-sponsored and societally-enforced discrimination.

Racialized Distrust: Knowledge-Based, Not Paranoid-Schizophrenic

Anthropologist John Jackson offers an intriguing discussion about the strong influence of racial construction in the United States on what he calls "racial paranoia," or "distrustful conjecture about purposeful race-based maliciousness and the 'benign neglect' of racial indifference" (2008, 3). In Jackson's view, racial paranoia plagues all racial groups because of the centering of race in historical and conflictual race-based interests. He also links racial distrust to racial paranoia:

> Distrust is one of the most important features of racial paranoia. Without it, racism and racial discrimination would have little social traction. And this distrust feeds our doubts. Employers fear that black workers will be

lazy and confrontational, which is part of the reason why they may pass them over for jobs or promotions. White law school applicants fear that less-qualified minorities will get accepted to schools that deny them entry, which propels some to file lawsuits claiming reverse discrimination. And we can complicate this picture even further by admitting that individuals sometimes internalize the fears and distrust others attribute to their own ostensible racial group. For example, African Americans can also readily cross the street when they see other African Americans approaching. What do we make of claims that black cab drivers are not that much more likely to stop for black would-be passengers than their white counterparts? This fear can characterize relations across racial lines or within racial camps. Either way, we have a lack of trust that racial paranoia feasts on.

And this distrust is not just cognitive. It is also intuited, felt, sensed, which is an incredibly important part of racial paranoia's power. (16–17)

As I have noted previously, I take the view that blacks' distrust is grounded in their socialized, experienced, and perceptual foundations about race. My view suggests that blacks' fear of discrimination is not oriented in paranoid-schizophrenic symptoms likened to a health condition. Like Jackson, I suggest that there is something "real" about the fear of race affecting one's livelihood. Choosing not to use the language of "paranoia," I suggest that there may not be an excessive emphasis on race as an explanation for one's treatment because of the extent to which race has been historically "overemphasized" as a marker for ill-treatment for black group members. Even in Jackson's conjecture, just because de jure discrimination no longer exists does not eliminate the possibility of de facto discrimination occurring post–Jim Crow. This is why in my conception of racialized distrust, I am interested in racial uncertainty and what this means for the perceived likelihood that certain racial groups may or may not discriminate against a trustor in the future.

Examining blacks' distrust based on the race of the person being assessed, therefore, should account for the influence of the several indicators that I have submitted. Later in this chapter, I analyze these indicators as determinants of racialized trust and as factors influencing differences in trust in racial groups. Trust scholars in political science, notably, often conceptualize trust without accounting for possible distinctions in trust levels based on the race of the actor being perceived. These studies, additionally, emphasize trust in actors within specific contexts, in this case political contexts. While this remains an important inquiry, still there is a dearth of information about how blacks principally trust in racial groups.

Most of the literature on blacks' cultural mistrust focuses on blacks' perceptions of whites, exclusively. What has been done in political science also focuses on blacks' political trust in other blacks and in whites or the assessment of differing trust levels among racial groups (Avery 2006). Rarely do these studies explore blacks' mistrust of other groups, such as Asian Americans and Latinos. Racial trust studies, therefore, should be broadened to include perceptions of both white and nonwhite groups.

Accordingly, blacks' trust in various racial groups receives further attention and analysis in this chapter. I return to an analysis of how blacks perceive these groups specifically in social and political contexts in chapter 6 and chapter 7, respectively. Here, using data from the 2007 NPSS and the 2000 SCBS, I build on the analysis in chapter 4 on blacks' racial processing to determine the effects of racial socialization, perceptions of discrimination, and stereotyping on racial trust. While the cultural mistrust literature offers us a glimpse of blacks' attitudes toward whites, the literature on blacks' racial attitudes foregrounds hypotheses regarding blacks' racial trust in nonwhites, as well. I discuss this literature in the next section.

Black Racial Attitudes toward Whites, Latinos, and Asian Americans

In a recent survey released by the Pew Research Center (2010c), both blacks (76 percent) and whites (79 percent) overwhelmingly stated that blacks and whites get along "very" or "pretty" well. Blacks and Latinos, however, viewed their relationships differently. Blacks were more positive, claiming mostly that blacks and Latinos get along "pretty well" (54 percent), whereas a plurality of Latinos (32 percent) claimed that they get along with blacks "not too well." Still, blacks in the survey were more likely to see an increasing Latino population as bad for blacks than they were to say that it is a good thing. In fact, Latinos also perceived their relations with whites in more negative terms, reporting more maladaptive relations than what whites viewed. Nevertheless, Latinos (20 percent) were twice as likely as whites (10 percent) to see their relations as getting along "very well."

Blacks with negative attitudes toward their own group members, additionally, possess more negative attitudes toward nonblack groups (Cummings and Lambert 1997), and blacks subscribing to more negative stereotypes about Latinos also sense more threat from Latinos who are immigrants (McClain, Lyle, Carter, et al. 2007). Scott Cummings and Thomas Lambert (1997) also find that blacks have more positive attitudes about Latinos than about whites; yet blacks' attitudes toward Asian Americans are indistinguishable from those of whites.

These studies of black public opinion are among the few that focus on blacks' interracial attitudes, for research on interracial attitudes generally focuses on whites' attitudes toward nonwhites. Research that has been done on blacks' attitudes toward other groups finds blacks having more positive attitudes toward Latinos than Latinos offer in return (Mindiola, Niemann, and Rodriguez 2002; McClain, Carter, et al. 2006). Blacks' attitudes toward Asian Americans have been regarded as less favorable, as have Asian Americans' attitudes toward blacks (Kim 2000); however, this finding depends on the concentration of both groups in a locality. In general, however, with increased racial isolation, blacks adopt more negative attitudes toward groups other than their own (Gay 2004; Marschall and Stolle 2004; Oliver and Wong 2003). Blacks often perceive whites negatively, with evidence suggesting that increased interracial contact lessens this negativity (D. Harris 1995). Yet there also is general conflicting evidence in the literature about the effect of increased contact between groups on building more positive or negative attitudes between them (Hewstone and Brown 1986; Huddy 2004). Regardless of the amount of contact between groups, evidence suggests that blacks feel closer to racial and ethnic minorities (particularly, Spanish-speaking peoples, Asian Americans, and American Indians) than they do to whites, and overall, blacks feel closer to their own racial group members (D. Harris 1995).

Positive attitudes toward Latinos and Asian Americans can be mitigated by perceived economic competition between blacks and these groups when socioeconomic gains and losses are viewed in zero-sum terms (Bobo and Hutchings 1996; Gay 2006). These attitudes dampen the potential for positive intergroup relations. Perceived or reality-based asymmetrical relations between groups heighten racial threat and retard the potential for trust. Numerous studies, additionally, point to the perceived effect of racial economic threat couched in attitudes about immigration that could potentially decrease trust between blacks and Latinos and Asian Americans, two groups that are often affected by immigration politics.

For example, Michael Thornton and Yuko Mizuno (1999) analyzed black adults' attitudes during the 1980s toward Hispanic and West Indian groups. Using data in the 1984 and 1988 National Black Election Study, they tested blacks' feelings of closeness to Latinos, West Indians, and whites. Their analysis found that African Americans felt closest to the groups in the following order: whites, West Indians, and Latinos. Black men felt closer to these groups than black women did. Younger blacks felt less close to whites than older blacks did. As well, blacks who lived in urban areas felt less close to whites than did those who lived in more rural areas. Regional influences mattered only in that blacks who lived in the South felt less close to Latinos. Women who worried about immigrants taking jobs away from blacks also felt less close to whites.

In a study of Los Angeles residents, James Johnson, Walter Farrell, and Chandra Guinn (1997) found that blacks and non-Hispanic whites are more likely than Latinos and Asian Americans to feel that there will be a negative effect of immigration on their well-being. Roughly one-half of the non-Hispanic white and black respondents expressed that they would have less political and economic influence than they currently have if immigration continued at the present rate. A majority of blacks surveyed also agreed that more good jobs for Asians and Latinos would result in less good jobs for blacks. Nevertheless, Latinos viewed their competition in employment as being primarily with Asians.

In the Johnson, Farrell, and Guinn study, racial groups also expressed negative stereotypes of one another. For example, Asian Americans in the study viewed blacks and Latinos more negatively, associating both groups with being less intelligent than Asians and preferring to live on welfare. While whites also expressed negative attitudes toward Latinos, they viewed Asian Americans less negatively than they viewed Latinos. Latinos viewed Asian Americans more negatively than they viewed all other groups. However, Asian Americans viewed whites more negatively than they viewed all other groups. A majority of blacks and Latinos in the study expressed that almost all non-Hispanic whites are prone to discriminate against members of their group. Among Asian Americans, Korean and Japanese Americans were more likely than Chinese Americans to view non-Hispanic whites as likely perpetrators of discrimination against their groups. Blacks, whites, and Latinos viewed Asian Americans as being difficult to get along with.

Other scholars have found evidence of tensions between blacks and Asian Americans in the context of neighborhood stores, in major cities such as Los Angeles (Diaz-Veizades and Chang 1996) and New York City (Kim 2000), where blacks are mostly customers and Asians (Korean Americans) are mostly store owners. Case studies document black-Korean tensions during the 1980s and 1990s, which stemmed from blacks' perceived persecution by Korean store owners who seemingly followed them as criminal suspects in their stores or offered them poor, discriminatory service (Abelmann and Lie 1995; Kim 2000).

In a study of a San Francisco housing project, Patricia Guthrie and Janice

Hutchinson (1995) also found evidence of blacks' possessing stereotypical attitudes toward Asian Americans. Blacks commonly ignored ethnic differences among Asians, referring to them as "Chinese," regardless of their actual ethnicity, and referred to them as "immigrants" without clear knowledge of their citizenship status. Furthermore, with respect to employment, blacks perceived that employers prefer employing Asians over blacks. Therefore, negative attitudes toward immigrants in general, perceived competition with Asian Americans, and perceptions of discrimination by Asian Americans can decrease blacks' trust in this group.

Just as with Asian Americans, blacks' attitudes about Latinos may be tempered by attitudes about immigration. Localities with large concentrations of nonwhite immigrants can potentially become sites for racial conflict. In 1994, the controversial Proposition 187 was a California ballot initiative that sought to restrict undocumented immigrants' access to social services, health services, and public education. Although the proposition initially passed, it was later found unconstitutional by the state supreme court. The proposition developed in a context in which whites no longer constituted the majority population in the state and in which immigrants were potentially perceived as undocumented residents who were either "free riding" on or competing for the resources of taxpayers. Despite the potential for racial conflict even among racial and ethnic minorities, in a study of blacks', whites', and Asians' attitudes toward Proposition 187, Irwin Morris (2000) found that blacks were on average less supportive of Proposition 187 than were whites and Asian Americans.

Aside from the West, where there is a high concentration of immigration, especially in California, more recently, the South has become a context for potential racial conflict over immigration. Paula McClain and colleagues studied immigration attitudes in the South, where Latino immigration has changed the demographic landscape of a formerly black-white context. In many southern localities, Latinos now cohabitate or inhabit areas that historically were occupied by blacks. Such demographic changes are believed to heighten blacks' perception that Latinos are socioeconomic competition (Mohl 2003; McClain, Lyle, Carter, et al. 2007; McClain, Carter, Perez, et al. 2009), and evidence suggests that blacks perceive this competition with Latinos more than whites do.

In McClain and colleagues' studies of black, Latino, and white attitudes about Latino immigration in Durham, North Carolina (McClain, Lyle, Carter, et al. 2007; McClain, Carter, Perez, et al. 2009) and in Little Rock, Arkansas, and Memphis, Tennessee (McClain, Carter, Perez, et al. 2009), blacks' perceived economic threat and subscription to more negative stereotypes about Latinos increased their vexation about Latino immigration. For instance, 42 percent of black respondents expressed that Latinos were taking jobs away from blacks, compared to 49 percent who disagreed with this belief and another 9 percent who neither agreed nor disagreed (McClain, Carter, Perez, et al. 2009). Blacks also expressed greater anxiety about increased Latino immigration leading to fewer economic opportunities for their racial group members (McClain, Carter, Perez, et al. 2009).

Black attitudes about Latino immigration, especially in the South, appear to be in flux, perhaps reflective of the kinds of interactions blacks have with Latinos in their respective localities and the continued growth of the Latino population (McClain, Carter, Perez, et al. 2009). For example, in one study, blacks' greater contact with Latinos diminished their perceptions of economic threat from Latino immigrants and enhanced perceptions of greater economic opportunities (McClain, Carter, Perez, et al. 2009). In some instances, blacks even feel closer to Latinos than they do to whites (McClain, Carter, et al. 2006). Yet evidence indicates that both whites and blacks appear concerned about the effects of Latino immigration (McClain, Lyle, Carter, et al. 2007; McClain, Carter, Perez, et al. 2009), and in some instances whites are even more concerned than blacks, but with less concern about economic competition (McClain, Carter, Perez, et al. 2009).

Part of blacks' vexation appears to stem from their beliefs about the continuing denial of their democratic inclusion. With the immigration of another nonwhite group in the region, the denial of democratic inclusion seems compounded by perceptions that whites control the socioeconomic advancement of one group over another and have the power to marginalize blacks further in comparison to Latinos (Carter 2007). Moreover, evidence points to both political and economic competition between blacks and Latinos in areas where the two groups are heavily concentrated (McClain and Karnig 1990; McClain 1993; Johnson and Oliver 1994; McClain 2006). Thus, despite blacks' shared minority status with Latinos, negative attitudes about immigrants and negative views of their own economic standing will likely diminish their trust in Latinos.

Blacks' Racial Trust: Hypotheses about Intraracial and Interracial Trusts

As we have learned from the preceding review of literature, blacks feel closer to racial and ethnic minorities than they do to whites. Although blacks share racial minority status with Latinos and Asian Americans, regional context, immigrant attitudes, perceptions of likely discrimination, and economic conditions can potentially reduce the effect that shared status should have on increasing blacks' trust in these groups. Regionally, blacks in the South or the West live in greater proximity to Latinos and Asian Americans, and these regions have been potential sites for interminority conflict and for blacks' possessing more negative attitudes toward Latinos and Asian Americans. Blacks' negative attitudes toward immigrants and immigration and their perceived competition with groups that are either stereotyped as "immigrants" or that actually do constitute most of the immigrants in a locality also potentially conceal racial threat. Hence, negative attitudes toward immigration should reduce trust in Latinos and Asian Americans. Furthermore, blacks who are less satisfied with their current economic conditions potentially see Latinos and Asian Americans more competitively, thus reducing the likelihood for trust in these groups. In sum, blacks should racially trust in the following ways:

1. Blacks should trust other blacks more than they trust other racial groups.
2. Blacks should trust their own group members more than whites, Asian Americans, and Latinos trust blacks.
3. Blacks should trust whites less than they trust other groups.
4. Blacks should trust whites less than other groups do.
5. Blacks with negative attitudes about immigration should be more distrusting of Asian Americans and Latinos, as two groups commonly associated with immigration politics.
6. Black southerners should be more distrusting of whites and Latinos than blacks in other regions are.
7. Black westerners should be more distrusting of Asian Americans than blacks in other regions are.

Employing data from the NPSS, we can determine effects of race on blacks' general trust in others by examining a race and trust experiment. Using these data, we can also ascertain whether certain characteristics of trustworthiness determine trust in specific racial groups. Using data from the SCBS, we can compare blacks' racial trust with other racial groups'. We also can learn more about how blacks' attitudes toward immigration and how their perceived economic status influence their racial trust. The next few sections address the following inquiries: Do blacks trust differently depending on the race of the person to be trusted? Do factors of trustworthiness influence how much people of a certain race are trusted?

The Racial Nature of Generalized Social Trust: Results from the NPSS

As I mentioned previously, generalized trust measures often ask people how much they can trust people in general. In this section, I examine how race influences generalized trust by incorporating the race of the people to be trusted in general, and I analyze race and trust experiments to determine whether blacks trust differently depending on the race of the trustee.

In the NPSS, respondents were asked, "How much do you feel you can trust (race of target) people? Most (target) people can be trusted, or you can't be too careful in trusting (race of target) people," scaled 0 to 1. As noted in the previous survey experiments, the target race mentioned in each respondent's survey reflects a randomized equal-probability distribution for receipt of a survey mentioning one of five targets—people (the control group), blacks, whites, Asians, or Latinos. Any statistically significant differences determined in the comparative analysis of means indicate those influenced by the race of the target. Put more simply, statistically significant differences show that one racial group is trusted more or less than another group.

Results from a race and trust experiment in the NPSS and the comparisons of means for each target in the experiment are shown in table 5.2. In this experimental analysis, we can compare how blacks, whites, and Latinos in the NPSS trust in each group. These results exemplify that blacks trust people in general the least of all the targets, although whites are trusted second least. In other words, black respondents in the NPSS trust blacks, Asians, and Latinos more than they trust whites. In fact, among all the racial groups in which blacks can trust, whites are trusted the least. Contrary to expectation, blacks trust Latinos no differently than they trust Asian Americans. However, as expected, blacks trust their own group members more than they trust Asian Americans and Latinos.

In order to compare whether blacks trust distinctively compared to whites and Latinos, I also scrutinize the results of these groups' trust in other racial groups. For whites in the NPSS, we see that, similar to blacks, people in general are trusted the least of all the targets. In fact, whites' mean for trust in people in general is almost the same as blacks' mean, whereas Latinos' mean for trust in people in general is greater than both blacks' and whites'. With further inspection of the comparisons of means, whites trust all racial groups more than they do people in general. Contrary to expectation, whites trust blacks and Asians more than they do their own group members. Modest distinctions in the results also indicate that whites trust Asian Americans

TABLE 5.2

Comparisons of Means for Racial Groups' Generalized Racial Trust (Race and Trust Experiment)

Comparisons of means	Black respondents' trust	White respondents' trust	Latino respondents' trust
People/Blacks	.35/.89 (+)**** (n = 191)	.34/.88 (+)**** (n = 90)	.49/.91 (+)**** (n = 93)
People/Whites	.35/.56 (+)*** (n = 193)	.34/.65 (+)*** (n = 84)	.49/.65 (n = 86)
People/Asians	.35/.78 (+)**** (n = 181)	.34/.89 (+)**** (n = 83)	.49/.85 (+)**** (n = 89)
People/Latinos	.35/.76 (+)**** (n = 176)	.34/.72 (+)**** (n = 83)	.49/.91 (+)**** (n = 92)
Whites/Blacks	.56/.89 (+)**** (n = 182)	.65/.88 (+)**ᵃ (n = 80)	.65/.91 (+)*** (n = 81)
Whites/Asians	.56/.78 (+)*** (n = 172)	.65/.89 (+)**ᵃ (n = 73)	.65/.85(+)**ᵃ (n = 77)
Whites/Latinos	.56/.76 (+)*** (n = 167)	.65/.72 (n = 73)	.65/.91 (+)*** (n = 80)
Asians/Blacks	.78/.89 (+)**ᵃ (n = 170)	.89/.88 (n = 79)	.85/.90 (n = 84)
Asians/Latinos	.78/.76 (n = 155)	.89 (+)/.72 *ᵃ (n = 72)	.85/.91 (n = 83)
Latinos/Blacks	.76/.89 (+)**ᵃ (n = 165)	.72/.88 (+)*ᵃ (n = 79)	.91/.91 (n = 87)

Source: 2007 National Politics and Socialization Survey

Note: All statistically significant differences of means are indicated based on a p-value of at most .005, which is consistent with the Bonferroni adjustment method. The Bonferroni adjustment method for comparisons of means requires that the statistical significance of ten comparisons must be adjusted downward by dividing a .05 statistical significance level by the number of comparisons made to avoid Type I errors, or reporting statistically significant comparisons when they are, in fact, not significant. Therefore, the acceptable level of statistical significance for this analysis is $p \leq .005$. (+) indicates the group trusted most in the comparisons of means.
ᵃ Statistically significant without Bonferroni adjustment method, which offers a stringent standard of statistical significance
* $p \leq .10$; ** $p \leq .05$; *** $p \leq .01$; **** $p \leq .001$

slightly more than they do Latinos, and they trust blacks slightly more than they do Latinos. Notwithstanding whites' trusting Latinos less than they trust both Asian Americans and blacks, whites do not trust their own group more than they do Latinos, as the comparisons of means between these two groups are statistically indistinguishable.

Latinos in the NPSS, in contrast to whites, trust blacks, Asians, and fellow Latinos more than they trust people in general. They do not distinguish trust between people in general and whites. They also trust blacks, Asians, and Latinos more than they do whites. Latinos, interestingly, do not trust differently among Asian Americans, blacks, and Latinos, as their trust for these groups is statistically indistinguishable. Thus, similar to blacks, Latinos trust whites the least of all other racial groups. But, unlike blacks, they do not trust their own group more than they trust Asians and blacks.

The Effect of Racial Experiences and Attitudes on Racialized Trust

How do racial socialization experiences (racial consciousness messages and racial protectiveness messages), black identity, and expectations for prospective racial discrimination (racial uncertainty) influence trust? Through the NPSS analyses of trust in the respective target groups that we obtained for respondents who received surveys about a specific target in the race and trust survey, we are able to capture these effects. Of all the models analyzed, only one model was not statistically overdetermined: blacks' trust in people in general. Although the results are not featured here, only education and racial protectiveness messages were statistically significant, yet at only the 90 percent confidence level. Increased education enhanced trust in people in general. Of very important note is the inverse relationship between racial socialization about racial protectiveness messages and trust in people in general, which indicates that, as expected, with greater emphasis on racial protectiveness socialization messages, black respondents have less trust in people in general.

The Effect of Trustworthiness Characteristics on Racialized Trust

To what extent do certain aspects of trustworthiness predict trust in each racial group? I analyze NPSS responses of blacks', whites', and Latinos' trust in each group based on the respondents who received surveys featuring these specific targets in the race and trust experiment. (Results are not shown.) In most instances, specific trust characteristics do not predict general trust in groups of people. With two exceptions, people who feel that credibility and competence matter more in perceived trustworthiness are also more trusting of Asian Americans.

These ordered probit regression models also show whether white and Latino respondents are more or less trusting in racial groups than are black respondents in the NPSS. Results indicate that Latino NPSS respondents are more trusting than black respondents are in people in general, whites, and Asians. Whites and blacks in the NPSS, however, trust all groups similarly. That is, notably, whites are no more or less trusting than blacks are in each of the target groups in the experiment. This brings special attention to the fact, additionally, that black, white, and Latino respondents do not trust their own group more than other groups do.

Socioeconomic indicators such as education and income have different effects on trust in groups. On the one hand, more education has more liberalizing effects on increasing people's trust in people in general and in Latinos. Increased income, on the other hand, reduces trust in people in general and in blacks, while increasing trust in Asian Americans.

In models that were tested that were specific to black respondents' opinions only, trustworthiness characteristics mattered only in the model of trust in Asian Americans. For black respondents, those who felt more strongly that *credibility* matters more as an indicator of trustworthiness were also more trusting of Asian Americans, whereas those who felt more strongly that *competence* matters more as an indicator of trustworthiness were less trusting of Asian Americans. While the model comparing Latinos' and whites' attitudes to blacks' attitudes shows that, similar to the model for black respondents, *credibility* increases trust in Asian Americans, on the contrary, the model for only black respondents shows that more belief in *competence* as an indicator of trustworthiness decreases blacks' trust in Asian Americans.

Trusting Skin? How Blacks' Racial Trust Compares to Other Racial Groups'

In the NPSS, we saw that not only do blacks trust differently depending on the race of the person being evaluated, but so do whites and Latinos. The 2000 Social Capital Benchmark Survey (SCBS) allows us to compare blacks' racial trust to whites', Latinos', and Asian Americans' racial trust. The SCBS gives us a representative, national probability sample (N = 3,003) for models that compare whites' (n = 1,839), Asians' (n = 44), and Latinos' (n = 502) racial trust to blacks' (n = 501, the omitted racial category). Respondents are asked, "Generally speaking, how much would you say that you can trust (Asian people, African Americans or blacks, white people, or Hispanics or Latinos)?" The variables for trust in each racial group (*tr2wht* = trust in whites, *tr2asn* = trust in Asians, *tr2blk* = trust in blacks, *tr2his* = trust in Hispanics) have been recoded 0 = trust them not at all, 1 = trust them only a little, 2 = trust them some, 3 = trust them a lot.

In the SCBS, whites and Asian Americans are most likely to report trusting groups "a lot." While a very small percentage of people report trusting groups "not at all," Latinos report trusting groups "not at all" most frequently. This contrasts the findings in the NPSS, wherein Latinos, in particular, are more trusting in certain racial groups than blacks are. Latinos also are most distrusting of blacks and Asians.

As for blacks, while we may expect blacks to be most distrusting of whites, here, in contrast to the NPSS, larger percentages of blacks distrust Latinos and Asians. In fact, ordered probit regression models comparing blacks' racial trust to nonblacks' (not shown here) elucidate that blacks are less trusting of whites, Asian Americans, and Latinos than nonblacks are. Interestingly, blacks do not trust their fellow group members more than nonblacks do. When all the measures of racial trust in each racial group are combined into a single interracial trust scale (*racetcat*), blacks are still less trusting than nonblacks (results not shown). How do blacks trust these racial groups in comparison to how the other racial groups do?

Table 5.3 shows determinants of blacks', whites', Asian Americans', and Latinos' racial trust in several racial groups. The models control for demographic factors such as *race* (*ethnic4*, including dummy variables for whites, Asians, and Latinos in order to compare whether their trust is more or less than blacks' (the omitted category), *gender* (female = 1), *age, education, income,* and *region* (South = 1, in models for trust in blacks, whites, and Latinos; West = 1, in the model for trust in Asians, *censreg*), whether respondents feel that *their racial or ethnic group gives them a sense of community* (*grpeth*, the only comparable measure of racial identity in the survey), whether the respondent feels *economically satisfied* (yes = 1, *econsat*), whether the respondent feels *others view him or her dishonestly* (dishonestly = 1, *expdisc3*), and whether the respondent feels *immigrants are too demanding in their push for equal rights* (too demanding = 1, *immig2*, in models for trust in Latinos and Asian Americans only).

The model for solely black respondents' racial trust, shown in table 5.4, includes all the aforementioned variables, with the addition of an additive measure for whether the black respondent has white, Asian American, or Latino friends—*diversity of racial networks* (*bwht, basn, bhisp,* scaled 0–3; N = 494, with 21 percent having no friends of another race, 35 percent with one friend, 24 percent with two friends, and 20 percent with three friends), with higher scores indicating more diverse racial networks.

TABLE 5.3

Determinants of Groups' Racial Trust in Black, White, Latino, and Asian Groups

Covariates	Trust in blacks	Trust in whites	Trust in Asians	Trust in Latinos	Interracial trust index
White	.1816***	.2532****	.4337****	.4035****	.4121****
	(.0695)	(.0696)	(.0760)	(.0749)	(.0751)
Asian	.1282	.4113*	.6978***	.2469	.4641
	(.2152)	(.2217)	(.2277)	(.2183)	(.2242)
Latino	−.3622****	−.1170	−.0778	.2501	−.0056
	(.0843)	(.0841)	(.0929)	(.0882)	(.0919)
Female	.0900*	−.0239	−.0649	−.0038	.0317
	(.0508)	(.0506)	(.0541)	(.0529)	(.0532)
Age	.0087***	.0112****	.0069****	.0069****	.0083****
	(.0016)	(.0016)	(.0018)	(.0018)	(.0018)
Education	.0332**	.0137	.0280*	.0432****	.0205
	(.0153)	(.0152)	(.0166)	(.0163)	(.0163)
Income	.0288*	.0234	.0355**	.0251	.0276*
	(.0149)	(.0149)	(.0159)	(.0157)	(.0157)
South	−.0738	−.0782	—	−.1015*	−.1165***
	(.0511)	(.0509)		(.0519)	(.0584)
West	—	—	.0215	—	−.0642
			(.0668)		(.0717)
Sense of community from R's ethnic group	.1631*	−.0088	.0373	.0683	.0686
	(.0948)	(.0942)	(.1001)	(.0984)	(.0983)
Economic satisfaction	.1485****	.1613****	.1716****	.1900****	.1473****
	(.0415)	(.0411)	(.0440)	(.0434)	(.0435)
R feels others view R as dishonest	−.1567****	−.1645****	−.1667****	−.1524****	−.1505****
	(.0282)	(.0280)	(.0305)	(.0299)	(.0306)
Immigrants' push for equal rights too demanding	—	—	−.4309****	−.5019****	−.5215****
			(.0561)	(.0552)	(.0552)
Cut 1	−1.175	−1.401	−1.223	−1.311	−.2595
	(.1223)	(.1269)	(.1303)	(.1311)	(.1258)
Cut 2	−.3093	−.3870	−.3616	−.3086	1.328
	(.1166)	(.1160)	(.1245)	(.1242)	(.1282)
Cut 3	1.505	1.379	1.466	1.540	—
	(.1199)	(.1187)	(.1279)	(.1277)	
N	2145	2180	1876	1959	1960
Pseudo R²	0.05	0.05	0.08	0.07	0.08

Source: 2000 Social Capital Benchmark Survey

Note: Standard errors are indicated in parentheses.

* p ≤ .10; ** p ≤ .05; *** p ≤ .01; **** p ≤ .001

TABLE 5.4
Determinants of Blacks' Racial Trust in Black, White, Latino, and Asian Groups

Covariates	Trust in blacks	Trust in whites	Trust in Asians	Trust in Latinos	Interracial trust index
Female	−.1240	−.2373*	−.4219****	−.2128	−.2343*
	(.1279)	(.1284)	(.1432)	(.1365)	(.1387)
Age	.0126****	.0130****	.0118***	−.0011	.0076*
	(.0040)	(.0040)	(.0046)	(.0045)	(.0045)
Education	.0241**	−.0035	.1110**	.0976**	.0605
	(.0392)	(.0396)	(.0447)	(.0435)	(.0439)
Income	−.0026	−.0218	−.0376	.0187	−.0124
	(.0357)	(.0356)	(.0401)	(.0388)	(.0396)
South	.1167	.1996*	—	.0449	.0398
	(.1182)	(.1184)		(.1278)	(.1346)
West	—	—	−.3103	—	−.2781
			(.2561)		(.2675)
Sense of community from R's ethnic group	.0951	−.0026	−.1553	−.0173	−.2179
	(.1606)	(.0969)	(.1769)	(.1733)	(.1766)
Economic satisfaction	.2158**	.2084**	.4259****	.3217***	.3413****
	(.0966)	(.0969)	(.1064)	(.1037)	(.1056)
R feels others view R as dishonest	−.1457**	−.1456***	−.2071****	−.1246**	−.1942***
	(.0539)	(.0539)	(.0603)	(.0594)	(.0614)
Immigrants' push for equal rights too demanding	—	—	−.4107***	−.3845***	−.4909****
			(.1442)	(.1395)	(.1428)
Diversity of racial networks	.0831	.1774***	.2588****	.2672****	.3269****
	(.0592)	(.0593)	(.0665)	(.0646)	(.0660)
Cut 1	−1.065	−1.197	−.8069	−1.024	.2088
	(.2795)	(.2844)	(.2994)	(.3007)	(.2947)
Cut 2	−.0907	−.1254	.1649	−.0143	1.847
	(.2673)	(.2678)	(.2917)	(.2923)	(.3090)
Cut 3	1.696	1.588	2.159	1.948	—
	(.2778)	(.2776)	(.3126)	(.3086)	
N	378	376	312	328	331
Pseudo R²	0.04	0.04	0.10	0.08	0.10

Source: 2000 Social Capital Benchmark Survey

Note: Standard errors are indicated in parentheses.

* $p \leq .10$; ** $p \leq .05$; *** $p \leq .01$; **** $p \leq .001$

The results in table 5.3 show that, contrary to expectation, whites trust blacks, other whites, Asians, and Latinos more than blacks do. While Asian Americans and blacks equally trust blacks and Latinos, Asian Americans are moderately more trusting of whites than blacks are, and as can be expected in trusting one's own group, Asian Americans are more trusting of other Asians than blacks are. Latinos, however, are less trusting of blacks than blacks are. Blacks and Latinos, nevertheless, have statistically indistinguishable trust attitudes toward whites, Asians, and Latinos.

As for other influential covariates in the model for all racial groups' racial trust, women are moderately more trusting in blacks than men are. Older Americans of all races are more trusting in each of the racial groups than are younger people. More education increases trust in blacks, Asians, and Latinos, whereas higher income only increases trust in blacks and Asian Americans. Southerners are less trusting in Latinos, whereas living in the West has no effect on trust in Asians. Respondents' ethnic communal sensitivity matters only in trusting blacks, thus moderately enhancing trust in this group.

As we might think that economic satisfaction would influence whether groups think about other groups negatively or positively, especially as likely economic competitors, less economic satisfaction diminishes racial trust in each of the racial groups. As we are likely to expect that people who think that others view them as dishonest would be distrusting of others in general, this effect bears out, as heightened feelings of projected dishonesty diminish people's trust in all racial groups. Negative attitudes toward immigrants' demands for equality also decreases trust in both Asian Americans and Latinos, as expected.

Turning to the model of solely blacks' public opinion, in table 5.4 we see that black women trust whites and Asian Americans less than black men do. Older blacks trust other blacks, whites (unexpectedly, given their likely racial experiences with institutionalized racism), and Asian Americans more than younger blacks do. Contrary to what historical relationships might suggest, additionally, blacks in the South are more trusting of whites than are non-southerners. Blacks with more education are more trusting of other blacks, Asian Americans, and Latinos than are those with less education. Greater economic satisfaction increases trust across all racial groups. Projection of others' attitudes about one's being dishonest, conversely, decreases trust in all other racial groups. Believing that immigrants are too demanding in their quest for equal rights diminishes trust in Asian Americans and Latinos. Whereas there is no effect of diverse racial networks on trust in fellow blacks, as might be expected, having more diverse racial networks increases trust in whites, Asians, and Latinos.

Tables 5.3 and 5.4 also include the results from an ordered probit model of an additive measure of interracial trust, which includes trust in all racial groups, excluding trust in the SCBS respondents' racial group. This measure indicates a tripartite gradation of whether the respondents interracially trust at "low," "medium," or "high" levels.

Table 5.3 shows that of all comparisons between whites', Asian Americans', and Latinos' racial trust and blacks' racial trust in the SCBS, only whites are more interracially trusting than blacks are. With closer inspection of specifically black public opinion on interracial trust, we ascertain that black women are moderately less trusting than are black men and that age moderately influences blacks' interracial trust, with older blacks trusting other racial groups more than younger blacks do. Economic dissatisfaction decreases interracial trust, as does having fewer friends from other racial groups. Agreeing that immigrant demands for equality are too pushy also diminishes blacks' interracial trust.

Despite blacks' reported differences in trust in each of these racial groups, results from another measure that asked blacks directly whether they trust other racial groups more or less than their own show that overwhelmingly most say they trust these groups the same as their own. (Blacks' trust in whites is the same as their own group = 86 percent; equal trust in Asians = 83 percent; equal trust in Latinos = 84 percent.) Twice as many blacks trust Asians (13 percent) and Latinos (13 percent) less than their own group as those who trust whites (7 percent) less than their own group. These results contrast the findings in the NPSS, which through unobtrusive measures in the race and trust experiment indicate that blacks (1) distrust whites most and more than they do Asians and Latinos and (2) trust fellow blacks more than they trust whites, Asians, and Latinos.

A Note on Race, Trust, and Social Desirability

The unobtrusive experimental design in the NPSS was designed the way that it was in order to avoid the possibility that respondents may give socially desirable responses about racial trust when they are cognizant of questions that ask them within the frame of one survey (as in the SCBS) how much they trust each racial group. In this instance, respondents can become overly sensitive to questions about groups of which conventional knowledge may suggest they should be most distrusting. The race and trust experiment in the NPSS, in which respondents received survey questions about trust with respect to only one group, was employed in order to avoid this effect of social desirability and to lessen respondents' awareness that their responses about one racial group would be compared to their responses about another group. In the SCBS, without unobtrusive racial trust measures, unfortunately, it is impossible to avoid the potential for social desirability in racial trust comparisons. Therefore, some of the results from the SCBS may indicate socially desirable responses. However, we must still consider the import that the SCBS data offer because, unlike the NPSS, the survey includes a representative national sample with an oversample for blacks and Latinos. The NPSS's survey experiments, however, offer internal validity through randomized administration of the targets in the experiments.

Summary and Conclusion: Evidence of Racialized Trust

From the NPSS, we ascertained that, on one hand, whites are less likely than blacks to weigh fairness and appearance in their trust assessments. Latinos, on the other hand, are less likely than blacks to evaluate trust based on competence and reliability. Older Americans value fairness more in their trust assessments, whereas younger people value credibility more.

The results in the NPSS race and trust experiment showed that whites, Latinos, and blacks generally have negative assessments of people in general. However, when we ask groups more specifically how much they trust certain racial groups, they are much more trusting on average than they are when they are asked about people in general. This distinctive trust in people in general versus racial groups perhaps suggests more about how people characterize human behavior, in general. Racial classifications of the targets in the experiment appear to sensitize attitudes toward specific groups, perhaps giving them more dimensionality as everyday people. This, along with distinctive patterns of trust, may suggest that trust-associative knowledge facilitates reputations of racial groups, similar to Partha Dasgupta's (2000) claim that trust is based on reputation and observed behavior over time.

Even more important is the fact that, across all groups, the extent of distrust in people in general versus racial groups may suggest a need for researchers to consider the implications of trust measures that solely analyze trust of people in general. Results of such studies may be biased by whatever attributions people associate with the character of humankind rather than people they can associate with everyday, real-life experiences—here especially as applied to members of racial groups. Racial cueing also can affect racial groups' perceptions differently depending on the content of the cue (I. White 2007). Still, the racialized characterization of trust, although expected given the hierarchical racial structure of society, indicates that racial groups attribute more or less trust to others based on people's racial categorization. Furthermore, although evidence was limited to the model of trust in people in general, blacks who received greater emphasis on racial protectiveness were less trusting in people in general.

In view of the results from both the NPSS and the SCBS, we learned that blacks are not the only group that engages in racialized trust. As we learned from the NPSS, whites trust blacks and Asian Americans more than they trust other whites. Latinos in this survey trust people in general, whites, and Asians more than blacks do. Blacks and whites trust other racial groups in almost similar patterns. Blacks trust people in general and whites the least in their assessments of trust of all other groups. Interestingly, the arithmetic mean for blacks' trust in whites also is the least in comparison to white and Latino respondents' arithmetic means for trust in this group

Some results in the SCBS contradict those in the NPSS. In the NPSS, blacks have clearly more distrust of whites. However, in the SCBS, while blacks are more distrusting of whites, Asians, and Latinos than nonblacks are, nevertheless, twice as many black respondents trust Asians and Latinos less than their own group as those who trust whites less than their own group. Additionally, contrary to expectation, whites are more trusting than blacks are of all the racial groups, including even blacks. In the NPSS, however, trust in each of the groups is statistically indistinguishable between black and white respondents. In the SCBS model of interracial trust across all the groups, additionally, only whites were statistically more interracially trusting than blacks.

While Latinos do not trust blacks differently from the way blacks trust themselves in the NPSS, contrarily, in the SCBS, Latinos are less trusting of blacks than blacks are. Latinos in the NPSS also trust people in general, whites, and Asians more than blacks do; however, in the SCBS, blacks and Latinos trust whites, Asians, and Latinos similarly. For all racial groups, more economic satisfaction increases trust in each of the racial groups. Feeling that immigrants' demands for equality are excessive, however, reduces respondents' trust in Asian Americans and Latinos, specifically.

As for the model of specifically blacks' trust in the SCBS, we learned that black women are less trusting than black men are of whites, Asians, and all other racial groups combined. Feeling less economically satisfied, as expected, reduces trust in each racial group and all racial groups combined.

Blacks who feel that immigrant demands are excessive also are more racially distrusting. Blacks with more racially diverse friendship networks also are more racially trusting in whites, Asians, Latinos, and racial groups across the board. According to the SCBS, blacks and other racial groups mostly trust their own racial group no differently than they trust other racial groups. But when people are asked about their trust in specific racial groups, we see that this is not the case. Moreover, in the NPSS race and trust experiment, clearly blacks trust their own group more than people in general, whites, Asians, and Latinos. They also trust Asian Americans and Latinos similarly in this experiment; yet they trust these groups more than they do whites.

Regarding the hypotheses about black interracial attitudes, in sum, the results indicate the following:

1. Blacks should trust other blacks more than they trust other racial groups: Yes = NPSS.
2. Blacks should trust their own group members more than whites, Asian Americans, and Latinos do: No = NPSS, excluding the comparison between blacks and Asian Americans; in the SCBS, whites are actually more trusting of blacks than blacks are; Asian Americans' trust in blacks is indistinguishable from blacks'; and Yes, blacks trust blacks more than Latinos do.
3. Blacks should trust whites less than they trust other groups: Yes = NPSS; No = SCBS.
4. Blacks should trust whites less than other groups do: No = NPSS; Yes = SCBS.
5. Blacks with negative attitudes about immigration should be more distrusting of Asian Americans and Latinos, as two groups commonly associated with immigration politics: Yes = SCBS.
6. Black southerners should be more distrusting of whites and Latinos: No = SCBS; black southerners are actually moderately more trusting in whites than are nonsoutherners; there is no statistically significant relationship between being southern and distrusting Latinos.
7. Black westerners should be more distrusting of Asian Americans: No = SCBS; there is no statistically significant relationship between being a black westerner and distrusting Asian Americans.

From this chapter, we have discerned the racialized nature of trust. While some of the results in the NPSS and SCBS differ, we still witnessed the extent to which different racial groups perceive trust differently based on specific racial groups. We also learned that whether blacks are more or less distrusting in other racial groups depends on the group to which their attitudes are compared and the race of the trustee group. The next two chapters extend the analysis of racial trust to account for the ways that a trustee's race is interpreted in social or political contexts.

Part III

Racial Externalization

6

The Societal Context

Given blacks' discrimination experiences in almost every aspect of life, one might wonder why blacks would even trust at all. But do we see that there are specific social contexts wherein blacks are more socially trusting than in others? Furthermore, do blacks interpret the race of social actors differently in certain contexts? These inquiries guide the empirical analysis of this chapter.

Thus far, I have noted that much of the research on social trust finds that blacks are less socially trusting than other racial groups. To unpack how black Americans trust socially, this chapter scrutinizes blacks' social trust with respect to (1) their *generalized trust* in others as people in general, or strangers (see Uslaner 2000–2001, 2001; Seligman 1997), (2) their generalized trust in people in specific social contexts—neighborhoods, shopping places, workplaces, and religious institutions (see Putnam 2000b), also referred to here as *contextualized trust*, and (3) their trust in specific racial groups in the aforementioned contexts.

Considering the effects that racial socialization, racial discrimination, racial uncertainty, and disparate trust in racial groups seemingly have on blacks' internalization of race, we should expect that blacks navigate their social (and political) realities differently from other racial groups. Put simply, blacks should be more distrusting in social (and political) contexts than are other racial groups, with greater wariness in their interactions with non-blacks, especially whites.

To measure whether this is the case, this chapter first uses the SCBS to compare blacks' social trust to that of other racial groups to determine whether they are, in fact, less trusting. Second, this chapter uses the SCBS to determine whether blacks trust differently in certain social contexts and to identify spaces where blacks are more or less trusting. Finally, this chapter uses race and social context experiments in the NPSS to determine whether blacks trust racial actors differently in certain contexts. Data from the race and social context experiments are examined further to determine the effects on blacks' social trust of several factors: (1) black Americans' racial socialization experiences, (2) their racial identity, and (3) their racial uncertainty. In order to study blacks' social trust, it is important first to consider some of the complexities of examining social trust and race.

Conceptualizing Social Trust: What Exactly Do We Mean? How Do We Inscribe Race?

Trust reduces transaction costs in interpersonal relationships: the more one trusts, the less effort one takes in learning about another person's background or record of performance in completing tasks. Trust also enhances the bonds between and among citizens so that they are able to relate comfortably with one another in order to produce desired social or political outcomes (Uslaner 2000–2001; Fukuyama 1995). Despite recognizing the benefits of trust for individuals and society, the general literature on trust often grapples with defining the concept of trust (Hardin 2004, 2006; Cook, Hardin, and Levi 2005; Ostrom and Walker 2003; Uslaner 2002), as it appears to assume different purposes that affect how scholars interpret its meaning in society.

For one, scholars search for the central meaning of what we mean by *trust* and how the concept itself problematizes our understanding and measurement of trust (Lewis and Weigert 1985b; Seligman 1997; Lin 2001a, 2001b; Miller and Mitamura 2003). They also consider how people become agentic individuals in navigating their relations with others in increasingly complex environments with probabilistic risks (Luhmann 1979; Seligman 1997). Other scholars attempt to contextualize the origins of trust by considering the dynamic process of the concept as being either a natural occurrence as an outgrowth of primordial relations or as a systemically induced artifact (Lewis and Weigert 1985a; Seligman 1997). Yet other researchers consider to what extent social relations produce trust or, conversely, to what extent trust produces social relations and facilitates the organization of civil society (Lewis and Weigert 1985a, 1985b; Uslaner 2000–2001; Lin 2001a, 2001b). Some inquiries even focus on whether trust is value-oriented, manifesting society's normative structure and variegated modes of information transmission in certain spaces (Fukuyama 1995; Seligman 1997; Uslaner 2000–2001, 2002). Additional scholarship questions the objects that are entrusted and the extent to which they are trusted—whether they are institutions, media, agents, or trust in the idea of *trust* itself (Lewis and Weigert 1985a; Putnam 2000b). Still others consider whether trust is measurable at all, given that our greater interest should lie in the characteristic or quality of being *trustworthy* (Uslaner 2002; Hardin 2004).

Social trust, as Putnam (1995) conceives it, is a trust that improves the likelihood for building relationships and that reinforces previously established relationships by improving the likelihood for reciprocity. When people trust one another socially, they are able to build beneficial relationships in different contexts. Such relationships, for example, enhance the prospect for improved citizen-government relations because social trust influences how people behave politically (Brehm and Rahn 1997). Moreover, those who have higher levels of social trust and those who are more socially interactive also have higher levels of civic participation (Kwak, Shah, and Holbert 2004).

Despite what seems to be an evidentiary need for trust in society, as I have illustrated through the review of several conceptualizations of trust, how we come to understand what trust and, particularly, *social* trust is, is a contested terrain. Nevertheless, the different manifestations of trust elucidate the critical nature of the concept for understanding the human position, its relationship to abstract "others," and more broadly, its holism for society (Lewis and Weigert 1985a). A fortiori, it is befitting to understand how people navigate their social spaces, interpret the kinds of people (here, racial groups) who occupy these spaces, and assess trust based on the confluence of the context and the racial actor. This intersection of race and space is the raison d'être of this chapter. Here, I examine how social trust is reduced when respondents are asked more specifically, "In whom do you trust?" This examination inserts the race of the actor in a specific social context.

The study of social trust, however, is often narrowed to the examination of generalized trust in others, measured as a response to the question, "How much do you feel that you can generally trust others? You can't be too careful in trusting others, or generally, others can be trusted?" The 2000 SCBS (Putnam 2000b), however, does include measures of general trust in others in specific social contexts, along with measures of the conventional conception of generalized social trust. Literature on social trust, however, has been less particular about how citizens trust in the context of specific social spaces —neighborhoods, workplaces, shopping places, or religious institutions. To address this void, I examine these several spaces here.

While trust is often measured as generalized trust with respect to trusting in people, complicating trust more by empirically examining how people trust others differently depending on the *context* of their assessment offers greater detail about both cognitive and affective processing of trust in social contexts. This is an even greater research consideration given that neighborhoods, workplaces, shopping places, and religious institutions all have been contexts in which blacks have been discriminated, continue to be discriminated, and continue to use either their personal agency or group-centered politics to abate disparate treatment based on race (see Kelley 1994). These social spaces even become discursive spaces, where blacks exchange perspectives about black progress (Harris-Lacewell 2004). In this sense, these *social* contexts are dually *politicized* contexts, and as I have argued previously, the political science literature should recognize them as such.

More importantly, this chapter (followed by the next chapter on political trust) offers a transition from blacks' psychological processing of messages internalized about race into the externalization of their racial understandings in their social environs. It is in these social environs (and political environs, as I examine in the next chapter) that blacks link information about racial groups' discriminatory behavior to certain contexts and behaviors and that blacks trust in racial groups differently across contexts. So in my conceptualization of trust (social and political), it is both an attitude about how much a racial group member can be trusted to fulfill an act fairly or nondiscriminatorily and a perception about how much the group member is likely to diverge from the discriminatory group stereotype in a certain context. As Susan Welch et al. (2001) recognize, "race and place" are heavily interwoven in American history and politics.

I argue that social trust is reduced and variegated when respondents are asked more specifically *in whom they trust*, especially based on the race of the actor. With respect to blacks, as the theory of discriminative racial-psychological processing suggests, prior negative internalized messages about race should lead this group to trust discriminately and should reduce their trust in nonblack actors, especially whites.

In the next few sections, I review blacks' social trust trends. I also discuss their discrimination experiences in neighborhoods, shopping places, workplaces, and religious institutions. This elaboration contextualizes my expectations for blacks' social trust in specific racial actors in these contexts. Later, I turn to the 2000 SCBS and the 2007 NPSS to examine empirically how race operates in blacks' social trust, and I compare their social trust to whites', Asians', and Latinos' social trust.

Trends in Social Trust

Social trust in the United States has been declining for the past three decades (Putnam 1995, 2000a). In the 2006 Pew Social Trends Survey, which asks respondents, "Generally speaking, would you say that most people can be trusted or that you can't be too careful in dealing with people?" 45 percent of Americans responded that "most people can be trusted," compared to 50 percent who said, "you can't be too careful in dealing with people" (Pew Research Center 2007). A social trust index composed of three measures— most people can be trusted, most people try to be fair, and most people try to be helpful—indicates that most people fall into the low-level social trust category (38 percent), followed by the high-level social trust category (35 percent), and last, the moderate-level social trust category (22 percent). Blacks, however, are more likely to report low-level trust, as 61 percent of blacks fall into the low-level social trust category, compared to 53 percent of Latinos and only 32 percent of whites.

Other research on social trust among racial groups also finds that black Americans have lower levels of social trust (Brehm and Rahn 1997; Brehm 1998; Rahn and Transue 1998; Uslaner 2000–2001). Moreover, the probability that social trust will improve political trust is less among blacks than it is for other racial groups (Brehm and Rahn 1997). Between 1972 and 1994, only 17 percent of black respondents reported that "most people can be trusted," compared to 45 percent of whites and 27 percent of respondents of other races (Putnam 1995). Thus, low social trust among blacks is a trend that has been documented over a long period of time. By reviewing how blacks perceive trust in others in these specific social contexts, we can discern how trust may vary across these contexts.

Neighborhood Discrimination: Divided by the Picket Fence?

Before the passage of the Fair Housing Act of 1968, black Americans and other people of color were often segregated from living in the same neighborhoods as whites. Historically, government-sanctioned, race-specific loan practices and racially discriminatory real estate practices structured neighborhood residency in ways that not only segregated blacks from whites but also socioeconomically depressed their home values, sometimes structuring concentrated, racialized poverty (W. Wilson 1987, 1996; Massey and Denton 1993; Anyon 1997; Katznelson 2005) and other times suppressing the mobility of the black middle class in comparison to whites (Massey and Denton 1993; Pattillo-McCoy 1999).

Even today, blacks who feel that racially integrated neighborhoods are unwelcoming also are more likely to prefer living in environments with a larger concentration of black Americans (Farley et al. 1994). Whites, Latinos, and Asian Americans, conversely, express hesitance about living in neighborhoods with larger concentrations of blacks (Farley et al. 1994; Bobo and Zubrinsky 1996). Blacks' living in residential areas that are heavily concentrated with other blacks also tends to have specific effects on their psychological processing of relating to others and people in their environment: increasing racial solidarity (Bledsoe et al. 1995), increasing negative attitudes about other racial groups (Oliver and Wong 2003; Marschall and Stolle 2004), and detracting from generalized trust in others (Marschall and Stolle 2004). Yet, there is evidence indicating that blacks living in mixed-race neighborhoods also are most likely to perceive racial discrimination against other blacks (Welch et al. 2001).

Given the racial discrimination experiences of black Americans in living spaces, we would expect blacks to be less trusting of whites as neighbors because they have been more strategically segregated from this group in housing. With some of the tensions documented between blacks and Asian Americans in their shared living environments (Guthrie and Hutchinson 1995), we would also expect blacks to be less trusting of Asian American neighbors, although white neighbors should be distrusted most.

Shopping while Black: Blacks' Navigation of Race in Shopping Places

Before the passage of the 1964 Civil Rights Act, which protects people from discrimination in public accommodations on the basis of their race, gender, color, religion, or national origin, black Americans commonly were denied access to full services and equal treatment in public places. Blacks were segregated from business environments in such a way that many black businesses and black economic institutions developed to fill the need for services in the black community. Many blacks were forced to use black-only restrooms and to enter through black-only entrances in the back of stores and faced "no trial" policies in clothes purchasing and product testing (Myrdal 1944).

Despite social advances via the passage of the Civil Rights Act of 1964, discrimination in public spaces continues today (Feagin 1991; Fifield and O'Shaughnessy 2001; Williams, Henderson, and Harris 2001). In a 1988–1990 study of thirty-seven in-depth interviews from a larger study of 135 middle-class black Americans from Boston, Buffalo, Baltimore, Washington, D.C., Detroit, Houston, Dallas, Austin, San Antonio, Marshall, Las Vegas, and Los Angeles, 79 percent of the respondents reported experiences with discrimination in public accommodations in the form of "rejection or poor service"

(Feagin 1991). More recently, blacks also have filed lawsuits against several large retail chains—Dillard's, The Children's Place, Eddie Bauer, Avis Rent a Car, Holiday Universal, and Denny's—in order to challenge racial discrimination in public accommodations (Fifield and O'Shaughnessy 2001).

"Shopping while black," just like "driving while black," suggests that blacks are unfairly targeted and discriminated against as they are stereotyped as potential criminals—shoplifters in stores and fugitives as drivers. For example, the criminal stereotype associated with "shopping while black" may lead store clerks to follow black shoppers excessively around stores due to the stereotype that blacks (especially women) are likely to shoplift or cannot afford products and, therefore, will steal them. The criminal stereotype associated with "driving while black" may lead police officers to follow or even to pull over black drivers (especially men) due to suspicion that they are perhaps driving a stolen vehicle (especially if it is a high-priced vehicle that may be perceived as one that a black person cannot afford and, therefore, may have stolen), that they are in the process of leaving a crime scene, or that they are actively transporting drugs or other contraband. For both "shopping while black" and "driving while black," blacks' contemporary mistreatment stems from perceptions about their "place" and whether they appear to "fit" in their shopping or driving environment.

Considering the historical and contemporary experiences that blacks have with discrimination in public accommodations, we would expect them to be less likely than nonblacks to trust shopping clerks in shopping places. Blacks with more diverse racial networks should be more trusting of shopping clerks than those with less diverse networks. Having negative attitudes about immigrants also should decrease trust in store clerks, as such attitudes should contextualize relations with groups (especially Asian Americans as store clerks) who may be stereotyped as "immigrants" and perceived negatively as discriminatory toward blacks. Blacks should be less trusting of whites and Asian Americans as shopping clerks, as these are two groups with which blacks have had more negative relationships in their shopping experiences (J. Lee 2000; Kim 2000; Fifield and O'Shaughnessy 2001).

Blocking the American Dream: Racial Discrimination and the Workplace

Historically, employers commonly practiced racial discrimination, as they designated jobs as "black" or "white" only. Labor unions, which champion the rights and concerns of laborers, oftentimes segregated and excluded black workers from collective bargaining efforts (Litwack 1998; Lewis 1991; Georgakas and Surkin 1998). Until 1941, the federal government even participated in segregating its employees. It was not until President Franklin D. Roosevelt issued Executive Order 8802, which outlawed discrimination based on race, creed, color, or national origin in industry, that industries were desegregated.

To ensure equal access to employment without discrimination, during the 1960s, governments at all levels implemented affirmative action programs across the country to increase racial and ethnic minorities' access to employment opportunities. Nevertheless, blacks continue to perceive racial discrimination in the workplace as an impediment to their success and social mobility (Hochschild 1995). The urban black poor, likewise, face discrimination by their employers, who, in holding negative, stereotypical attitudes about black workers, prefer to hire other racial groups (W. Wilson 1996).

Given these experiences, we would expect blacks to be less trusting of their co-workers than are nonblacks. Blacks with more diverse racial networks, however, should be more trusting of their co-workers. With negative attitudes about immigrants, blacks should be less trusting of their co-workers, perhaps seeing such co-workers as economic competition. Nonetheless, blacks should be more distrusting of white co-workers than of any other racial group.

A Haven for (In)equality: Race and Religious Institutions in America

As a social space, historically, churches have been racially segregated, and many continue to be even today (Harris 1999). As a consequence of racial segregation, the "black church" developed as an important social space for black Americans' respite from racial injustice. The black church, with strong association to Baptist tradition and tenets, has been a space where blacks, male and female, have acquired leadership roles and voices that society otherwise would not allow them to have, given the legal sanctioning of a racial hierarchy (Higginbotham 1993). The black church has been, ever since, an integral part of the black experience, offering leadership, opportunities for spiritual and community involvement, and several types of networks: kinship, financial, and spiritual (Lincoln and Mamiya 1990; Chatters et al. 2002).

Blacks, furthermore, report high levels of religiosity (Taylor, Thornton, and Chatters 1987), and they out-participate whites in religious activities (R. Taylor et al. 2001). Church-based resources also increase blacks' political activism (Brown and Brown 2003; Harris 1999), especially for those who attend "political churches," or those churches that actively involve their congregants in political activities (McDaniel 2008; Calhoun-Brown 1996).

Because of the centrality of black churches in black Americans' lives historically and today, we would expect their trust in co-congregants to be higher than their trust in others in any other context. Given that the black church remains a predominantly black institution even today, it is also most likely that co-congregants will be fellow black Americans. As a result, race and social trust should function differently in this context, because black Americans should perceive the church as a place where they will feel less likely to be discriminated against by fellow parishioners, who are also black. Unlike other contexts, blacks should be more trusting than nonblacks are in their co-congregants. Blacks also should be more trusting of specifically black co-congregants than they are of co-congregants of other races.

Measuring Social Trust

As I mentioned previously in this chapter, I measure social trust as (1) generalized social trust, (2) social trust in actors in different contexts, including trust in neighborhoods, shopping places, workplaces, and religious institutions, here referred to as contextualized social trust, and (3) contextualized trust in specific racial actors. In the SCBS, *generalized social trust* is measured as the commonly used measure—whether "people can be trusted or you can't be too careful trusting others" (1 = trusted; 0 = careful; *trust2*).[1] Because generalized social trust is a dichotomous dependent variable, I use probit regression to analyze this model.

Contextualized social trust includes separate measures for trust in people in the context of *neighborhoods* (trust in neighbors where they live; *trs2nei*), in *shopping places* (trust in clerks in places where people shop; *trs2shop*), in *workplaces* (trust in co-workers; *trs2wrk*), and in *religious institutions* (trust in co-congregants; *trs2rel*).[2] Each of these items is scaled as 0 = not at all, 1 = a little, 2 = some, and 3 = a lot. Because each of the contextualized trust measures is an ordinal, categorical variable, I analyze them separately using ordered probit regression. Using the SCBS, I analyze models that (1) compare blacks' social trust to whites', Latinos', and Asian Americans' social trust and (2) account for blacks' social trust, solely.

Brehm (1998) and Brehm and Rahn (1997) have found that those who are less satisfied with life in general and those who less satisfied with their economic disposition are more distrusting of others. I include measures for *happiness* (0 = not at all happy, 1 = not very happy, 2 = happy, 3 = very happy;

happy) and whether respondents are *economically satisfied with their current financial situation* (0 = not at all satisfied, 1 = somewhat satisfied, 2 = very satisfied; *econsat*) to control for the effects of social and economic discontent. Those who are happier and more economically satisfied should be more trusting of others. Those who feel that they have a higher *quality of life* also should be more likely to trust in others, as we may expect that these people are more likely to feel comfortable in their own life's circumstances such that they relate this comfort to relationships with other people and have a more positive outlook on life (0 = poor, 1 = only fair, 2 = good, 3 = excellent; *qol*). Those who *feel that someone had discriminated against them because that person felt that they were dishonest* (0 = never, 1 = rarely, 2 = sometimes, 3 = often, 4 = very often; *expdisc3*) should be more distrusting of others. Black people with more diverse racial networks (an additive measure for whether the black respondent has white, Asian American, or Latino friends; *bwht, basn, bhisp*, scaled 0–3) should be more socially trusting.

The model for trust in one's neighbors includes several variables that account for factors that measure the extent of involvement people have with others in their neighborhood. *Length of residency,* or those who have lived in their communities longer, should be more familiar with their neighbors and, hence, more likely to trust them (1 = less than one year, 2 = one to five years, 3 = six to ten years, 4 = eleven to twenty years, 5 = more than twenty years, 6 = whole life; *livcom*). As well, those who have a vested interest in retaining healthy relationships and maintaining quality neighborhoods should be more trusting in their fellow neighbors. That is, those who are a *member of a neighborhood association* (1 = yes, 0 = no; *grpnei2*) and those who *visit their neighbors more often* (1 = never, 2 = once a year or less, 3 = several times a year, 4 = once a month, 5 = several times a month, 6 = several times a week, 7 = just about every day; *neisoc*) also should be more trusting in their neighbors.

In the model for trust in one's co-congregants, I account for the effect of religious participation. I include measures of *church or religious institutional membership* (1 = yes, 0 = no; *relmem2*), *attendance at religious services* (1 = yearly, 2 = few times per year, 3 = one to two times per month, 4 = almost weekly, 5 = weekly or more often; *relaten2*), *participation in church activities other than attending services* (1 = yes; 0 = no; *relpart2*), and *participation in an organization affiliated with religion* (1 = yes, 0 = no; *grprel*). I expect those who are members of religious institutions, more frequent attendants, more participatory in activities other than religious services, and more participatory in religious organizations to be more trusting of their co-congregants.

In the models of social trust in shopping places and workplaces, I include the variable *immigrants demands for equal rights are too pushy* (1 = too pushy; *immig2*), to control for attitudes toward immigrants that may suggest perceived competition by the group or stereotypical negative attitudes toward groups commonly stereotyped as immigrants through nativistic racism: Asians and Latinos. As I discussed in the literature review in the preceding chapter, these two groups also have been perceived as likely competitors of blacks. Believing that immigrants are too pushy in their demands for equal rights should reduce blacks' trust in store clerks and co-workers.

Standard control variables are included for *gender* (1 = female; 0 = male; *gender*); *education* (1 = less than high school; 2 = high school diploma; 3 = some college; 4 = associate's degree or specialized training; 4 = bachelor's degree; 5 = some graduate training; 6 = graduate and professional degree; *educ*), *age*, and *region* (South = 1, otherwise 0; West = 1, otherwise 0; *censreg*). As for the racial comparative models, I include dummy variables for whites (whites = 1), Asians (Asians = 1), and Latinos (Latinos = 1), leaving blacks as the excluded, comparative group.

In order to examine how black Americans trust in social actors with specific racial backgrounds, I also analyze data in the 2007 NPSS, which incorporates unobtrusive measures of social trust via several race and contextualized trust experiments. These experiments manipulate the race of several actors (white, black, Asian American, and Latino; people = control) across neighborhood, shopping, workplace, and religious contexts. The NPSS affords us the opportunity to see how both race and context influence blacks' social trust. I analyze unpaired comparisons of means to detect any statistically significant differences in social trust based on the race of the target in the contextualized social trust questions. Furthermore, because the NPSS includes measures of racial socialization, racial identification (black linked fate), and racial uncertainty (unlike the SCBS), we can measure their effects on blacks' trust in each of these contexts. In the models for trust in neighbors of different races, I also include a control for living in a predominantly black neighborhood, which should reduce blacks' trust in white neighbors. The NPSS social trust questions are all scaled 0 = never trust, 1 = rarely trust, 2 = sometimes trust, 3 = often trust, and 4 = very often trust.

Hypotheses: Race, Context, and Trust

To reiterate, blacks' social trust should be less than that of nonblacks in all contexts, with the exception of religious institutions, where blacks should trust their co-congregants more than nonblacks do. Negative attitudes toward immigrants should decrease blacks' social trust in the context of shopping places and workplaces. Having more racially diverse friendship networks should increase social trust. Furthermore, trust in respective social contexts should vary based on the race of the social actors. Of all the racial groups, blacks should trust whites the least. Furthermore, neighborhood insularity among blacks should increase their distrust in nonblack groups in the context of neighborhoods.

As for the effect of racial socialization on blacks' social trust, blacks who were socialized with emphasis on racial protectiveness messages should be more socially distrusting of other racial groups, including their own group members. Racial uncertainty should decrease blacks' trust in nonblack racial groups, especially in the context of places where blacks have historically encountered more discrimination: neighborhoods, workplaces, and shopping places. Having received greater emphasis on racial consciousness should increase blacks' trust in other blacks, Asians, and Latinos and decrease their trust in whites. Having more linked fate with other blacks should reduce blacks' trust in whites, in particular. Those blacks who were socialized with greater emphasis that race should matter less in blacks' lives should be more trusting of whites in several contexts. Emphasis on socialization about racial consciousness should enhance blacks' trust in the context of religious institutions. In sum, the hypotheses for this chapter are as follows:

Generalized Social Trust

H_1: Blacks will be less socially trusting in others than are nonblacks.

H_2: Blacks who have more racially diverse friendship networks should be more socially trusting in others, in general.

Contextualized Social Trust

H_1: Blacks' social trust in others will differ by social context.

Corollary A: Black Americans will be less socially trusting than nonblacks are in their neighbors, co-workers, and store clerks.

Corollary B: Black Americans will be more socially trusting than nonblacks are in their co-congregants.

H_2: Blacks who have more racially diverse friendship networks will be more socially trusting in social actors who are neighbors, co-workers, and store clerks, specifically.

H₄: Blacks' trust in others will depend on the race of the social actor in that context.

Corollary A: Black Americans will be less socially trusting of whites as neighbors, co-workers, store clerks, and co-congregants.

Corollary B: Black Americans will be less socially trusting of Asian Americans as store clerks.

Corollary C: Black Americans will be less socially trusting of Latinos as co-workers.

H₅: Blacks who have been socialized more negatively about race (racial protectiveness messages) should be less socially trusting.

H₆: Blacks who fear prospective racial discrimination (racial uncertainty) should be less socially trusting of nonblacks in various contexts.

H₇: Blacks who have been socialized more about racial consciousness messages should be more socially trusting of other blacks, Asians, and Latinos.

H₈: Blacks who feel greater linkages to other blacks should be more trusting in fellow blacks, Asians, and Latinos.

Generalized Social Trust: Do Blacks Trust Differently from Nonblacks?

In the SCBS, only 28.9 percent of blacks (N = 460) said they feel that "most people can be trusted," compared to 52.2 percent of nonblacks (N = 2,271). Overwhelmingly, 71 percent of blacks said they feel that "you can't be too careful in trusting other people." Results of a probit analysis (not shown) indicate that blacks are, in fact, less trusting than nonblacks are of most people.

Turning to table 6.1, we see that in comparing whites', Asians', and Latinos' generalized social trust to blacks', only whites and Asians are statistically more socially trusting than blacks are. Latinos and blacks share similar views about trust in others in general. Additionally, people who are older and more educated are generally more socially trusting, as are people who feel their ethnic group gives them a sense of community, who feel they have a better quality of life, and who are generally happier. Yet those who live in the South and those who perceive that others feel they are dishonest are less socially trusting.

TABLE 6.1
Probit Models of Generalized Trust in Others

Covariates	All racial groups	Blacks
Whites	.5385****	—
	(.0823)	
Asians	.7662****	—
	(.2291)	
Latinos	.0869	—
	(.1014)	
Female	−.0837	−.0342
	(.0585)	(.1549)
Age	.0040**	.0011
	(.0018)	(.0048)
Education	.1094****	.0402
	(.0176)	(.0468)
Income	.0236	.0229
	(.0173)	(.0434)
South	−.2263****	−.0795
	(.0584)	(.1439)
Group gives sense of ethnic community	.2144**	.3684**
	(.1085)	(.1802)
Economic satisfaction	.0171	−.0764
	(.0485)	(.1159)
R feels others perceive R as dishonest	−.1664****	−.1901***
	(.0351)	(.0746)
Quality of life	.2248****	.1768*
	(.0416)	(.0968)
Happiness	.3365****	.3808***
	(.0511)	(.1250)
Diversity of racial networks	—	.0241
		(.0721)
Constant	−2.125****	−1.851****
	(.1744)	(.4252)
N	2285	387
Pseudo R^2	0.14	0.07

Source: 2000 Social Capital Benchmark Survey
Note: Standard errors are indicated in parentheses.
* p ≤ .10; ** p ≤ .05; *** p ≤ .01; **** p ≤ .001

As for the model specific to blacks' social trust, none of the demographic variables is statistically significant. Just as in the model of all racial groups' social trust, however, blacks who feel their group gives them a sense of community are more socially trusting than those who do not feel a sense of community. Likewise, feeling one has a higher quality of life and feeling happier also increase blacks' social trust. Contrary to expectation, having more diverse racial networks does not increase blacks' generalized social trust in others, nor does it have an effect at all.

Contextualized Social Trust

As shown in table 6.2, blacks in the SCBS report more than do nonblacks (whites, Asians, and Latinos) that they trust in people as neighbors, store clerks, and co-workers only "some." The one place that blacks are more trusting is in the context of their religious institutions. Yet, while 54 percent of blacks trust their co-congregants "a lot," still almost one-third of blacks report trusting in their co-congregants "some." At least one-fifth of blacks report that they trust in their neighbors, store clerks, and co-workers "a little."

Also notable is the fact that twice as many blacks as nonblacks report that they "do not at all" trust their neighbors, store clerks, co-workers, and co-congregants. Blacks' largest reported distrust, or the greatest incidence of their "not at all trusting" others, is in the context of neighborhoods (12 percent) and shopping places (14 percent). With 14 percent of blacks reporting they do "not at all" trust store clerks where they live, shopping places appear to be the social context where blacks are most distrusting. Interestingly, just as many nonblacks as blacks (47 percent) report that they trust store clerks only "some"; however, twice as many nonblacks as blacks trust store clerks "a lot."

The largest difference between blacks and nonblacks in attitudes about trusting "a lot" within a social space is in the context of the workplace: 29 percent fewer black respondents than nonblack respondents report trusting in their co-workers "a lot." Neighborhoods appear to be the context with the next-largest difference between blacks' and nonblacks' trusting in others "a lot": twice as many nonblacks as blacks trust their neighbors "a lot."

Figure 6.1 shows a comparison of the arithmetic means of blacks', whites', Asians', and Latinos' trust in their neighbors, local store clerks, co-workers, and co-congregants. Judging from these results, all racial groups are more socially trusting of people in the context of religious institutions. Contrary to expectation, blacks are not the most socially trusting of all racial groups in their co-congregants. However, blacks are more socially trusting in their

TABLE 6.2

Comparison of Blacks' and Nonblacks' Contextualized Social Trust

	Neighbors			Store clerks			Co-workers			Co-congregants		
	Black (%)	Nonblack (%)	% diff.	Black (%)	Nonblack (%)	% diff.	Black (%)	Nonblack (%)	% diff.	Black (%)	Nonblack (%)	% diff.
Not at all	12	6	6	14	7	7	9	4	5	4	2	2
A little	24	11	13	24	16	8	23	10	13	9	6	3
Some	39	34	5	47	47	0	41	31	10	32	20	12
A lot	25	50	−25	15	30	−15	26	55	−29	54	72	−18
Total N	482	2,397		483	2,374		432	1,955		463	2,009	

Source: 2000 Social Capital Benchmark Survey

Note: Diff. = differences between blacks and nonblacks in percentage reporting; negative sign indicates that blacks report percentage points less than nonblacks. Percentages may not add up to 100 percent due to rounding.

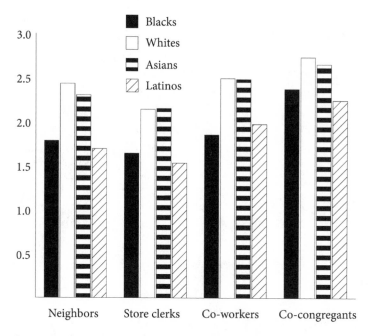

Fig. 6.1. Arithmetic means of racial groups' contextualized social trust

co-congregants than they are of others in any other context, as expected. What also is notable is that blacks are the least trusting compared to whites, Latinos, and Asians only in the context of workplaces. Still, for blacks, the context in which they trust the least is in shopping places. As opposed to blacks' being the least socially trusting racial group, it appears that Latinos are the least trusting compared to all racial groups in the context of their neighborhoods, shopping places, and religious institutions. To determine whether these racial differences are statistically significant, it is important to compare the racial groups' contextualized social trust using multivariate models.

The ordered probit results (not shown here) indicate that black Americans are less trusting of people than are nonblacks (all other groups combined) in the context of shopping places, workplaces, and even religious places. In the ordered probit regression models, when we compare blacks' social trust to that of other racial groups separately, in table 6.3 we see that blacks are less trusting than are whites and Asians, in particular, as far as trusting their neighbors, store clerks, co-workers, and co-congregants. There is only one

TABLE 6.3
Ordered Probit Regressions of Racial Groups' Contextualized Trust

Covariates	Neighbors	Store clerks	Co-workers	Co-congregants
Whites	.5238****	.3904****	.6363****	.5684****
	(.0678)	(.0709)	(.0772)	(.0794)
Asians	.6054***	.8631****	.7556****	.6369**
	(.1958)	(.2306)	(.2371)	(.2788)
Latinos	−.0081	−.0545	.1943**	−.1280
	(.0795)	(.0843)	(.0895)	(.0903)
Female	.0097****	.0109	−.0993	−.0117
	(.0497)	(.0502)	(.0564)	(.0609)
Age	.0097****	.0152****	.0111****	.0024
	(.0017)	(.0017)	(.0021)	(.0020)
Education	.0369**	.0091	.0325*	−.0004
	(.0152)	(.0154)	(.0176)	(.0184)
Income	.0422***	−.0425***	−.0020	−.0208
	(.0149)	(.0151)	(.0172)	(.0182)
South	.0137	−.0416	−.0001	.0471
	(.0501)	(.0508)	(.0577)	(.0610)
Group gives sense of	−.0032	.0972	−.0646	−.0350
ethnic community	(.0924)	(.0920)	(.0988)	(.1072)
Economic satisfaction	.0186	.0525	.0800*	.0460
	(.0414)	(.0419)	(.0475)	(.0503)
R feels others perceive	−.0724***	−.0812***	−.1297****	−.1080****
R as dishonest	(.0270)	(.0281)	(.0300)	(.0309)
Quality of life	.4703****	.2443****	.1695****	.2220****
	(.0346)	(.0354)	(.0393)	(.0413)
Happiness	.2621****	.2965****	.2675****	.3021****
	(.0433)	(.0439)	(.0498)	(.0516)
Participate in neighborhood	.0590	—	—	—
organization	(.0624)			
Frequency R visits neighbors	.1064****	—	—	—
	(.0134)			
Length of residency in	.0395**	—	—	—
community	(.0177)			
R feels immigrants' push for	—	−.1363***	−.1415**	—
equal rights too demanding		(.0518)	(.0582)	
Church membership	—	—	—	.2826****
				(.0734)
Frequency of church	—	—	—	.1153****
attendance				(.0259)
Participates in religious	—	—	—	.1308*
activities besides				(.0733)
church services				

TABLE 6.3 (*continued*)

Covariates	Neighbors	Store clerks	Co-workers	Co-congregants
Participates in organization affiliated with religion	—	—	—	.1562*
				(.0857)
Cut 1	1.416	.3362	−.0632	−.2338
	(.1565)	(.1507)	(.1703)	(.1770)
Cut 2	2.283	1.216	.7828	.5202
	(.1580)	(.1505)	(.1678)	(.1728)
Cut 3	3.541	2.696	1.886	1.589
	(.1651)	(.1569)	(.1713)	(.1747)
N	2,380	2,098	1,804	2,045
Pseudo R^2	0.16	0.09	0.09	0.13

Source: 2000 Social Capital Benchmark Survey
Note: Standard errors are indicated in parentheses.
* $p \leq .10$; ** $p \leq .05$; *** $p \leq .01$; **** $p \leq .001$

instance in which blacks are less trusting than Latinos are, and that is with respect to their co-workers.

In the model for *trust in one's neighbors*, which sets all continuous variables to their means and all dichotomous variables to the value of 1 (excluding gender, which is set to 0 for males, and race, which is set to 1 depending on the racial group of interest), as table 6.4 illustrates, whites have a .21 greater probability than blacks of trusting their neighbors "a lot," whereas Asians have a .23 greater probability. Latinos have the same probability as blacks in trusting their neighbors "a lot." Both Latinos and blacks are also more than twice as likely as whites and Asians to trust their neighbors only "a little."

The model including all racial groups also shows us that women, older Americans, and those with higher education levels and incomes are more trusting of their neighbors. Feeling that one has a greater quality of life, being happier about one's life, having more contact with one's neighbors, and living longer in one's community also enhance trust in one's neighbors. When people feel that others view them as dishonest, this, however, reduces their trust in their neighbors.

In the model of black public opinion shown in table 6.5, we see that of all the demographic variables, only age affects blacks' trust in their neighbors: older blacks trust their neighbors more than younger blacks do. The effects of quality of life, happiness, contact with one's neighbors, and length of residency consistently increase blacks' trust in their neighbors, as they do in the model for all racial groups. Unlike the model of trust in neighbors among all

TABLE 6.4

Comparisons of Probabilities from Ordered Probit Models of
Racial Groups' Contextualized Trust

	Not at all	A little	Some	A lot
Trust in neighbors				
Blacks	.05	.17	.46	.31
Whites	.01	.08	.39	.52
Latinos	.05	.17	.46	.31
Asians	.01	.08	.37	.54
Trust in store clerks				
Blacks	.09	.22	.53	.16
Whites	.04	.15	.53	.28
Latinos	.09	.23	.52	.15
Asians	.01	.08	.45	.46
Trust in co-workers				
Blacks	.08	.20	.42	.30
Whites	.02	.09	.34	.55
Latinos	.05	.17	.41	.37
Asians	.02	.08	.31	.59
Trust in co-congregants				
Blacks	.01	.05	.24	.70
Whites	.002	.01	.12	.86
Latinos	.01	.06	.27	.65
Asians	.002	.01	.12	.87

Source: 2000 Social Capital Benchmark Survey
Note: Ordered probit regression probabilities are estimated using Clarify (Tomz, Wittenberg, and King 2003). Probability estimates represent a model controlling for a racial group member who is a southern male, of mean age, education, and income, with mean attitudes about their economic satisfaction, perceptions that others view them as dishonest, quality of life, and happiness. The model for trust in neighbors also indicates a respondent with mean length of residency in their community, a mean number of visits to his or her neighbors, and who is a member of a neighborhood association. The models for trust in store clerks and trust in co-workers also includes attitudes for those who feel immigrants are too pushy in their demands for rights. The model for trust in co-congregants includes a respondent's being a church member, with mean church attendance, and participation in religious activities aside from church services.

TABLE 6.5

Ordered Probit Regressions of Blacks' Contextualized Trust

Covariates	Neighbors	Store clerks	Co-workers	Co-congregants
Female	−.0357	−.1223	−.2131	−.1878
	(.1205)	(.1278)	(.1343)	(.1375)
Age	.0067*	.0138****	.0159****	.0069
	(.0041)	(.0040)	(.0049)	(.0042)
Education	.0306	.0444	−.0097	.0028
	(.0375)	(.0395)	(.0439)	(.0414)

TABLE 6.5 (*continued*)

Covariates	Neighbors	Store clerks	Co-workers	Co-congregants
Income	.0110	−.0203	.0436	−.0391
	(.0341)	(.0357)	(.0391)	(.0377)
South	.1392	.2006*	.0352	.0904
	(.1140)	(.1204)	(.1284)	(.1263)
Group gives sense of ethnic community	−.1541	.0157	−.0941	−.1812
	(.1525)	(.1564)	(.1634)	(.1688)
Economic satisfaction	.1594*	.0325	.0699	.1126
	(.0936)	(.0969)	(.1066)	(.1039)
R feels others perceive R as dishonest	.0191	−.1018*	−.1456**	−.0537
	(.0510)	(.0535)	(.0567)	(.0551)
Quality of life	.4929****	.1842**	.0626	.1780**
	(.0778)	(.0780)	(.0820)	(.0842)
Happiness	.2747***	.2056**	.2251**	.2507**
	(.0938)	(.0970)	(.1050)	(.1021)
Participate in neighborhood organization	−.0360	—	—	—
	(.1370)			
Frequency R visits neighbors	.0704**	—	—	—
	(.0277)			
Length of residency in community	.0855**	—	—	—
	(.0409)			
R feels immigrants' push for equal rights too demanding	—	.0899	.1133	—
		(.1281)	(.1369)	
Church membership	—	—	—	.1212
				(.1657)
Frequency of church attendance	—	—	—	.0701
				(.0602)
Participates in religious activities besides church services	—	—	—	.3336**
				(.1580)
Participates in organization affiliated with religion	—	—	—	.0336
				(.1464)
Diversity of racial networks	.1304**	.1565***	.1114*	.0706
	(.0566)	(.0592)	(.0631)	(.0616)
Cut 1	1.557	.4175	−.1606	−.3194
	(.3507)	(.3447)	(.3771)	(.3605)
Cut 2	2.538	1.353	.8003	.3734
	(.3608)	(.3486)	(.3773)	(.3586)
Cut 3	3.691	2.760	1.995	1.463
	(.3749)	(.3627)	(.3859)	(.3630)
N	402	352	310	386
Pseudo R^2	0.10	0.05	0.05	0.06

Source: 2000 Social Capital Benchmark Survey
Note: Standard errors are indicated in parentheses.
* $p \leq .10$; ** $p \leq .05$; *** $p \leq .01$; **** $p \leq .001$

racial groups, having greater economic satisfaction also moderately increases blacks' trust in their neighbors. Additionally, racially diverse friendship networks increase blacks' trust in their neighbors.

The model in table 6.3 comparing whites', Asians', and Latinos' trust in store clerks elucidates that only whites and Asian Americans have a greater probability of trusting store clerks than blacks do. In fact, holding all continuous variables at their means and all dummy variables at 1, with the exception of 0 for "male" and the manipulation of race based on the racial group of interest, while whites have a .08 higher probability than blacks of trusting store clerks "a lot," Asians have a .30 higher probability than blacks of trusting store clerks "a lot." In fact, of all racial groups, Asian Americans have the greatest probability of trusting store clerks "a lot." As expected, negative attitudes about immigrants reduces trust in store clerks. Based on this model, for blacks, negative attitudes about immigrants increases the probability that one trusts store clerks "not at all" by .02 probability and reduces the probability that one trusts store clerks "a lot" by .04 probability.

Looking at the model of exclusively blacks' trust in store clerks, both being older and living in the South increase trust in store clerks (though only moderately so for living in the South), as do feeling that one has a greater quality of life and greater happiness in life. Both the model comparing racial groups' trust in store clerks and the black public-opinion model indicate that projections of dishonesty reduce trust. Unlike the racial comparative model, however, the black public-opinion model does not indicate a statistically significant relationship whatsoever between blacks who have negative attitudes about immigrants and trust in their store clerks. Having more racially diverse friendship networks, however, increases blacks' trust in their store clerks.

With respect to *trust in the workplace*, once again, the model comparing whites', Asians', and Latinos' trust in their co-workers to blacks' trust shows that each of these groups is more trusting of their co-workers than blacks are. In fact, as table 6.4 illustrates, while blacks have a .30 probability of trusting their co-workers "a lot," whites have a .25 higher probability and Asians have a .29 higher probability of trusting their co-workers "a lot," compared to blacks. While Latinos have only a .07 higher probability of trusting their co-workers "a lot" compared to blacks, this still translates into a 23 percent higher probability of falling in the "a lot" category than blacks. Blacks also have a 60 percent higher probability than Latinos of falling in the "not at all" category of trusting their co-workers. Believing that immigrants are too pushy in their demands for equal rights also reduces trust in one's co-workers, decreasing blacks' probability of trusting their co-workers "a lot" by .05 probability.

Turning to the model of blacks' attitudes about their co-workers, we see that of all the demographic variables, only age matters in blacks' trust in their co-workers. That is, older blacks are more trusting in their co-workers than younger blacks are. Only feeling greater happiness and having more diverse friendship networks increase blacks' trust in their co-workers. Trust in co-workers is reduced by only one factor: the perception that others think one is dishonest. Negative attitudes about immigrants do not have a statistically significant influence on blacks' trust in their co-workers, and neither does a black person's perceived quality of life.

As for *trust in co-congregants*, despite the role the church has played in blacks' liberation and the fact that blacks trust their church co-congregants more than they trust others in any other context, table 6.3 shows that, nevertheless, whites and Asian Americans trust their co-congregants more than blacks do. Despite blacks' having the highest probability of all contexts of trusting their co-congregants "a lot" (.70 probability), whites and Asians, respectively, have a 23 percent and 24 percent higher probability than black do of trusting co-congregants "a lot." Yet there are no statistically significant differences between blacks' and Latinos' trust in their co-congregants. All the measures of religious activism—church membership, frequency of church attendance, participating in religious activities other than church services, and participation in an organization affiliated with religion—increase trust in one's co-congregants.

For the model of black public opinion, specifically, only three variables increase trust in one's co-congregants: feeling one has a better quality of life, feeling happier, and participating in religious activities outside regular church services. Unlike in the models for trust in neighbors, store clerks, and co-workers, having diverse racial networks does not influence blacks' trust in their co-congregants; perhaps this is because of the greater likelihood that blacks are in a racially homogeneous religious institution where interracial attitudes likely matter less in blacks' interactions with other blacks. To determine the extent to which the race of a social actor influences blacks' trust in others in specific contexts, I examine race and contextualized trust experiments in the NPSS.

Social Trust in Racial Actors: Results of NPSS Race and Contextualized Trust Experiments

Table 6.6 shows the arithmetic means for blacks' contextualized trust in racial actors as neighbors, store clerks, co-workers, and co-congregants. On

TABLE 6.6

Arithmetic Means of Blacks' Contextualized Trust
(Race and Social Trust Experiments)

Social actors	People	Blacks	Whites	Asian Americans	Latinos
Neighbors	2.3	2.4	2.3	2.4	2.3
Store clerks	2.2	2.4	2.2	2.2	2.3
Co-workers	2.4	2.6	2.3	2.4	2.4
Co-congregants	2.6	2.5	2.4	2.6	2.7

Source: 2007 National Politics and Socialization Survey

average, we see that across the several racial groups and contexts, blacks mostly trust these social actors "sometimes." Similar to the SCBS, the highest means for blacks' social trust are in the context of religious institutions. The NPSS helps us to compare blacks' trust in racial groups in the race and contextualized trust experiments (1) to determine the extent to which some groups are trusted more than others in certain contexts, (2) to compare whether their contextualized trust is distinct from that of white and Latino respondents in the survey, and (3) to determine the effect of their internalized racial knowledge and attitudes on their social trust.

Table 6.7 shows the results of the NPSS's race and contextualized trust experiment for *trust in one's neighbors*. For blacks, there is only a statistically significant difference in the means of trusting people in general and trusting blacks as neighbors. While black respondents in the NPSS trust blacks more than people in general as neighbors, they do not trust blacks more than they trust any other group of racial actors as neighbors. For whites in the NPSS, they trust Asians as neighbors more than they trust people in general, and they trust Asians more as neighbors than they trust blacks. Interestingly, Latinos trust Asians more as neighbors than they do both whites and their own group members.

When we look at the results of an ordinary least squares model (table 6.8) that controls for several demographic variables and two measures of socialization, black linked fate, and racial uncertainty, we can determine, specifically, the extent to which blacks' racial internalization influences their social trust in their neighbors, per target in the race and contextualized trust experiment. Only models of trust in neighbors regarding people in general and Asians have statistically significant covariates. In the model of trust in people in general as neighbors, racial consciousness socialization reduces trust in people, whereas black linked fate increases trust. As for blacks' trust in Asians as neighbors, socialization emphasis on racial protectiveness decreases trust. These results, however, must be interpreted cautiously, given the statistically insignificant F-statistics.

When we review the results of the race and contextualized trust experiments for *trust in store clerks* in table 6.9, we see that blacks trust other blacks

TABLE 6.7
Comparisons of Arithmetic Means for Racial Groups' Trust in Neighbors (Race and Social Trust Experiment)

Comparisons of means	Black respondents' trust	White respondents' trust	Latino respondents' trust
People/Blacks	2.3/2.4 (+)*a	2.4/2.4	2.5/2.4
	(n = 202)	(n = 99)	(n = 99)
People/Whites	2.3/2.3	2.4/2.5	2.5/2.4
	(n = 204)	(n = 97)	(n = 98)
People/Asians	2.3/2.4	2.4/2.7 (+)*a	2.5/2.7
	(n = 196)	(n = 92)	(n = 93)
People/Latinos	2.3/2.3	2.4/2.4	2.5/2.4
	(n = 188)	(n = 92)	(n = 95)
Whites/Blacks	2.3/2.4	2.5/2.4	2.4/2.4
	(n = 204)	(n = 100)	(n = 101)
Whites/Asians	2.3/2.4	2.5/2.7	2.4/2.7 (+)*a
	(n = 198)	(n = 93)	(n = 77)
Whites/Latinos	2.3/2.3	2.5/2.4	2.4/2.4
	(n = 190)	(n = 93)	(n = 97)
Asians/Blacks	2.4/2.4	2.7/2.4 (+)*a	2.7/2.4
	(n = 196)	(n = 79)	(n = 96)
Asians/Latinos	2.4/2.3	2.7/2.4	2.7(+)/2.4*a
	(n = 182)	(n = 88)	(n = 92)
Latinos/Blacks	2.3/2.4	2.4/2.4	2.4/2.4
	(n = 188)	(n = 95)	(n = 98)

Source: 2007 National Politics and Socialization Survey

Note: Variables are scaled from 0 = never trust to 4 = very often trust. (+) indicates the group trusted most in the comparisons of means. Statistically significant differences of means are indicated based on a p-value of at most .005, which is consistent with the Bonferroni adjustment method. The Bonferroni adjustment method for comparisons of means requires that the statistical significance of ten comparisons must be adjusted downward by dividing a .05 statistical significance level by the number of comparisons made to avoid Type I errors, or reporting statistically significant comparisons when they are, in fact, not significant. Therefore, the acceptable level of statistical significance for this analysis is p ≤.005.

a Statistically significant without Bonferroni adjustment method, which offers a stringent standard of statistical significance

* p ≤ .10; ** p ≤ .05; *** p ≤ .01; **** p ≤ .001

TABLE 6.8

OLS Regression Model of Blacks' Contextualized Trust in Neighbors (Results of Race and Social Trust Experiments)

Social trust in neighbors	Mostly black neighborhood	Racial consciousness socialization	Racial protectiveness socialization	Black linked fate	Racial uncertainty	Constant	F prob.	Adj. R²	N
People	-1.069 (.6068)	-.1112** (.02056)	.0761 (.0378)	.4461* (.1529)	-.2556 (.1767)	-3.557 (1.301)	0.10	0.87	13
Blacks	.4302 (.3244)	.0172 (.0168)	.0286 (.0298)	-.1213 (.1477)	-.0540 (.1331)	1.089 (1.190)	0.73	-0.17	23
Whites	-.5537 (.4359)	-.0094 (.0177)	.0107 (.0338)	-.3065 (.2133)	-.0246 (.1833)	2.709 (1.398)	0.58	-0.05	28
Asians	.0026 (.3945)	.0099 (.0219)	-.0589** (.0264)	-.0356 (.2060)	.2105 (.2128)	-.51539 (1.889)	0.14	0.30	23
Latinos	-.2391 (.7127)	.0078 (.0223)	-.0294 (.0825)	.1897 (.3923)	-.3164 (.4603)	.9807 (3.753)	0.82	-0.46	16

Source: 2007 National Politics and Socialization Survey

Note: Standard errors are indicated in parentheses. Results of the models featured in the table include only the variables of interest. The full model also includes demographic variables for control variables.

* p ≤ .10; ** p ≤ .05; *** p ≤ .01; **** p ≤ .001

more than they trust people in general, whites, and Asian Americans as store clerks. Whites, interestingly, trust blacks more than they trust people in general, Latinos, and even their own group members as store clerks. Latinos' trust in store clerks only is distinct between blacks and whites as store clerks: blacks are trusted most.

Turning to the ordinary least squares models of blacks' social trust in store clerks in table 6.10, we see that black linked fate increases trust in people in general as store clerks. Black linked fate, however, has the reverse effect on whites as store clerks, in effect reducing trust in them. Having received

TABLE 6.9

Comparisons of Arithmetic Means for Racial Groups' Trust in Store Clerks (Race and Social Trust Experiment)

Comparisons of means	Black respondents' trust	White respondents' trust	Latino respondents' trust
People/Blacks	2.2/2.4 (+)**a (n = 203)	2.3/2.6 (+)*** (n = 100)	2.3/2.5 (n = 100)
People/Whites	2.2/2.2 (n = 207)	2.3/2.4 (n = 97)	2.3/2.2 (n = 99)
People/Asians	2.2/2.2 (n = 200)	2.3/2.5 (n = 92)	2.3/2.4 (n = 95)
People/Latinos	2.2/2.3 (n = 200)	2.3/2.3 (n = 92)	2.3/2.3 (n = 96)
Whites/Blacks	2.2/2.4 (+)**a (n = 204)	2.4/2.6 (+)*a (n = 101)	2.2/2.5 (+)*a (n = 101)
Whites/Asians	2.2/2.2 (n = 201)	2.4/2.5 (n = 93)	2.2/2.4 (n = 96)
Whites/Latinos	2.2/2.3 (n = 193)	2.4/2.3 (n = 93)	2.2/2.3 (n = 97)
Asians/Blacks	2.2/2.4 (+)**a (n = 197)	2.5/2.6 (n = 96)	2.4/2.5 (n = 97)
Asians/Latinos	2.2/2.3 (n = 186)	2.5/2.3 (n = 88)	2.4/2.3 (n = 93)
Latinos/Blacks	2.3/2.4 (n = 189)	2.3/2.6 (+)*a (n = 96)	2.3/2.5 (n = 98)

Source: 2007 National Politics and Socialization Survey
Note: (+) indicates the group trusted most in the comparisons of means. Variables are scaled from 0 = never trust to 4 = very often trust. Statistically significant differences of means are indicated based on a p-value of at most .005, which is consistent with the Bonferroni adjustment method.
a Statistically significant without Bonferroni adjustment method, which offers a stringent standard of statistical significance
* p ≤ .10; ** p ≤ .05; *** p ≤ .01; **** p ≤ .001

TABLE 6.10

OLS Models of Blacks' Contextualized Trust in Store Clerks (Results of Race and Social Trust Experiments)

Social trust in store clerks	Racial consciousness socialization	Racial protectiveness socialization	Black linked fate	Racial uncertainty	Constant	F prob.	Adj. R²	N
People	.0062 (.0071)	-.0130 (.0143)	.2144** (.0847)	-.0231 (.0997)	.8336 (.7479)	0.30	0.03	68
Blacks	.0014 (.0067)	.0189 (.0132)	-.0900 (.0681)	-.1008 (.0653)	2.425**** (.5650)	0.19	0.05	80
Whites	.0025 (.0081)	-.0117 (.0191)	-.1926* (.0993)	.0187 (.0963)	3.226**** (.8645)	0.66	-0.03	77
Asians	.0128 (.0093)	-.0378** (.0152)	.0129 (.1004)	-.0848 (.0967)	1.816** (.8467)	0.08	0.09	75
Latinos	.0169* (.0088)	.0133 (.0203)	.1725 (.1151)	-.1915 (.1208)	2.050** (.9047)	0.10	0.11	56

Source: 2007 National Politics and Socialization Survey

Note: Standard errors are indicated in parentheses. Results of the models featured in the table include only the variables of interest. The full model also includes demographic variables for control variables.

* $p \leq .10$; ** $p \leq .05$; *** $p \leq .01$; **** $p \leq .001$

greater emphasis on racial protectiveness socialization messages, additionally, reduces blacks' trust in Asian store clerks, whereas having received greater emphasis on racial consciousness socialization messages moderately increases trust in Latino store clerks.

When we turn to the results for the comparisons of means among blacks', whites', and Latinos' *trust in co-workers*, in table 6.11, we see that blacks are more trusting of black co-workers than they are of people in general, whites, and Latinos. Interestingly, whites trust blacks more as co-workers than they

TABLE 6.11

Comparisons of Arithmetic Means for Racial Groups' Trust in Co-workers
(Race and Social Trust Experiment)

Comparisons of means	Black respondents' trust	White respondents' trust	Latino respondents' trust
People/Blacks	2.4/2.6 (+)*[a]	2.6/2.8	2.5/2.7
	(n = 202)	(n =94)	(n = 99)
People/Whites	2.4/2.3	2.6/2.5	2.5/2.4
	(n = 204)	(n = 91)	(n = 97)
People/Asians	2.4/2.4	2.6/2.6	2.5/2.6
	(n = 196)	(n = 86)	(n = 93)
People/Latinos	2.4/2.4	2.6/2.8	2.5/2.7
	(n = 191)	(n = 88)	(n = 93)
Whites/Blacks	2.3/2.6 (+)***[a]	2.5/2.8 (+)*[a]	2.4/2.7 (+)*[a]
	(n = 202)	(n = 97)	(n = 102)
Whites/Asians	2.3/2.4	2.5/2.6	2.4/.2.6
	(n = 196)	(n = 89)	(n = 96)
Whites/Latinos	2.3/2.4 (+)	2.5/2.8	2.4/2.7 (+)*[a]
	(n = 191)	(n = 91)	(n = 96)
Asians/Blacks	2.4/2.6	2.6/2.8	2.6/2.7
	(n = 194)	(n = 92)	(n = 98)
Asians/Latinos	2.4/2.4	2.6/2.8	2.6/2.7
	(n = 183)	(n = 86)	(n = 92)
Latinos/Blacks	2.4/2.6 (+)**[a]	2.8/2.8	2.7/2.7
	(n = 189)	(n = 94)	(n = 98)

Source: 2007 National Politics and Socialization Survey
Note: (+) indicates the group trusted most in the comparisons of means. Variables are scaled from 0 = never trust to 4 = very often trust. Statistically significant differences of means are indicated based on a p-value of at most .005, which is consistent with the Bonferroni adjustment method.
[a] Statistically significant without Bonferroni adjustment method, which offers a stringent standard of statistical significance.
* $p \leq .10$; ** $p \leq .05$; *** $p \leq .01$; **** $p \leq .001$

TABLE 6.12

OLS Models of Blacks' Contextualized Trust in Co-workers (Results of Race and Social Trust Experiments)

Social trust in co-workers	Racial consciousness socialization	Racial protectiveness socialization	Black linked fate	Racial uncertainty	Constant	F prob.	Adj. R^2	N
People	.0045	-.0171	.0533	-.1081	2.672***	0.93	-.09	67
	(.0080)	(.0162)	(.0953)	(.1134)	(.8363)			
Blacks	.0061	-.0131	-.0528	-.0283	2.043***	0.33	0.02	79
	(.0073)	(.0142)	(.0749)	(.0719)	(.6181)			
Whites	.0036	-.0248	-.1955	.0166	3.079	0.63	-0.03	76
	(.0095)	(.0221)	(.1177)	(.1164)	(.9998)			
Asians	.0022	-.0373**	.1603	-.1537	2.251**	0.06	0.11	72
	(.0100)	(.0154)	(.1027)	(.0994)	(.8851)			
Latinos	.0113	-.0139	.2588**	-.1199	.9286	0.16	0.08	58
	(.0083)	(.0189)	(.1072)	(.1123)	(.8194)			

Source: 2007 National Politics and Socialization Survey

Note: Standard errors are indicated in parentheses. Results of the models featured in the table include only the variables of interest. The full model also includes demographic variables for control variables.

* p ≤ .10; ** p ≤ .05; *** p ≤ .01; **** p ≤ .001

do whites as co-workers. Latinos, on the other hand, trust blacks and other Latinos as co-workers more than they trust whites.

The regression models in table 6.12 indicate that only one of the racial socialization variables predicts blacks' trust in their co-workers. Blacks who have received greater emphasis on racial protectiveness socialization are more distrusting of Asians in the workplace. Black linked fate increases blacks' trust in Latino co-workers.

In the race and contextualized trust experiments for blacks' *trust in co-congregants* in table 6.13, we see that blacks trust Latinos as co-congregants

TABLE 6.13

Comparisons of Arithmetic Means for Racial Groups' Trust in Co-congregants (Race and Social Trust Experiment)

Comparisons of means	Black respondents' trust	White respondents' trust	Latino respondents' trust
People/Blacks	2.6/2.5 (n = 203)	2.6/2.4 (n =100)	2.5/2.8 (n = 101)
People/Whites	2.6/2.4 (n = 207)	2.6/2.6 (n = 96)	2.5/2.2 (n = 99)
People/Asians	2.6/2.6 (n = 196)	2.6/2.7 (n = 88)	2.5/2.6 (n = 89)
People/Latinos	2.6/2.7 (n = 197)	2.6/2.8 (n = 92)	2.5/2.7 (n = 96)
Whites/Blacks	2.4/2.5 (n = 202)	2.6/2.4 (n = 100)	2.2/2.8 (+)***a (n = 102)
Whites/Asians	2.4/2.6 (n = 195)	2.6/2.7 (n = 88)	2.2/2.6 (+)**a (n = 90)
Whites/Latinos	2.4/2.7 (+)**a (n = 196)	2.6/2.8 (n = 92)	2.2/2.7 (+)**a (n = 97)
Asians/Blacks	2.6/2.5 (n = 191)	2.7/2.4 (n = 92)	2.6/2.8 (n = 92)
Asians/Latinos	2.6/2.7 (n = 185)	2.7/2.8 (n = 84)	2.6/2.7 (n = 87)
Latinos/Blacks	2.7(+)/2.5*a (n = 192)	2.8 (+)/2.4*a (n = 96)	2.7/2.8 (n = 99)

Source: 2007 National Politics and Socialization Survey

Note: (+) indicates the group trusted most in the comparisons of means. Variables are scaled *from* 0 = never trust to 4 = very often trust. Statistically significant differences of means are indicated based on a p-value of at most .005, which is consistent with the Bonferroni adjustment method.

a Statistically significant without Bonferroni adjustment method, which offers a stringent standard of statistical significance.

* p ≤ .10; ** p ≤ .05; *** p ≤ .01; **** p ≤ .001

TABLE 6.14

OLS Models of Blacks' Contextualized Trust in Co-congregants (Results of Race and Social Trust Experiments)

Social trust in co-congregants	Racial consciousness socialization	Racial protectiveness socialization	Black linked fate	Racial uncertainty	Constant	F prob.	Adj. R^2	N
People	.0042 (.0083)	-.0237 (.0169)	-.1506 (.0999)	.0874 (.1175)	3.119**** (.8438)	0.32	0.02	68
Blacks	.0230*** (.0078)	.0179 (.0154)	-.1173 (.0796)	-.0101 (.0763)	1.576 (.6602)	0.002	0.20	80
Whites	.0091 (.0091)	-.0215 (.0216)	-.2359** (.1123)	-.0183 (.1103)	2.608*** (.9723)	0.28	.03	75
Asians	-.0043 (.0109)	-.0297* (.0170)	-.0436 (.1146)	-.0991 (.1083)	3.035*** (1.002)	0.41	0.01	69
Latinos	.0093 (.0078)	.0173 (.0180)	.3194*** (.1040)	-.1286 (.1084)	.6882 (.8186)	.005	0.37	58

Source: 2007 National Politics and Socialization Survey

Note: Standard errors are indicated in parentheses. Results of the models featured in the table include only the variables of interest. The full model also includes demographic variables for control variables.

* $p \leq .10$; ** $p \leq .05$; *** $p \leq .01$; **** $p \leq .001$

more than they trust both whites and their own group members. Whites trust Latinos more than they trust blacks as co-congregants. Latinos trust blacks, Asians, and Latinos more than they trust whites as co-congregants.

As table 6.14 elucidates, blacks in the NPSS who were socialized with more emphasis on racial consciousness socialization are more trusting in blacks as co-congregants. Having received greater emphasis on racial protectiveness socialization messages reduces blacks' trust in Asian Americans as co-congregants. Feeling greater linked fate with other blacks, on the one hand, reduces blacks' trust in whites as co-congregants; yet, on the other hand, it increases their trust in Latinos as co-congregants.

Summary and Conclusion: Race and Blacks' Social Trust

This chapter has examined the influence of race on blacks' social trust; compared their social trust to whites', Asians', and Latinos'; compared their trust in different racial actors in separate social contexts; and ascertained the influence of blacks' internalized racial knowledge and attitudes on their social trust.

In the SCBS, when blacks' generalized social trust and contextualized social trust (in neighbors, store clerks, co-workers, and co-congregants) are compared to those of nonblacks (all nonblack racial groups combined), blacks are less socially trusting than are nonblacks, and contrary to expectation, having diverse racial networks does not increase blacks' generalized social trust. In view of specific comparisons of blacks' social trust to separate racial groups, moreover, we see that blacks have less generalized trust in others than do whites and Asians, specifically. There is no statistically significant difference, however, between blacks' and Latinos' generalized social trust.

With respect to contextualized trust, whites and Asians are more trusting of their neighbors, store clerks, co-workers, and co-congregants than blacks are. Latinos are only more socially trusting than blacks are regarding their co-workers. In fact, looking at blacks' contextualized trust, both shopping places and workplaces are the contexts where blacks are the most distrusting of others. While the hypothesis is confirmed that blacks trust others the most in the context of religious institutions, nevertheless, they still trust their co-congregants less than other racial groups do, that is, with the exception of Latinos. This is to say that both blacks and Latinos share in being low, socially trusting groups.

What seems counterintuitive is that, regarding blacks' trust in their neighbors, store clerks, and co-workers, older blacks are more socially trusting than are younger blacks. We might expect that older blacks, who are more likely to have had personal discrimination experiences and de jure experiences with racial discrimination, would have less trust in people in these contexts because of the historical circumstances in which blacks were treated poorly. In the SCBS, at least, that is not the case. Because the SCBS does not include measures of racial socialization, racial discrimination or uncertainty, or racial identity, we are unable to use this data set to determine possible effects of different internalization of race on blacks' perceptions of their social environments and the racial actors in them. Thus, the NPSS offers import with the inclusion of these measures, and the race and contextualized experiments that can assist us in determining additional factors that influence blacks' externalization of racial attitudes and, particularly, their social trust. Controlling for these measures in addition to demographic variables can help us determine whether blacks' socialization and personal experiences with race affect their contextualized social trust.

In the NPSS, black, white, and Latino respondents' contextualized trust can be compared across racial actors. For all racial groups, some racial groups are trusted more than others. As in the SCBS, blacks have the highest arithmetic means of social trust in the context of religious institutions. Overall, the highest arithmetic mean is trust in Latinos as co-congregants (2.7 mean); this result indicates that blacks said they trust Latinos as co-congregants more often than they said that about other groups. In fact, blacks trust Latino co-congregants more than they do black co-congregants (2.5 mean).

Considering other contexts, in the ten possible means comparisons per context in the NPSS, rarely did blacks trust distinctly in one group more than another. Regarding neighbors, there is only one instance of statistically distinguishable trust: blacks trust people in general less than they trust other blacks. For store clerks, there are three instances: blacks trust other blacks more than they trust people in general, whites, and Asians, confirming the expectation that Asians would be trusted less but disconfirming the expectation that they would be trusted less than Latinos. In the context of the workplace, there also are only three instances: blacks trust people in general, whites, and Latinos less than they trust blacks as co-workers, thus confirming the expectation that blacks would be distrusting of whites and Latinos in the workplace. With respect to co-congregants, there are only two instances: blacks trust Latinos more than they trust whites and blacks as co-congregants.

The pattern of trust seems to suggest that within the context of neighborhoods, shopping places, and workplaces, blacks are likely to distinguish their trust in social actors on the basis of whether they are members of their own racial group or members of groups that perhaps hark back to stereotypes or maybe to memories of racial discrimination or competition in these contexts. This finding supports the hypothesis that blacks' contextualized trust depends on attitudes regarding specific racial groups and social contexts. Blacks in the NPSS, however, do not trust whites the least of all racial groups in social contexts. Nor do they often distinguish trust between nonblack groups, and the same can be said for whites and Latinos in the survey. Blacks, however, perceive trust in groups distinctly from whites and Latinos as trustors, as these groups trust certain racial actors more or less than blacks in various contexts. Even more noticeable is that there is not a large difference in the extent to which blacks trust their own group members more than they trust the other groups, despite statistically significant differences in means.

In the separate models of trust in racial actors for each social context, racial socialization messages influence blacks' contextualized trust only in the following contexts: trust in people in general as neighbors (more emphasis on racial consciousness messages reduces trust); trust in Asians as neighbors (more emphasis on racial protectiveness messages decreases trust); trust in Asians as store clerks (more emphasis on racial protectiveness messages reduces trust); trust in Latinos as store clerks (more emphasis on racial consciousness increases trust); trust in Asians as co-workers (more emphasis on racial protectiveness messages reduces trust); trust in blacks as co-congregants (more emphasis on racial consciousness increases trust); and trust in Asians as co-congregants (more emphasis on racial protectiveness messages reduces trust).

Black linked fate has the effect of both increasing and decreasing contextualized trust in certain targets of the experiments. On the one hand, black linked fate increases trust in social actors: people in general as neighbors and store clerks, and Latinos as co-workers and co-congregants. On the other hand, black linked fate reduces trust in whites as store clerks and co-congregants. Despite evidence in the literature that supports the notion that discrimination experiences decrease social trust, here, a related concept— racial uncertainty, or the fear of being discriminated against in the future —has no effect whatsoever on blacks' contextualized trust. Thus, we see that blacks' prospective concerns for being racially discriminated against do not factor into their contextualized social trust.

From the analysis in this chapter, we learn that blacks are generally less socially trusting than are other racial groups, with the exception of Latinos. Moreover, people in general, not just blacks, distinguish their trust in social actors on the basis not only of the context but also of the person's race. The results in this chapter lend support to Alan Miller and Tomoko Mitamura's (2003) contention that people interpret trust based on both whom they trust and whom they deem suspicious. For blacks, this suspicion does not come from racial uncertainty but rather from familial messages that have socialized them about racial protectiveness to avoid mistreatment by racial groups. In the next chapter, we discern how blacks perceive racial actors in the context of the political sphere. From this analysis, we can learn more about how a political actor's racial background influences blacks' political trust in that person and to what extent internalized information about race plays a role in blacks' political trust. Moreover, we can determine the extent to which blacks (compared to other groups) trust differently in politics than they do in their social spaces.

7

The Political Context

In chapter 6, I examined the effects of internalized racial knowledge on blacks' navigation of their social contexts. Whereas racial socialization experiences influenced some perceptions of racial actors, racial uncertainty had no influence whatsoever on blacks' social trust. We learned that blacks trust people more in some social contexts than in others. While group-centric assessments of social trust were evident, nevertheless, there were no instances in which blacks overwhelmingly trusted their own group members more than they trusted nonblack groups. Blacks who received more emphasis on racial protectiveness messages, however, were more likely to socially distrust certain racial groups. Black consciousness also increased trust in some groups and not in others. So how does internalized racial knowledge influence trust in racial actors in the political context? This and the analysis of blacks' political trust are the focus of this chapter.

While blacks' quotidian social experiences have historically influenced their push for equality in politics, the greater meaning of their exclusion can be seen in their inability to be a part of political decision-making that affects every aspect of their lives. Turning to an examination of blacks' political trust, this chapter helps us to assess how blacks process trust in a realm in which they have been historically denied access and in which they continue to face the real-life consequences of decision-making that may or may not be responsive to their needs.

Communities define their own vision of political representation. How this vision is defined and how the political system responds to this vision relates to the way that communities are treated and the way that these communities feel that their interests are incorporated into political agendas. Aside from political incorporation, while policy responsiveness is a salient attribute of government accountability, communities that lack identifiable representation by their own chosen leaders or by people who look like them, who otherwise may have been barred from political participation because of these looks, may feel political alienation and underrepresentation. The mere presence of a look-like-me political actor similarly can boost excluded communities' sense of legitimacy not only in the political system or political institution but also in the politics of their communities. In a democracy, inclusion is important for the purpose of articulating interests. A system without outlets for vocal expression violates the norms of democracy and invites distrust on behalf of the voiceless (M. Williams 1998). History elucidates race-related restrictions on blacks' electoral voice and choice. The psychological effects of these restrictions continue to be the focus of political trust studies and inquiries about race and representation.

In a similar vein, this chapter examines the influence of race on blacks' political trust. It broadens the analysis of race and representation beyond the traditional black-white dichotomy, additionally, by examining multiracial comparisons of blacks' trust in black, white, Asian American, and Latino political actors and by controlling for these representatives' partisanship. Several inquiries guide the analysis in this chapter. How do black Americans process race, coalitional potential, and partisanship of political actors in their political trust? Do they trust the federal and local levels of government differently compared to other racial groups? Do their internalized racial experiences influence their perceptions? Furthermore, do they feel that certain racial groups can be trusted more in federal and local governments to do what is right for blacks' interests? This chapter addresses these research inquiries by using data in the 2000 SCBS and the split-sample survey experiments in the 2007 NPSS to compare blacks' trust in political actors with different racial backgrounds, partisan leanings, and responsibilities in federal and local governments.

Black Politics: Institutionalized Distrust?

Historian Rayford Logan (1965) describes "The Nadir" (1877–1901) as the low point in African Americans' relationship with their government. Much of this "low point," however, predates even this era. The United States Constitution protected the institution of slavery and the trade of black human bodies in several ways: prescribing that no law could outlaw the slave trade before the year 1808 (Article I, Section 9), that runaway slaves initially had to be lawfully returned to their owners (Article IV, Section 2), and that slaves could be counted three-fifths a person toward the population count used to determine the number of representatives per state in the House of Representatives (Article 1, Section 2). Territories were also admitted to the Union as states on the basis of whether they would allow or disallow slavery as an institution.[1]

Black subjugation, hence, was institutionalized into the fabric of the nation. Subsequently, the power of owning slaves influenced the political power structure of the presidency and the House of Representatives for much of the antebellum period, as white southern politicians had a stronghold on these two political institutions through the disproportionate location of chattel property in their region, which inadvertently facilitated their election (Walton and Smith 2008).[2] Despite the power that slaves' presence provided to their region, their own personal political influence was obliterated by their widely believed subhuman status and their failure to be included as formal participants in the American political system.

Even the Supreme Court did not recognize blacks as humans with rights that the Court should protect, codifying into public policy via the *Dred Scott* case (1857) what was conventionally practiced in everyday black life: rampant racial oppression, limited social mobility, and virtual exclusion from political representation. The question of blacks' status as slaves propelled the nation into war during the Civil War (1861–1865), and only at the conclusion of the war did many black slaves acquire freedom, through the passage of the Thirteenth Amendment.

Reconstruction-era laws expanded black rights to include access to citizenship and the franchise through the passage of the Fourteenth and Fifteenth Amendments, respectively. Along with these rights, blacks acquired newfound agentic, political influence through the election of representatives who supported their inclusion in society, many of whom were Republican representatives, including a slew of black representatives elected under the Republican Party banner. In fact, because of many blacks' admiration for President Abraham Lincoln's abolition of slavery, during Reconstruction, the Republican Party became the party that blacks' perceived as considerate of their interests during this period, leading them to become heavily Republican supporters (Weiss 1983; Fauntroy 2007). Freedmen's Bureau programs during this era also offered blacks services that integrated them into society as new-entrant, functioning, and resourceful citizens.

After a roughly twelve-year window of expanded opportunities, "The Nadir" of the first Reconstruction era commenced. More specifically, through the manipulation of Republican presidential candidate Rutherford B. Hayes's dealings with southern, white congressmembers in order to break the tie in his 1876 presidential election bid against Samuel Tilden, the Compromise of 1877 removed troops from the South. These troops were responsible for protecting blacks from post–Civil War, Confederate rage and disorder (Logan 1965). Subsequently, southern white redemption reconstructed the region into a Solid South that recaptured whites' antebellum domain and racial power (Woodward 1974).

With this power transition, Black Codes defined blacks' second-class citizenship, as the first foray into what eventually became a formalized legal structure recognized by the Supreme Court in the *Plessy* case (1896) as constitutionally acceptable "separate but equal" laws that were practiced socially in various ways across the southern region as "Jim Crow" mores (Woodward 1974). By 1910, most black men had been disenfranchised in southern states, with many states having changed their constitutions to prescribe this disempowerment (Woodward [1951] 1999; Wynes 1961; Litwack 1998). Taxes requiring blacks to pay to vote at the polls, primaries exclusive to whites only, clauses restricting the right to vote to those with grandfathers who had voted, districts constructed to dilute the black vote, and sheer intimidation toward those who attempted to vote constricted black electoral participation practically to nil, thus marginalizing most blacks out of politics (Key 1949). Amid political exclusion, blacks' interests were negotiated between black leaders and paternalistic whites who sought control over black social and political equality. Therefore, blacks' political interests faced immeasurable political uncertainty, left to the behest of white benefactors or representatives who capriciously decided to support blacks' interests depending on the counterbalance of their personal volition and whites' group interests. With blacks' disenfranchisement and conventionally recognized lower-rung status in the racial hierarchy, their interests carried much less weight, contributing even more to their voicelessness and practical invisibility in American politics at this time.

Within a hundred-year period following the conclusion of the Civil War (1865–1965), blacks were relegated to invisible political actors within the white public sphere, championing their own interests through their black institutional developments and personal exchanges within intraracial social networks in the confines of the black public sphere (Lewis 1991; Dawson 2001). Others established cross-racial social and political networks with whites, depending on their personal ideologies about black progress, and established intermittent auxiliary organizations with their white-dominated local governments (Logan 1965; Dawson 2001). Insurgent attitudes facilitated blacks' communal engagement, which served as a "quasi-governmental" development of the black community (McAdam 1982).

As W. E. B. Du Bois ([1903] 1990) noted, blacks acquired a "double consciousness," in which they knew that their status as Americans was fragilely defined by their dual status as Negroes. Nevertheless, through the aegis of black civic and civil rights organizations and black individuals united in protest against their second-class citizenship status during the modern civil rights movement, blacks influenced the scope of second-era reconstruction policies (*Brown v. Board of Education* case, 1954; Civil Rights Act of 1964; Voting Rights Act of 1965; and Fair Housing Act of 1968), which redefined blacks' presence in the American sociopolitical structure in the mid-twentieth century and beyond (Morris 1984).

With the historical political exclusion of blacks by various political institutions, blacks experienced a tumultuous political relationship with their government, nationally and locally, and their choices for political representation had been limited by candidate options (Key 1949), racialized party structures and platforms (Woodward 1974; Frymer 1999; Fauntroy 2007), and racialized composition of voting districts that influenced electoral outcomes, public policies, and, ultimately, policy responsiveness to their group interests (Parker 1990; Dawson 1994; Canon 1999). Moreover, with limited periods of expanded rights and overwhelming historical experiences with disparaging racial projects (Omi and Winant 1994), low political trust among blacks seemed likely and effactually institutionalized.[3] Protest politics during the mid-twentieth century facilitated a second reconstruction era and renewed blacks' interest in acquiring the full right to the franchise and electoral participation, and the government responded with the passage of the Voting Rights Act of 1965 (Keyssar 2000).

While the passage of the Voting Rights Act of 1965 proved to be a major milestone in black Americans' political participation, still issues remained regarding the ability of blacks to become incorporated into the political system. These issues focused on black Americans' ability to elect representatives who presumably could best represent their interests and offer them more policy responsiveness. As far as building a more trusting political relationship, *black* representatives were viewed as the more trustable representatives for black interests. Racial kowtowing to the electorate between the two major political parties over civil rights policies during the 1960s also led to the realignment of the two major parties, shifting most blacks' and many whites' partisanship because of racial policy preferences that addressed blacks' historical discrimination (Carmines and Stimson 1989).

Increased black electoral participation after passage of the Voting Rights Act of 1965 also ushered in a new era of black politics, in which the ballot, once again, proved useful for advocating black political interests, especially as black elected officials were increasingly elected by the black electorate (Tate 1993). By 1969, blacks elected to Congress united to form the Congressional Black Caucus as a symbolic means to influence national politics through collectivized black interests across representatives from different voting districts. Black mayors were increasingly elected as leaders in cities across the country. For the first time since Reconstruction, blacks acted as major electoral players in the American political system, locally and nationally. Political transitions between white mayors and black mayors seemingly increased blacks' political trust (Howell and Fagan 1988). Black political leadership in conventional political apparatuses also appeared to offer blacks a glimmer of hope for political change, inclusion, and incorporation in government (Browning, Marshall, and Tabb 1984).

Despite these tremendous political gains, to date, blacks' political trust still remains lower than that of other Americans. Longstanding political distrust among blacks in comparison to other Americans, however, remains to be fully understood (Brehm and Rahn 1997; Rahn and Transue 1998; Putnam 2000b; Tate 2003). Yet the decline in blacks' political trust has been a part of a larger trend among Americans and people in many democracies, in general (Pew Research Center 2010b; Catterberg and Moreno 2005; Putnam 2000b; Pharr 1997). Thus, the downward trust trend has perplexed many scholars who have searched for explanations: was it social disorder, limited policy responsiveness, lackluster institutional performance, or dislike of incumbents?

For blacks, historical discrimination and political exclusion dictated the likelihood of all these things being explanations. More centrally, institutionalized racism influenced all of the above. Anecdotal evidence suggests that blacks' experiences with the political system foreshadowed their political distrust. For scholars studying black political behavior, inquiries thus focus on *how* race influences blacks' relationships with the political system and, more specifically, their political trust.

Explaining Blacks' Political Distrust: The Influence of Race

Burgeoning scholarship on race and representation examines how black Americans are best incorporated into the political system, using Pitkin's (1967) conceptualization of representation as either *descriptive* representation (congruent racial group membership between the representative and constituents), *substantive* representation (congruent political interests between the representative and constituents), or *symbolic* representation (representation without substantive benefit but psychological benefit to the constituent group's interests) (Tate 2003; Mansbridge 1999; M. Williams 1998; Lublin 1997; Whitby 1997; Guinier 1995; Swain 1993; Browning, Marshall, and Tabb 1984). A leading way to incorporate black interests into the political system was thought to be the election of a black representative, hence descriptive representation. But what good would descriptive representation be without the election of a representative who also offered substantive representation of black group interests? Scholars thus considered whether only black representatives could best represent black interests or whether white representatives with similar policy interests and partisan congruence could represent black interests equally well (Canon 1999; Swain 1993; Tate 2003).

Initially, many of these inquiries indirectly pointed to the significance of race and representation in blacks' political trust, offering generally two explanations of blacks' political distrust. On one hand, scholars suggest that systemic structures influence blacks' political distrust by institutionally imposing limitations on blacks' voting choice, particularly, the election of representatives who share their racial background (Bobo and Gilliam 1990; Swain 1993; Guinier 1995; Gay 2002; Tate 2003). Scholars consider systemic ways to incorporate representation of black group interest, for example, through the construction of majority-minority districts or other voting systems that enhance political minorities' influence on electoral outcomes. Researchers then investigated whether voting districts with larger black populations enhanced or hurt black representation, either by increasing the likelihood of the election of a (black) Democratic political representative from the district or by creating substantive representation for blacks at the cost of increasing the number of Republican-leaning districts, which could lead to a Republican majority in the legislature (Canon 1999; Lublin 1997).

On the other hand, scholars suggest that blacks' psychological orientations (political socialization, racial consciousness, and political efficacy) about the political system affect their relationships and broader perceptions of the political system (Shingles 1981; Miller et al. 1981; Avery 2006, 2009). The perceived lack of responsiveness to black political interests induced discussions about how to increase and enhance black political representation in the American political system, and the weight of this focus landed on the responsibility of representatives to be accountable to black group interests (Guinier 1995). For example, Katherine Tate (2003) investigates how black Americans perceive the effectiveness, responsiveness, and trustworthiness of representatives with different racial backgrounds (black or white). This strain of research also introduces the importance of political trust in the race and representation debate, as Tate inquires whether substantive or descriptive representation enhances blacks' political trust. The two explanations—systemic and psychological influences—are not necessarily mutually exclusive, as they both emphasize the importance of blacks' acquiring either descriptive or substantive representation or both. Another aspect of analyzing how blacks perceive race and representation is to examine how close blacks feel to other racial groups in their ideas and feelings about politics, as these groups are likely coalition partners or political actors with whom blacks may interact politically, and thus, blacks may consider whether to trust them in some political capacity, despite incongruent racial representation.

Racialized Political Proximity: How Close Do Blacks Feel to Other Racial Groups?

The NPSS asked black respondents how close they feel to blacks, whites, Asians, and Latinos in their ideas and feelings about politics (scaled 0 = not close at all to 4 = very close). Sixty-seven percent of blacks (N = 513) expressed that they feel "very close" to other blacks in ideas and feelings about politics, followed by 27 percent who feel "fairly close." As for feeling close in ideas and feelings to whites, 23 percent of blacks (N = 509) feel "very close," followed by 49 percent of blacks who feel "fairly close." And 26 percent of blacks feel "not too close" to whites. Regarding closeness to Asians, the highest percentage of blacks expressed that they feel "not too close" to this group, or 38 percent (N = 498). This group is followed by 30 percent of blacks who reported that they do not feel close at all with Asian Americans. Forty-three percent of blacks said they feel "fairly close" to Latinos (N = 502), compared to another 27 percent who feel "not too close" to Latinos. There were an equal number of blacks who feel "not close at all" and "very close" to Latinos (15 percent). Thus, it appears that blacks feel the least close to Asian Americans of all the racial groups in ideas and feelings about politics. But what factors contribute to these attitudes toward these groups?

To determine factors that influence how blacks feel about these groups, several multivariate models are tested for each racial group. Race and politics have affected all blacks in the United States, regardless of their ethnicity as African Americans or otherwise. To control for possible differences in perceived politics of black people among ethnic groups, however, it is important to include a control variable for "non–African American," identifying blacks (those who identify as West Indian or African) who may view politics differently from blacks who identify as "African American." Blacks living in predominantly black neighborhoods should feel greater proximity to other blacks and less proximity toward nonblack groups. Having received more emphasis on racial consciousness socialization should increase blacks' proximal feelings with Asian Americans and Latinos as fellow racial and ethnic minorities. Having received more emphasis on black protectiveness socialization messages should decrease blacks' feelings of closeness to all groups. Black linked fate should increase feelings of closeness to fellow blacks and diminish feelings of closeness to whites. Democratic partisanship should increase blacks' feelings of proximity to Latinos, as this group shares similar socioeconomic disparities with blacks and many Latinos (with the exception of Cuban Americans, who identify more with the Republican Party) mostly identify with the Democratic Party (McClain and Stewart 2006).

In table 7.1 we see the results of the several multivariate models for feelings of closeness in ideas and feelings in politics for blacks, whites, Asians, and Latinos. These models include controls for several demographic variables (including a variable that controls for differences between blacks who identify as African American or either West Indian or African), two racial socialization messages (racial consciousness and racial protectiveness), racial uncertainty (expectation for future racial discrimination), black linked fate, and partisan identification.

In the model of blacks' feelings of closeness to other blacks in ideas and politics, we see that blacks who identify as either West Indian or African feel less political closeness to other blacks than African Americans do. As expected, greater emphasis on racial consciousness socialization messages and feeling greater linkages to other blacks increases blacks' political proximity to other blacks. Interestingly, the only instance in which greater emphasis on racial protectiveness socialization messages influences feelings of political closeness to other groups is in the case of closeness to other blacks. Having received emphasis on such messages reduces feeling of political closeness to other blacks. Living in a predominantly black neighborhood reduces feelings of political closeness to whites, as does identifying more strongly with the Democratic Party. The only factor that influences blacks' feelings of political proximity to Asian Americans is black linked fate: with a greater feeling of linkage to other blacks, black respondents in the NPSS feel moderately more political closeness to Asian Americans.

As for political proximity to Latinos, older blacks feel less close to Latinos than younger blacks do. Having received more emphasis on racial consciousness socialization, however, increases blacks' feelings of political proximity to Latinos. Feeling more linked fate with other blacks also increases

TABLE 7.1

*Blacks' Feelings of Political Closeness to Black, White,
Latino, and Asian Groups*

Covariates	Blacks	Whites	Asians	Latinos
Non–African Americans	−.7751****	−.3477	−.0456	.0180
	(.1846)	(.2458)	(.2546)	(.2445)
Female	.1309	.0673	−.2219	.0910
	(.1388)	(.1862)	(.1927)	(.1849)
Age	−.0513	.0339	−.0507	−.1059**
	(.0392)	(.0534)	(.0552)	(.0532)
Income	.0196	−.0092	−.0193	.0014
	(.0451)	(.0596)	(.0620)	(.0596)
Education	−.0124	.0130	.0347	.0037
	(.0362)	(.0483)	(.0508)	(.0491)
South	.1482	−.1288	.0251	.1278
	(.1404)	(.1861)	(.1944)	(.1850)
R lives in predominantly	.1638	−.2989*	−.0765	−.0211
black neighborhood	(.1347)	(.1801)	(.1866)	(.1795)
Racial consciousness	.0182***	.0104	.0101	.0218***
socialization	(.0062)	(.0084)	(.0088)	(.0083)
Racial protectiveness	−.0248**	−.0169	−.0157	−.0106
socialization	(.0116)	(.0159)	(.0165)	(.0158)
Expectation of future	−.0153	−.1295	−.1418	.0378
racial discrimination	(.0627)	(.0833)	(.0860)	(.0825)
Black linked fate	.1575**	.0408	.1565*	.1705*
	(.0678)	(.0897)	(.0927)	(.0890)
Party identification	−.0368	−.1198*	−.0715	−.1422**
(strong Republican to	(.0542)	(.0719)	(.0758)	(.0712)
strong Democrat)				
Constant	1.773***	1.923**	1.167	.9563
	(.6208)	(.8342)	(.8691)	(.8442)
N	106	104	102	103
F Prob.	0.00	0.32	0.62	0.04
R^2	0.32	0.13	0.10	0.21

Source: 2007 National Politics and Socialization Survey
Note: Standard errors are indicated in parentheses.
* $p \leq .10$; ** $p \leq .05$; *** $p \leq .01$; **** $p \leq .001$

feelings of political closeness to Latinos. On the contrary and counter to my anticipation, being a strong Democrat decreases blacks' perceived political closeness to Latinos, which dispels the hypothesis that Democrats would be more proximal with this group. If black Democrats have disparate views about Latinos, it is then important to gauge how blacks trust representatives and political officials who are Latinos (and other racial group members) and members of the two major parties. Studying such attitudes also helps us gauge the preferences that black respondents in the NPSS have for either race or partisanship or both in their political trust.

Trust Based on Descriptive and Substantive Representation: Either or Both?

The accumulated race and representation literature thus suggests that black Americans often face a Hobson's choice. Both race and partisanship vitally affect the quality of the political relationship that black Americans experience as a majority Democratic voting bloc with their representatives and the political system. Paul Frymer (1999) even describes black Americans as a "captured group" that lacks political alternatives to the Democratic Party, in part because of the historically concerted effort to push black Americans away from the Republican Party post-1964 and the failed viability of third parties in the American political system. At the least, the race of a political actor can enhance the psychological connection that black Americans feel toward the political system. Similarly, the partisanship of a political actor can be important in influencing policy outcomes from which black Americans benefit. Thus, both race *and* partisanship weigh heavily in black Americans' faith in the political system's policy responsiveness (M. Williams 1998).

So far, research on whether black or white political representatives deliver the most psychologically satisfying representation for blacks offers mixed results (Tate 2003; Swain 1993). Despite findings that indicate that black Americans' political trust does not increase with representation by a black representative compared to representation by a white representative, other findings show that the race of the political representative makes a difference in the perceived quality of the relationship that black Americans feel to the political system (Tate 2003). For example, black Americans give higher approval ratings to black legislators than to white legislators, even after controlling for partisanship. As Tate notes,

A full 60 percent strongly approved of their legislator's performance when that legislator was a Black Democrat as opposed to only 36 when the legislator was a White Democrat. In contrast still, only one-quarter of the respondents represented by White Republicans strongly approved of their performance, while nearly 30 percent strongly disapproved. (2003, 119)

Black Americans represented by black Democrats also are more likely than those represented by white Democrats to believe that their representatives do something "special" for their districts (Tate 2003). Furthermore, Tate finds that those blacks who perceive that there are more blacks in Congress are more trusting of Congress as an institution. Other research also finds that blacks are more likely to contact their representatives if he or she is black than if he or she is white (Gay 2002). Thus, descriptive representation seems to offer blacks some enhanced psychological connection to the political system.

The Democratic Party, since 1964 and its support of civil rights legislation, has offered a political platform seemingly more in sync with black Americans' political interests than the one offered by the Republican Party (Fauntroy 2007; Dawson 1994; Carmines and Stimson 1989). After 1964, black Americans have overwhelmingly supported the Democratic Party, even voting for Democratic presidential candidates with as much as 90 percent electoral support (McClain and Stewart 2006). In contrast, the Republican Party has been viewed more negatively as the party much less likely to "work hard" on black Americans' political interests (Dawson 1994).

Historically, the Republican Party also has been known to use race baiting against black Americans' interests in order to attract southern, white voters (Fauntroy 2007; Mendelberg 2001; Gilens 1999), and it continues to make less attractive appeals to the black American electorate (Fauntroy 2007; Philpot 2004; Wielhouwer 2000). James Glaser (1995) also finds that black Americans are more likely than whites to perceive partisan differences between the two parties on issues, in general, and more particularly, on racial issues. In fact, results in the NPSS support this finding. When black respondents in the NPSS were asked which major party they feel works the hardest on issues affecting blacks, 67 percent stated the Democratic Party, compared to only 1 percent who stated the Republican Party. Interestingly, another 32 percent of black respondents stated that neither the Democratic Party nor the Republican Party works the hardest on issues of major concern for blacks.

Considering that political parties serve as heuristic cues for party platforms and political issues (Rahn 1993), knowing the partisanship of political representatives is likely to make a difference in how black Americans perceive policy congruency between political parties and black group interests. Similarly, the perception that the Democratic Party is the party that "works hardest on black issues" should increase political trust in Democratic representatives and decrease political trust in Republican representatives.

Because black Americans overwhelmingly identify as Democrats (McClain and Stewart 2006), we should expect that a nonblack political representative with a Democratic partisanship would be trusted more than a black Republican. But is this always the case? That is, do black Americans trust nonblack Democrats (white, Asian American, or Latino) more, less, or equal to the way that they trust black Democrats or black Republicans? How do black Americans trust Republicans of various races? Do they trust black Republicans more than they trust other Republicans? Does substantive representation matter more in political trust than descriptive representation does? If so, then under what circumstances does it matter more? When does race matter and when does it not matter in black Americans' political trust? In other words, does race trump partisanship, does partisanship trump race, or do both matter in black Americans' political trust?

These questions raise important considerations when we turn to blacks' trust assessments in the context of political spaces. In low-information elections, race is a salient cue for voters' electoral decision-making (McDermott 1998), even leading black candidates to run deracialized campaigns to avoid electoral backlash from white voters who associate their skin color with a set policy agenda perceived as prescribed for blacks only (Gillespie 2010; McCormick and Jones 1993). While black Americans in the NPSS trusted Asian Americans and Latinos more than they did whites and in ways more similar to the way they trust other blacks, these distinctions were not noticeable with respect to social trust. Furthermore, the political realities that blacks face as far as perceived competition with Asian Americans and Latinos may diminish how blacks perceive trust in political actors with these racial backgrounds. Therefore, it is pertinent to test how blacks perceive political actors as members of both major political parties to determine how race and partisanship affect their political trust.

Blacks' Trust in Black Political Actors Compared to White, Asian, or Latino Political Actors

Individual blacks perceive political interests connected with the larger black racial group because of historical experiences with racial discrimination and black institutional cues that continue to emphasize race as a politically mobilizing agent (Dawson 1994; Tate 1993). Having a black political representative also enhances blacks' political empowerment and trust in the political system (Bobo and Gilliam 1990). We, therefore, should expect that the race of a political actor will be another important cue in black

Americans' political trust, and shared racial membership between them and a political actor should enhance their political trust. Blacks should perceive black political actors as enhancing their political linkage to the political system, leading to more political trust. Using race as a cue alone, blacks should perceive many white political actors on the basis of their historical reputation. White political actors, accordingly, should be trusted less than black political actors are.

Because partisanship also serves as another salient heuristic for evaluations of political actors, race and partisanship should not be mutually exclusive in blacks' political trust. As such, blacks should be more trusting of black Democrats than they are of white Democrats. Because white Democrats offer more substantive representation than black Republicans do, blacks should trust white Democrats more than they do black Republicans. Black Republicans, however, should be trusted more than white Republicans are.

Analyses of descriptive and substantive representation are often limited to an analysis of black and white political actors. Such an analysis does not account for how blacks might assess trust in political actors who are either Asian American or Latino. This information would prove valuable in multiracial contexts where such political actors are likely to represent black voters.

Demographically, Latinos now constitute the largest racial and ethnic minority group in the Unites States, and the presence of this group has increased in large numbers across the country in areas (especially the Midwest and the South) where, historically, the group had not had a presence (McClain, Carter, et al. 2006). Intergroup attitudes between Latinos and blacks appear to be asymmetrical, as blacks view Latinos as a group more positively than Latinos view blacks (McClain, Carter, et al. 2006; Mindiola, Niemann, and Rodriguez 2003). Studies also indicate that in areas with at least a 10 percent population of blacks and Latinos in cities with a population over twenty-five thousand, political incorporation is more competitive between these groups (McClain and Karnig 1990; McClain 2006). Political competition between Latino and black Americans is likely to increase, as these groups share and contest common political spaces for more political incorporation. Despite potential political conflict between blacks and Latinos over political incorporation, their shared nonwhite status should enhance trust between these groups, especially in comparison to white political actors. Blacks should trust Latino political actors (Democrat or Republican) more than they do white political actors of the same party.

Asian Americans are a smaller demographic group than Latinos are, and the Asian American population is concentrated mostly on the West Coast (McClain and Stewart 2006). Within the western context, black-Asian relations have been strained by blacks' perceived discrimination by Asian Americans as social actors in grocery stores and the service industry (Abelmann and Lie 1995). Blacks also view Asian Americans as socioeconomic competitors (Bobo and Hutchings 1996). Despite the negative interactions that have been documented between blacks and Asians, blacks should trust Asian American political actors (Democrat or Republican) more than they trust white political actors. Because of the differences in socioeconomic status between Asians and Latinos and blacks' prospective, perceived linkages between this difference and political interests, such that Latinos' socioeconomic status is more proximate to blacks, blacks should trust Asian political actors less than they trust Latino actors yet more than they trust white actors. Black political actors should be trusted more by blacks than are both Asian American and Latino actors with the same partisanship.

Black Americans as Racial Partisans: Results from the NPSS

Data from the NPSS split-sample experiments for race and partisanship are analyzed using unpaired and paired comparisons of arithmetic means. Unpaired comparisons analyze how blacks trust, for example, Asian American Democrats compared to black Democrats. Paired comparisons of means comparatively analyze how blacks trust Asian American Democrats compared to Asian American Republicans. Respondents were asked to rate their level of agreement with the following statements:

1. "It is hard for me to trust (people, blacks, whites, Asians, Latinos) who are elected officials and representatives of the Democratic Party."
2. "It is hard for me to trust (people, whites, blacks, Asians, or Latinos) who are elected officials and representatives of the Republican Party."

Responses are scaled from 0 = very true/low trust to 4 = not at all true/high trust.

To reiterate, it is expected that blacks should trust Democratic political actors more than they trust Republican political actors. They should trust black political actors more than they trust white, Latino, or Asian American political actors of the same political party. Blacks should trust white political actors (Democrat or Republican) least compared to black, Latino, or Asian

American political actors with the same partisanship. Asian political actors should be trusted less than are Latino political actors of the same party.

Of the 471 black respondents in the NPSS who reported their partisan identification, 72 percent (n = 338) identify as Democrats, compared to 5 percent (n = 26) who identify as Republicans and 23 percent (n = 107) who claimed to be independents. This partisan identification is mostly consistent with surveys that generally report that blacks identify solidly with Democrats, although here there is a smaller percentage of blacks who identify as Republicans (traditionally the figure is 11 percent) and a larger percentage of independents, who identify with neither of the major parties (see McClain and Stewart 2006).

According to univariate statistics (not shown), most of the black NPSS respondents reporting about their trust in "people in general" and "whites" as Democrats state that they are "somewhat" distrusting of these groups. The most trusted group of Democrats was black Democrats: 48 percent of black respondents who received this target expressed that it was "not at all true" that it is hard for them to trust black Democrats as elected officials and representatives. Black Democrats also were the most trusted group of public officials across the board, including Democrats of all races and Republicans of all races.

The comparisons of means (unpaired; means featured in table 7.2) also indicate that, for blacks, people in general and whites are trusted least as Democrats, and in the comparison of the means between people in general and whites, there is no statistically significant difference. This perhaps suggests that perceptions of people in general and whites as representatives are synonymous. As expected, black, Latino, and Asian American Democrats are trusted more than white Democrats are. Contrary to expectation, however, there are no statistically significant differences between trust in black Democrats and in Asian American Democrats. Thus, black Democrats are not trusted more than all nonblack Democrats. Additionally, Latino Democrats are not trusted more than Asian American Democrats are. As anticipated, however, black Democrats are trusted more than Latino Democrats are.

As for blacks' perceptions of Republicans, the univariate statistics (not shown) also indicate that NPSS respondents appear to be less trusting of people in general and whites as Republicans than they are of these same targets as Democrats. More respondents reported that they consider it is "very true" or "somewhat true" that it is hard for them to trust these groups as Republicans. Table 7.2 also includes the comparisons of means for each of the Republican targets. As hypothesized, white Republicans are trusted less than

TABLE 7.2

Comparisons of Arithmetic Means for Blacks' Trust in Democrats and
Republicans (Race and Partisanship Trust Experiment)

Comparisons of means	Trust in Democrats	Trust in Republicans
People/Blacks	2.0/3.2 (+)****	1.2/2.5 (+)****
	(n = 199)	(n =200)
People/Whites	2.0/2.0	1.2/1.5
	(n = 203)	(n = 205)
People/Asians	2.0/2.9 (+)****	1.2/2.4 (+)****
	(n = 183)	(n = 179)
People/Latinos	2.0/2.8 (+)****	1.2/2.4 (+)****
	(n = 188)	(n = 186)
Whites/Blacks	2.0/3.2 (+)****	1.5/2.5 (+)****
	(n = 196)	(n = 201)
Whites/Asians	2.0/2.9 (+)****	1.5/2.4 (+)****
	(n = 180)	(n = 180)
Whites/Latinos	2.0/2.8 (+)****	1.5/2.4 (+)****
	(n = 185)	(n = 187)
Asians/Blacks	2.9/3.2	2.4/2.5
	(n = 176)	(n = 175)
Asians/Latinos	2.9/2.8	2.4/2.4
	(n = 185)	(n = 161)
Latinos/Blacks	2.8/3.2 (+)***[a]	2.4/2.5
	(n = 181)	(n = 182)

Source: 2007 National Politics and Socialization Survey
Note: (+) indicates the group trusted most in the comparisons of means. Variables are scaled
from 0 = never trust to 4 = very often trust. Statistically significant differences of means are
indicated based on a p-value of at most .005, which is consistent with the Bonferroni adjustment method.
[a] Statistically significant without Bonferroni adjustment method, which offers a stringent standard of statistical significance
* p ≤ .10; ** p ≤ .05; *** p ≤ .01; **** p ≤ .001

black Republicans are, and notably a full point less. For Republicans, there
also is no statistically significant difference in the means between blacks'
trust in whites and in people in general as Republican political actors. Blacks,
Latinos, and Asians as Republican political actors all are trusted more than
are whites and people in general. However, unlike Democrats, there are no
statistically significant differences between blacks and Asians and blacks and
Latinos as Republicans.

Overall, as table 7.3 elucidates, black respondents in the NPSS trust each
of the Republican targets less than they trust the Democrat targets. Of special

TABLE 7.3

Comparisons of Arithmetic Means for Blacks' Trust in Democrats versus Republicans (Race and Partisanship Trust Experiment)

Comparisons of means	Blacks' trust (Democrats/Republicans)
People	2.0 (+)/1.2****
	(n = 102)
Blacks	3.2 (+)/2.5****
	(n = 95)
Whites	2.0 (+)/1.5****
	(n = 100)
Asians	2.9 (+)/2.5****
	(n = 75)
Latinos	2.8 (+)/2.4****
	(n = 84)

Source: 2007 National Politics and Socialization Survey
Note: (+) indicates the group trusted most in the comparisons of means. Variables are scaled from 0 = never trust to 4 = very often trust. Statistically significant differences of means are indicated based on a p-value of at most .005, which is consistent with the Bonferroni adjustment method.
[a] Statistically significant without Bonferroni adjustment method, which offers a stringent standard of statistical significance
* $p \leq .10$; ** $p \leq .05$; *** $p \leq .01$; **** $p \leq .001$

note is the fact that the means for people in general and whites as Democrats are less than those for blacks, Asians, and Latinos as Republicans. It appears that while partisanship is an important factor in blacks' trust in political actors, compared to their trust in other racial groups, blacks perceive white Democrats and white Republicans more suspiciously.

In the NPSS, what factors influence how much blacks trust in each racial target as a political actor in the two major parties? Furthermore, do racial socialization messages, black linked fate, racial uncertainty, or thoughts about the importance of the vote for black people to get what they want in politics (a black voting ethic) influence blacks' trust in these political actors? To test these inquiries a model of political trust is analyzed for each race and trust target in the survey. These political trust models control for common demographic factors (gender, age, income, education, and region), racial socialization messages (racial consciousness and racial protectiveness), strength of partisanship (strong Republican to strong Democrat), black linked fate (an important predictor in Dawson's 1994 models of African American partisanship), the expectation of future racial discrimination (racial uncertainty), black voting ethic, and whether one is registered to vote (1 = yes).

Considering these factors, it should follow that blacks who received greater emphasis on racial consciousness messages should be more trusting of black, Asian, and Latino Democratic political actors and less trusting of white Democratic political actors. Having received greater emphasis on racial protectiveness messages also should detract from blacks' trust in nonblack political actors. Blacks who identify more strongly with the Democratic Party should be less trusting of Republican political actors. Blacks with higher levels of linked fate, however, should be more distrusting of white political actors, specifically, and more trusting of black political actors.

As table 7.4 illustrates, black women are more trusting than black men are of Latino Republicans. Older blacks trust white Republicans more than younger blacks do. Higher-income blacks also are more trusting than lower-income blacks of Asian Americans as both Democrats and Republicans. Black consciousness socialization messages moderately increase trust in black Republicans. Yet having received greater emphasis on black protectiveness messages reduces political trust in Asian American and Latino Democrats and Republicans. Counter to expectation, black linked fate does not influence political trust in black Democrats. It does, however, decrease political trust in white Democrats. Racial uncertainty has no statistically significant effect on political trust in any of the political actors. Partisanship, additionally, only predicts three of the ten targets: trust in black Democrats, trust in people in general as Republicans, and trust in Latino Republicans. More specifically, blacks with stronger Democratic partisanship are more trusting in black Democrats and less trusting in people in general and Latinos as Republicans. Controlling for blacks' partisanship does not predict their trust in black Republicans, specifically. Even more notable is that blacks' partisanship does not decrease their trust in white Republicans. Black Republican respondents, however, are less trusting of black Democrats. Having a black voting ethic increases trust in people in general as Democrats. Despite the relevance of these results for interpreting determinants of blacks' political trust based on race and partisanship, many of the models must be interpreted cautiously due to the statistically insignificant F statistics. The next section examines how race influences trust in federal and local government actors to do what is right, in general, and to do what is in the best interest of blacks.

TABLE 7.4

Regression Models of Blacks' Political Trust Based on the Race and Partisanship Experiment

Covariates	People as Democrats	Black Democrats	White Democrats	Asian American Democrats	Latino Democrats	People as Republicans	Black Republicans	White Republicans	Asian American Republicans	Latino Republicans
Female	-.1511	.3219	-.1382	-.0175	.3827	.2946	.3752	.0979	.1566	1.075**
	(.2855)	(.2758)	(.2709)	(.3225)	(.3248)	(.2791)	(.3213)	(.3065)	(.3460)	(.4455)
Age	.0236	-.1090	.1231	-.0808	.1276	-.0428	-.1209	.1940**	-.0246	.1670
	(.0828)	(.0870)	(.0819)	(.0964)	(.0902)	(.0809)	(.1080)	(.0932)	(.1132)	(.1232)
Income	.0607	.0062	.0339	.1772**	.0933	.0066	-.1073	.0386	.2801***	.1159
	(.0752)	(.0691)	(.0785)	(.0867)	(.0797)	(.0735)	(.0842)	(.0895)	(.0969)	(.1089)
Education	-.1289	-.0292	-.0184	.0299	.1120	-.0137	-.0948	-.0487	.0298	-.0821
	(.0792)	(.0664)	(.0715)	(.0774)	(.0833)	(.0774)	(.0804)	(.0810)	(.0863)	(.1138)
South	.0008	.1610	-.2031	.0273	.3155	-.3910	.2568	-.0978	-.1743	.5382
	(.3167)	(.2816)	(.3086)	(.3080)	(.2957)	(.3097)	(.3415)	(.3505)	(.3373)	(.4053)
Black consciousness socialization	.0021	.0154	-.0155	.0024	.0071	.0139	.0246*	-.0032	.0050	.0020
	(.0115)	(.0109)	(.0105)	(.0182)	(.0107)	(.0112)	(.0133)	(.0119)	(.0183)	(.0146)
Black protectiveness socialization	-.0125	-.0280	.0024	-.0505*	-.0534**	.0080	-.0314	-.0173	-.0758**	-.0701*
	(.0226)	(.0215)	(.0251)	(.0262)	(.0262)	(.0221)	(.0258)	(.0276)	(.0297)	(.0358)
Black linked fate	-.0735	.1748	-.2403*	.0627	.1112	.1274	.1848	-.0806	-.1032	-.1335
	(.1395)	(.1107)	(.1269)	(.1710)	(.1422)	(.1364)	(.1363)	(.1447)	(.1857)	(.1941)
Expectation for future racial discrimination	-.1500	.0195	.0438	-.0962	.1597	-.1371	.1211	-.0198	-.0159	.2300
	(.1864)	(.1108)	(.1314)	(.1564)	(.1456)	(.1823)	(.1296)	(.1458)	(.1712)	(.1993)

Party identification (strong Republican to strong Democrat)	-.0681 (.1345)	.2873** (.1239)	.1813 (.1480)	.0037 (.1618)	.0442 (.1500)	-.4403*** (.1315)	.0142 (.1437)	-.1460 (.1685)	-.1741 (.1836)	-.4464** (.2049)
Black voting ethic	.3214** (.1406)	.1545 (.1114)	-.0607 (.1539)	-.0498 (.1651)	.1840 (.1429)	.1363 (.1361)	.0809 (.1322)	-.0726 (.1734)	-.1004 (.1793)	.0468 (.1948)
Registered to vote	.2901 (.4795)	-.3167 (.4264)	.3710 (.5376)	.0050 (.5455)	-.6106 (1.081)	.0153 (.4688)	-.6162 (.5217)	.3228 (.6130)	.0783 (.5937)	-.6356 (1.474)
Constant	2.387* (1.225)	1.087 (1.032)	2.009 (1.209)	2.855* (1.695)	-.8506 (1.447)	1.878 (1.198)	2.640 (1.247)	1.918 (1.378)	2.819 (1.790)	3.718* (1.975)
F Prob.	0.51	0.12	0.66	0.38	0.01	0.23	0.25	0.76	0.01	0.21
Adjusted R^2	-0.01	0.09	-0.04	0.02	0.30	0.06	0.04	-0.06	0.24	0.08
N	64	77	71	61	53	64	80	72	60	52

Source: 2007 National Politics and Socialization Survey

Note: Standard errors are indicated in parentheses. Results indicate regression analyses of black Americans who received questions about each racial target.

* $p \leq .10$; ** $p \leq .05$; *** $p \leq .01$; **** $p \leq .001$

Trust in Federal and Local Governments to Do What Is Right: Results from the SCBS

As I mentioned previously, the literature finds that blacks tend to be more trusting of national government than whites are. It is believed that this is in part due to the legal protections that the federal government eventually offered to blacks during the civil rights movement, as blacks faced egregious discrimination by their state and local governments. Therefore, it is expected that blacks should be more trusting of federal government than are non-blacks generally and than are specific nonblack racial groups. Furthermore, blacks should trust local government less than other racial groups do. To determine differences in political trust based on the levels of government, I turn to the SCBS to analyze univariate analysis and multivariate models of trust in government.

As shown in figure 7.1, when respondents were asked, "How much do you trust the government in Washington to do what is right?" most blacks and other racial groups said they trust this level of government "some of the time." In fact, with regard to those respondents who reported that they trust federal government "hardly ever," whites reported this level of distrust more than any other racial group did. Asian Americans reported more frequently than any other group that they trust the federal government "most of the time" and "just about always."

To account for the determinants of trust in federal government (*tgovnat2*), I regress a model of trust in federal government, including covariates such as *race* (black = 0, white = 1, Latino = 1, Asian = 1, *ethnic4*; black = 1, else = 0, *racblack*), *gender* (female =1; *gender*), *age, education, income, region* (South = 1; *censreg*), *participation in an ethnic, nationality, or civil rights organization* (yes = 1; *grpeth*), *registered voter* (yes = 1; *regvote*), *level of political interest* (*polint*), *economic satisfaction* (*econsat*), *perceived impact of making one's community a better place to live* (*effcom*), and *perceived quality of one's life* (*qol*). I regress ordered probit models comparing whites', Latinos', and Asians' trust in federal/local government to blacks'. I also regress a separate ordered probit model of black public opinion solely. This model also includes a measure for the effect that having *racially diverse networks* (an additive measure of the number of friends blacks have of another race: *bwht, basn, bhisp*, scaled 0–3).

People who are members of an ethnic, nationality, or civil rights organization are expected to be more trusting of government, in part, because of the role of the national government in enforcing federal laws over states'-rights

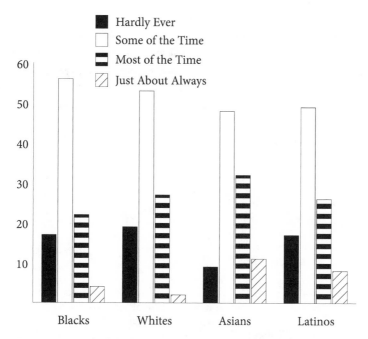

Fig. 7.1. Trust in the federal government

claims that they could discriminate against citizens, especially during Jim Crow. People with higher economic satisfaction and more positive perceptions of their life's circumstances should be more trusting of federal government, as they will be comfortable with their lives and not see government as intruding on their lives. People who have greater interest in politics should be more trusting in government, as well. Feeling a sense of communal efficacy also should enhance one's view that one can make a difference and influence the politics of government even at the national level. Diverse racial networks should enhance blacks' trust in government, as they would feel more comfortable with people who have diverse backgrounds making decisions that will affect their lives.

In a model for trust in federal government comparing blacks' trust to nonblacks' (combined) trust, contrary to expectation, blacks do not trust federal government more than do all nonblack groups combined. (Results are not shown.) However, the model for trust in federal government in table 7.5 shows that there are differences in trust between separate racial groups.

TABLE 7.5
Models of Trust in Federal and Local Governments to Do What Is Right

Covariates	Trust in federal government		Trust in local government	
	All racial groups	Black	All racial groups	Black
White	−.1775**	—	.2122***	—
	(.0807)		(.0806)	
Asian	.4798**	—	.3449	—
	(.2325)		(.2332)	
Latino	.0619	—	.1446	—
	(.0968)		(.0969)	
Female	.0890	−.1147	−.0340	−.1251
	(.0579)	(.1459)	(.0577)	(.1441)
Age	.0000	.0086*	.0050***	.0076
	(.0019)	(.0047)	(.0019)	(.0046)
Education	.0294	.0008	.0273	−.0315
	(.0181)	(.0465)	(.0181)	(.0458)
Income	−.0390**	−.0439	−.0366**	−.0185
	(.0174)	(.0424)	(.0174)	(.0416)
South	−.0509	−.0305	−.0354	.2314*
	(.0588)	(.1411)	(.0588)	(.1406)
Participation in ethnic,	−.1028	.1306	−.1046	.0715
nationality, or civil rights group	(.1058)	(.1859)	(.1055)	(.1868)
Registered to vote	−.0550	−.1556	−.1967**	−.1977
	(.0764)	(.1906)	(.0763)	(.1871)
Political interest	.1145****	.2337****	.1298****	.1933***
	(.0274)	(.0635)	(.0274)	(.0624)
Perceived effect on community	.0537	.0942	.0667*	.0867
	(.0362)	(.0888)	(.0362)	(.0882)
Economic satisfaction	.1479***	.0508	.0914**	.0884
	(.0466)	(.1123)	(.0464)	(.1118)
Quality of life	.1782****	.2442***	.3150****	.3221****
	(.0396)	(.0923)	(.0400)	(.0925)
Diversity of racial networks	—	−.1242*	—	−.0330
		(.0694)		(.0682)
Cut 1	.1572	.2705	.2784	.4933
	(.1809)	(.4505)	(.1807)	(.4522)
Cut 2	1.576	1.902	1.743	1.949
	(.1841)	(.4622)	(.1845)	(.4616)
Cut 3	2.882	3.085	3.110	3.295
	(.1935)	(.4789)	(.1929)	(.4858)
N	1529	269	1527	270
Pseudo R²	0.03	0.07	0.05	0.010

Source: 2000 Social Capital Benchmark Survey
Note: Standard errors are indicated in parentheses.
* p ≤ .10; ** p ≤ .05; *** p ≤ .01; **** p ≤ .001

While whites are less trusting of federal government than blacks are, Asian Americans are more trusting than blacks are. But there are no significant differences between Latinos' and blacks' trust in federal government.

Table 7.6 provides the predicted probabilities of trust in both federal and local governments based on the race of the respondents. The probabilities are calculated based on persons having a mean age, education, income, level of political interest, sense of communal efficacy in making their community a better place to live, and economic satisfaction, as well as being from the South, feeling a sense of community among their ethnic group, and being registered to vote. The coding for race is changed depending on the racial group for which we are interested in assessing the probability of trust. In assessing probabilities of trust for whites and Asians, compared to blacks, we see that whites have a .07 higher probability of falling in the "hardly ever" trusting national government category than blacks do, whereas Asian Americans are approximately .17 less likely to fall in this same category when compared to blacks.

The only factor that reduces trust in federal government is having a higher income. Increased interest in politics, feelings of economic satisfaction, and perceptions of a better quality of life enhance one's belief that the federal government can be trusted to do what is right. Unlike the model for all racial groups' trust, the model relative to blacks' trust in the federal government indicates that older blacks are more trusting of the federal government than are younger blacks. Economic satisfaction has no influence on blacks' trust in the federal government. Furthermore, contrary to expectation, blacks' having more diverse racial networks among friends actually reduces their trust in the federal government.

TABLE 7.6

Predicted Probabilities of Trust in Federal and Local Governments (Comparisons of All Racial Groups)

Level of trust in government	Blacks		Whites		Asians		Latinos	
	Federal	Local	Federal	Local	Federal	Local	Federal	Local
Hardly ever	0.40	0.40	0.47	0.32	0.23	0.28	0.37	0.35
Some of the time	0.48	0.48	0.44	0.51	0.51	0.52	0.48	0.51
Most of the time	0.12	0.11	0.09	0.15	0.23	0.19	0.13	0.14
Just about always	0.01	0.01	0.004	0.01	0.03	0.02	0.01	0.01

Source: 2000 Social Capital Benchmark Survey
Note: Probabilities are calculated using the Clarify statistical program.

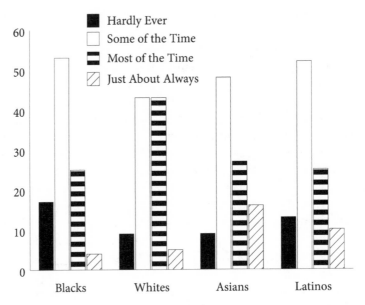

Fig. 7.2. Trust in local government

As for trust in local government (*tgovloc2*), in figure 7.2 we see that, with the exception of whites, who are equally trusting of local government both "some of the time" and "most of the time," most racial groups trust government "some of the time." Blacks are more likely than any other racial group to report trusting local government "hardly ever." In order to discern the determinants of trust in local government, I model the same covariates as those used in the model of trust in the federal government.

As hypothesized, blacks trust local government less than do all nonblack groups combined. (Results are not shown.) Table 7.5 indicates, more specifically, that whites are more trusting of local government than blacks are. In fact, as noted in table 7.6, whites are .08 less likely than blacks are to fall in the "hardly ever" category of trust in local government. There are no significant differences between blacks and Asian Americans or Latinos as far as trust in local government, however.

Unlike the model for trust in the federal government for all racial groups, a person's age, being a registered voter, and perceiving that one has influence in one's community affect trust in local government. Older Americans trust local government more than younger ones do. Registered voters are actually less trusting in local government. Perceiving that one can influence one's community moderately enhances one's trust in local government. As for the model of blacks' trust in local government, surprisingly, southern blacks are more trusting in local government than are nonsoutherners, although only moderately. Perhaps this finding has to do with who is serving in public office in that region. Unfortunately, the SCBS does not offer measures specific to the characteristics of the public officials in local government. There are only two other statistically significant covariates—political interest and quality of life—that also increase trust in local government.

The questions about trust in the levels of government in the SCBS were asked five years before the tragic outcomes of Hurricane Katrina. In the context of the city of New Orleans, the nation witnessed multiply-layered failures of federal, state, and local governments to respond expeditiously to assist residents stranded after the city's levees broke, flooding and submerging 80 percent of the city. With a predominantly black population and a heavy concentration of poverty in the city, a disproportionate number of persons affected by this natural disaster were black. Public opinion about the response to the natural disaster indicates that blacks were more disconcerted than whites were about the response to the disaster. For example, in a 2005 Pew Research Center survey, 70 percent of blacks (n = 211), compared to 46 percent of whites (n = 712), felt angry about the response to the disaster, and 73 percent of blacks, compared to 55 percent of whites, felt depressed about the response. As for the quality of the federal government's response and the response of President George W. Bush's administration, in particular, a strong majority of blacks (77 percent) felt the federal government responded "only fair/poor," compared to 55 percent of whites, and only 48 percent of blacks, compared to 51 percent of whites, felt the state and local government responded "only fair/poor." Blacks also felt more than whites did that the race of the victims made a difference in how quickly the government responded: 66 percent of blacks felt the response would have been faster had the victims been white, compared to 17 percent of whites who felt this. This event shows how both levels of government and political leaders affect how people perceive actions of government. It is highly likely that blacks' trust in the federal government waned during this critical period.

The effect of the response to Hurricane Katrina stands in contrast to blacks' trust in the federal government in an era after the election of the nation's first African American president, Barack H. Obama. A recent Pew Research Center report (2010b) shows blacks' trust outpacing both whites' and Latinos', as 37 percent of blacks trust government in Washington to do what is right, compared to 20 percent of whites and 26 percent of Latinos. Notably, despite blacks' having the highest level of trust in the federal government, 59 percent of blacks report that they trust the federal government only "some of the time/never."

These findings may lend some evidence to the trust that blacks have in political actors who share both their racial and partisan attributes. It also leads to an important inquiry: How much does the race of a political actor influence how blacks trust in different levels of government? To what extent do blacks trust these political actors based on a perception that they will do what is right for black interests, in particular? Although the SCBS helps to ascertain the determinants of trust in federal and local governments, it lacks measures that help to gauge, more specifically, the effects of race on respondents' perceptions, whether because of their racial internalization or the effect of the race of political actors. I now turn to the analysis of data in the NPSS to offer empirical evidence to examine these relationships.

Trust in Federal and Local Governments to Do What Is Right for Blacks: Results from the NPSS

In the NPSS, respondents were asked, "How much do you feel you can trust (people, blacks, whites, Asian Americans, or Latinos) in the (federal or local) government to do what is right for *blacks* and their interests?"[4] As a part of a split-sample survey experiment, each respondent received questions about trust in one of the race targets in the context of (1) the federal government and (2) the local government. Results of the race and trust experiment in levels of government are shown in table 7.7.

As for political actors in the federal government, blacks trust all racial groups more than they trust the control group, people in general. They also trust black political actors in the federal government more than they do all other racial groups to do what is right for blacks' interests. Whites are trusted least of all the racial groups to represent blacks' interests. While black respondents in the NPSS trust Latino political actors in the federal government more than they trust whites to do what is right for blacks' interests, they do not distinguish trust in Latino and Asian political actors.

Looking at the results for the experiment on race, trust, and the local government, the results are similar to the ones for the federal government experiment, with the exception that blacks do not trust whites more than they trust people in general, as they did in the federal government experiment. Clearly, blacks also see fellow blacks in local government as most likely

TABLE 7.7

Comparisons of Arithmetic Means for Blacks' Trust in Federal and Local Governments to Do What Is Right for Blacks (Race and Political Trust Experiment)

Comparisons of means	Trust in federal government	Trust in local government
People/Blacks	1.7/2.6 (+)**** (n = 200)	1.8/2.6 (+)**** (n =199)
People/Whites	1.7/1.9 (+)**ᵃ (n = 204)	1.8/1.9 (n = 203)
People/Asians	1.7/2.2 (+)**** (n = 179)	1.2/2.4 (+)**** (n = 179)
People/Latinos	1.7/2.3 (+)**** (n = 188)	1.8/2.3 (+)**** (n = 184)
Whites/Blacks	1.8/2.6 (+)**** (n = 198)	1.9/2.6 (+)**** (n = 198)
Whites/Asians	1.9/2.2 (+)*** (n = 177)	1.9/2.2 (+)*** (n = 180)
Whites/Latinos	1.9/2.3 (+)**** (n = 184)	1.9/2.3 (+)**** (n = 183)
Asians/Blacks	2.2/2.6 (+)*** (n = 173)	2.2/2.6 (+)*** (n = 172)
Asians/Latinos	2.2/2.3 (n = 159)	2.2/2.3 (n = 157)
Latinos/Blacks	2.3/2.6 (+)**ᵃ (n = 180)	2.3/2.6 (+)*ᵃ (n = 179)

Source: 2007 National Politics and Socialization Survey

Note: (+) indicates the group trusted most in the comparisons of means. Variables are scaled from 0 = never trust to 4 = very often trust. Statistically significant differences of means are indicated based on a p-value of at most .005, which is consistent with the Bonferroni adjustment method.

ᵃ Statistically significant without Bonferroni adjustment method, which offers a stringent standard of statistical significance

* p ≤ .10; ** p ≤ .05; *** p ≤ .01; **** p ≤ .001

to do what is right for black people, and again, whites are trusted least of all the racial groups to fulfill this prospective representation.

Summary and Conclusion: Race and Blacks' Political Trust

When blacks in the NPSS were asked whether they feel close in ideas and politics with whites, Asian Americans, and Latinos, most black respondents expressed greater political proximity to Latinos. While blacks expressed less propinquity with whites, they were even more likely to report feeling less close to Asian Americans in ideas and politics. This, however, did not translate into similar views as far as descriptive and substantive representation by partisan political actors.

So, do blacks trust nonblack Democrats (white, Asian American, or Latino) more, less, or equal to the way that they trust black Democrats? According to the results from the NPSS, as anticipated, blacks trust white Democrats less than they trust black Democrats. However, contrary to expectation, they trust Asian American and Latino Democrats equally as they do black Democrats. Their political trust in whites and people in general as Democrats is indistinguishable, and both these groups are the least trusted of all Democrats.

How do black Americans trust Republicans? As anticipated, all Republicans are trusted less than are Democrats of the same race. But as to the question of how blacks' trust in white Democrats compares to their trust in black Republicans, interestingly, the level of trust in black Republicans is higher than the level of trust in white Democrats. Thus, although black Republicans (as likely black conservatives) face sanctioning in the black community because of their outlying views about black group interests and progress (Harris-Lacewell 2004), in the NPSS, blacks perhaps still sense some level of racial identification with them that white Democrats are unable to offer. As for answering the question of whether substantive representation ever matters more in political trust than descriptive representation does, there appear to be some limitations in the extent of substantive representation. Blacks in the NPSS seem to limit their political trust in white Democrats, while making some concessions to trust black Republicans (as fellow group members) at levels higher than those for white Democrats (as likely fellow partisans).

Under what circumstances does substantive representation matter more? It appears that substantive representation matters more in the comparisons of black, Asian American, and Latino Democrats, as blacks have higher trust levels in all these groups than they do in white Democrats and as their trust in Asian American and Latino Democrats is mostly indistinguishable from their trust in black Democrats. It also matters more in the comparison of whites or people in general as Democrats to whites or people in general as Republicans. Descriptive representation, on the other hand, matters more when black Republicans are trusted more than white Democrats are. Similar to the results for Democrats, blacks' trust in Asian American and Latino Republicans does not differ from their trust in black Republicans. Racial protectiveness messages decreased blacks' political trust in Latino Democrats,

Asian American Republicans, and Latino Republicans. Black linked fate reduced blacks' political trust in white Democrats. Stronger Democratic partisanship increased their political trust in black Democrats; however, partisanship did not have a consistent effect on blacks' political trust across the several targets.

Examining trust in federal and local governments, compared to all racial groups combined, blacks are not less trusting than these groups in the federal government; however, they are less trusting in local government than are all nonblacks combined. More specifically, blacks are more trusting in the federal government than whites are and less trusting than Asians are. With respect to local government, blacks are less trusting than whites are, with no discernible differences in blacks' trust compared to Asians and Latinos. When layering the analysis to include controls for race and political trust in both levels of government as far as believing that racial actors will do what is right for blacks' interests, whites are trusted least of all the racial groups, Democrat or Republican. Blacks trust white Democrats at levels less than they trust black Republicans, suggesting that blacks in the NPSS have a higher regard and possibly deeper psychological connection through descriptive representation when they consider political actors and the extent to which they will do what is right for blacks' interests. They are more leery of whites (and people in general) as political actors in both federal and local governments, whether they are Democrat or Republican.

The results of this analysis have broader implications for how black Americans may think about race and trust with respect to race and representation. Can we say that black Americans will translate their political trust in white Democrats versus black Republicans into electoral outcomes that favor black Republicans? This will depend on the context of the political competition and the discourses surrounding the policy stances that both candidates take. For example, Tyson King-Meadows (2010) describes how black Republicans such as Michael Steele (former chairman of the Republican National Committee) appeal to black Democrats in their political campaigns by sustaining their black identities and casting the Republican Party as an option for blacks to avoid one-party-loyalist politics and indifference to black interests, meanwhile campaigning as Republicans who can appease the conservative interests of white Republicans.[5] Nevertheless, the seemingly increased movement of the Republican Party toward the ideological right, its support of policies that seem adverse to blacks' interest (such as staunch opposition to health care reform in 2010), and the implicitly racist undertones of Republican Party messages can prove to be partisan deterrents for blacks.[6]

Moreover, the extent to which political trust, in general, translates into electoral decisions also depends on how much voters weigh political trust in their electoral decision-making. Perhaps this "paradox in representation" between black Republicans and white Democrats illustrates how much more we need to interrogate the concept of representation with respect to race, political choice, political context, political information, and political knowledge. Maybe *ideologies* about black progress and work on issues related to black American interests matter in blacks' perceptions of black Republicans' and white Democrats' accountability in representing black interests. This is to say that black ideologies, as described by Michael Dawson (2001), may influence how blacks perceive the role of government (active or inactive, as related to the perspectives of black conservatives or black nationalists) and whites (active or inactive, as related to coalitional partners) and whether either of these entities should be involved in their political struggles whatsoever.

Conventional research mostly focuses on political trust and race and representation debates based on the analysis of blacks' perceptions of the quality of representation and trust in black or white legislators. Through analyzing black trust attitudes about blacks, whites, Asian Americans, and Latinos as political actors, this chapter offers a comparative analysis of political trust in other racial groups that moves beyond the traditional black-white paradigmatic studies. Such a study is pertinent because Asian Americans and Latinos can become representatives of black Americans in areas of the country where demographic changes are increasingly pushing politics beyond the traditional and historical black-white relations. The results of this study also indicate how perceptions of potential coalition partners, race *and* partisanship, and trust in racial actors at different levels of government influence how blacks politically trust.

The split-sample survey experiment method has commonly been used as an unobtrusive method to gauge whites' racial attitudes in order to overcome respondents' social desire to hide antiblack animus (Sniderman, Brody, and Tetlock 1991). This same principle is used in this study to overcome any nonblack animus among black American attitudes. By adding people in general as a control group in this study, we also see that trust attitudes about blacks, Latinos, and Asian Americans are distinguished from the attitudes about people in general, whereas attitudes about whites are not. Thus, methodologically, we learn that merely asking respondents to consider how much they trust only people in general to represent their interests, without specification of the race of the political actor, excludes very important information about how race factors into black Americans' (and possibly other Americans') psychological processes and their conceptions of what William Bianco (1994) defines as a "constituent-representative" trusting relationship.

This study becomes even more relevant as a study of black Americans' political trust because research continues to support that black Americans are less politically trusting than are other racial groups (Tate 2003; Brehm and Rahn 1997). However, by analyzing, more specifically, differences in blacks' trust compared to that of separate racial groups, we can determine distinctions otherwise unnoted by the comparison of blacks to only nonblacks as a whole. There are still unanswered questions about how blacks perceive racial likeness and what value descriptive representation offers them. That is, do blacks still feel a stronger psychological connection to members of their own racial group than to members of other racial and ethnic groups (Asian Americans and Latinos), despite their perception that Asian Americans and Latinos can be trusted in ways similar to blacks as partisans? If so, how is this "connection" perceived? Does it change in political contexts when black-Latino and black-Asian relationships are more competitive? This seems likely. More attention should be paid to carefully defining and operationalizing this connection. In addition, how do black Americans feel a connection to black Republicans, perhaps such as Colin Powell, who share similar racial backgrounds but different substantive policy interests? Are moderate Republicans trusted more than more conservative Republicans? Do these ideological differences influence trust in Democrats?

Given that the NPSS was fielded prior to the 2008 presidential primaries commencing in January 2008, the results in this analysis also offer some implications for how black Americans, at the least, may have thought about race (not necessarily race *and* gender) with respect to political trust in representatives from either the Democratic or the Republican Party. In fact, the results in this study that indicate blacks' suspicion of white Democrats as representatives could have been predictive in describing support that black Americans gave to Barack Obama (a black Democratic candidate) over Hillary Clinton (a white Democratic candidate) during the 2008 presidential primary season. This is especially important inasmuch as Hillary Clinton stood to gain political capital among black Americans because Bill Clinton enjoyed large community support among black Americans and had been described by the black American renowned, Nobel Prize–winning author Toni Morrison as being the first "black" president. This suggests that in some way, Bill Clinton and Hillary Clinton could transcend their whiteness to become "black" and, possibly, more trustworthy among black Americans as white political representatives. But by arguably making political moves to appeal to white voters, the Clintons appeared to squander away the trust that black Americans had in them as white Democratic representatives.

Several of these racialized missteps during the presidential primary season, arguably, led to Barack Obama overwhelmingly winning the vote share among black Americans. Elsewhere, I have explored blacks' trust in Hillary Clinton and Barack Obama as Democratic candidates to represent the interests of blacks, and prior to the racialized discourse during the height of the presidential primary season, blacks trusted candidate Obama more than candidate Clinton to represent their racial group's interests and the racial and gendered interests of black women (S. Nunnally 2008).

This study's results suggest that black Americans do not think about race and representation willy-nilly and that their level of political trust varies depending on the race *and* partisanship of political actors in whom they are asked to trust. Black Americans are *racial partisans* for this reason. They trust disparately yet deliberately based on the race *and* partisanship of political representatives. Descriptive representation is not always preferred over substantive representation. Neither is substantive representation always preferred over descriptive representation. There is something about a representative's race, perhaps even voters' opinions about race, representation, and racial groups in general, that warrants more empirical investigation.

Scholars such as Andra Gillespie (2010) explore these complexities of race, representation, and cross-racial appeal with respect to the intricacies that candidate Barack Obama and other black candidates like him in modern-day, post-civil-rights black politics face in appearing "connected enough" to black communities and "attractive enough" to white communities to cross-racially appeal to both electoral groups. Further research, additionally, should explore these qualitative complexities as far as people's perceptions of blacks and whites, in particular, as political actors and how people perceive what their representation means for black American political interests. In fact, the analysis in this chapter shows us the extent to which racialized trust seems more psychologically operative and meaningful for blacks in distinguishing their trust racially in actors in the political context than in the social context. This presents a dilemma for how much blacks perceive race as an integral factor in how people make decisions about who gets what, when, where, why, and how in the context of politics. It stands to reason that blacks are concerned about how race and distrust affect the perceived politics and representation of their group's interests and make judgments on the basis of the race and partisanship of the representative and whether these two identifiers are congruent with their own identities. In the concluding chapter, I explore what political distrust means for black politics and, ultimately, what the presidency of now, President Barack Obama, will mean for blacks' perceived connectedness to the American political system and to society in general.

8

Conclusion

In Whom Do Black Americans Trust?

The Vestiges of Race: Past and Present

Trust is supposedly the glue that makes democracy work. Normatively, citizens who trust connect with other citizens and participate politically in ways that build stronger linkages to government. Democratic theory supports this relationship, predicting that popular sovereignty enhances government accountability and responsiveness to citizens' inputs. In practice, however, as I have detailed extensively, democracy has functioned less equitably for some citizens, as institutionalized racism historically has corrupted the American political process and deemed nonwhite racial groups as inhuman and second-class citizens without equal protection of the law.

One such group experiencing the limitations of democratic functioning is blacks in America. Historically, this group was denied equal access to citizenship, the franchise, and free choice among political representatives that would otherwise enhance their relationship with government. Not only did blacks' race inhibit their access to social, economic, and political networks that would facilitate their participation in democracy, but also racial discrimination in their everyday life experiences historically constrained their free societal functioning for generations. Consequently, blacks' sociopolitical identities have been shaped by the imposition of a stigmatized race, and through their agency and civic and political activism, this racial group has championed fuller democratic inclusion. Race has been their legacy, and part of their struggle has been to shed imposed, negative racial attributes that continually disparage them in uncertain ways in their everyday lives.

Psychologically, this has meant that black group members have had to navigate the boundaries of their race with other racial groups, especially whites, who are situated atop the racial hierarchy in America. They also have had to negotiate their blackness in social and political spaces in order to protect themselves from the harm that a stigmatized race can carry (Fanon [1952] 1967, 1963; Link and Phelan 2001). This navigation assumes unknown, probabilistic risks, which, as I have argued herein, black group members attempt to avoid as harmful to them. In this way, race influences trust, as black Americans seek to maximize safe personal relations and to minimize racial harm on the basis of the perceived trustworthiness of racial actors with whom they interact. From this perspective, black group members have to be aware of the biases of race and to incorporate this knowledge into their daily social and political exchanges with others. To trust in this way involves assessing others as members of racial groups. Race is a heuristic through which behavioral characteristics are ascribed and attributed based on a collection of racial knowledge and experiences that are internalized in black group members' psyches and externalized via their trust in racial actors in social and political spaces.

In this book, I have offered a theory of discriminative racial-psychological processing that accounts for how racial internalization translates into racial externalization of lower trust levels among black group members. My theory, unlike general trust scholarship, attempts to explain beyond anecdotal evidence how and why blacks have lower social and political trusts compared to other racial groups. While my theory builds on the conventionally accepted explanation that blacks' sociopolitical experiences as a historically marginalized group contribute to this distrust, I explicate variation in blacks' historical and contemporary experiences by describing how blacks are exposed to information about race in variegated ways and, therefore, process race differently depending on these orientations. For me, studying blacks' trust includes an understanding of their perceptions in both political and social spaces, as social spaces have been historically politicized in blacks' efforts to challenge inequality in every aspect of their lives. To this extent, I devote attention to both social trust and political trust in order to capture how black Americans navigate trust in these spaces.

To reiterate, my theory of discriminative racial-psychological processing of trust argues that there are six ways that race affects blacks' sociopolitical perceptions through racial internalization: (1) their racial socialization experiences, (2) their racial homogenization of group behavior, (3) their perceptions of racial uncertainty about the prospect of being racially discriminated against, (4) their actual personal experiences with racial discrimination, (5) their racialized trust in specific racial groups, and, through racial externalization, (6) their racial-contextual perceptions of racial groups in social and political contexts. It is how race is internalized that affects blacks' levels of social and political trust.

Each chapter of the book has walked you through this racial-psychological processing among black Americans to examine empirically and to answer several critical inquiries about the influence of race on this group's trust. How do blacks learn about race? How does this information affect their racial perceptions and the perceived likelihood for discrimination? Does socialization about blacks' discriminatory historical relationships affect trust in both social and political spaces? Can we attribute blacks' distrust to *historical* discrimination experiences alone? That is, how do *contemporary*, personal experiences with racial discrimination affect trust? Does racialized distrust lower social and political trust? From these inquiries and the empirical analysis of data in the 2000 Social Capital Benchmark Survey and the 2007 National Politics and Socialization Survey, we have ascertained that race, in fact, does influence blacks' social and political trusts in various ways.

Racial Internalization

In chapter 3, I examined how blacks learn about race through their racial socialization. Most blacks learn about race from their families, and among ten messages about racial socialization, socialization about blacks' history of racial discrimination receives the most emphasis, and socialization about skin-color discrimination receives the least emphasis. As for messages about race relations, black Americans mostly receive medium-level emphasis on building positive interracial relations with whites, Asian Americans, and Latinos. Fewer people receive high emphasis on messages inculcating interracial distrust. Nevertheless, most blacks receive medium-level emphasis on this message. Blacks are more likely to report that they receive messages about *dis*trusting whites, whereas they report having received "no emphasis at all" on messages about distrusting Asian Americans and Latinos. More blacks receive low-level emphasis on intraracial distrust than they receive on interracial distrust.

Most notably, however, in an analysis of latent factors underlying the several racial socialization messages, two factors emerged: racial consciousness messages and racial protectiveness messages. These two factors undergird much of the analysis in the book about blacks' psychological processing. In fact, in chapter 4, I tested the effect of these messages on blacks' racial predispositions. The focus of that chapter, however, is on how blacks feel their knowledge affects their relations with black and nonblack racial groups, how they subscribe to racial stereotypes, how frequently they report personalized racial discrimination experiences, and how they perceive the likelihood for being racially discriminated against in the future (racial uncertainty).

While there is not overwhelming consensus that racial discrimination knowledge affects blacks' interracial relations, most blacks feel that their relations with whites have been affected by their racial knowledge, whereas this is not necessarily the case for their relations with Asians and Latinos. Having received emphasis on racial protectiveness messages also increases blacks' belief that their racial knowledge affects their attitudes and relations with nonblacks. Black linked fate enhances blacks' belief about the effect of racial knowledge on their relations with whites and Asians, specifically. We also discerned that blacks subscribe to both positive and negative stereotypes about racial groups, notably attributing negative stereotypes such as bossiness, selfishness, and prevarication to whites and people in general more than they attribute these attributes to other racial groups. Black linked fate increases blacks' subscription to positive stereotypes about Latinos, and having experienced more racial discrimination lessens blacks' negative stereotyping about Latinos.

Despite the historical relevance of racial discrimination for black group experiences, individually, most blacks contemporarily report having experienced racial discrimination "sometimes" in their lives, and greater linked fate increases the likelihood of their reporting such experiences. Blacks also are most likely to perceive whites and people in general as likely perpetrators of racial discrimination, and Asian Americans are perceived in more racially uncertain ways than Latinos are. Black linked fate, furthermore, increases blacks' negative attitudes toward whites and Asians, specifically. Racial protectiveness socialization messages also increase blacks' negative attitudes toward nonblack groups, in general.

Chapter 5 explored how perceiving others' race affects blacks' trust in others more generally and in specific groups. Fairness and appearance are two important characteristics of blacks' assessments of trust. While appearance is not clearly identified as "race" per se, it still suggests that there is a physicality associated with blacks' trust assessments. In the analysis of generalized trust in others, we confirmed that blacks are less trusting than nonblack groups are. We also witnessed that asking black, white, and Latino respondents about trust in people in general elicits the lowest level of trust. As for a specific racial group that blacks report distrusting the most, clearly it is whites. Further analysis of aspects of trustworthiness also indicated that beliefs about the importance of certain characteristics affects trust in specific racial groups.

Notably, between black respondents in the SCBS and those in the NPSS, there was a disconnection as far as trust in whites. While SCBS black respondents were more trusting of whites, NPSS respondents were less trusting. Comparing blacks' racial trust to that of other racial groups in the SCBS, we also ascertained the extent to which blacks trust other racial groups compared to whites', Asians', and Latinos' racial trust assessments. Negative attitudes toward immigrants reduces blacks' trust in Asian Americans and Latinos. However, as a general finding in the NPSS, blacks view whites more negatively than they view Asian Americans and Latinos. In the SCBS, we also determined that black women are less trusting in nonblack groups than black men are. The same finding does not hold for the NPSS. In the SCBS, additionally, having racially diverse friendship networks also increases blacks' trust in nonblack groups.

In sum, while there are discrepancies between the SCBS and the NPSS in their reporting of the way blacks trust certain groups more than others, it is evident that blacks (and even whites, Latinos, and Asian Americans) trust differently depending on the race of an actor. The NPSS used unobtrusive measures to elucidate how trust variation occurs depending on the race of an actor. Much of the analysis in chapter 5 supports that blacks view whites more warily than they view Asian Americans and Latinos, and definitely, blacks trust whites less than their own group members. Some evidence in the NPSS even suggests that blacks perceive Asian Americans and Latinos through a shared-minority lens, especially in comparison to whites. The question remains, are these perceptions consistent for racial groups in all contexts? Or do race and context interact to affect how blacks' perceive trustworthiness in these groups? It is through racial externalization that I have argued these attitudes are manifested in blacks' everyday life circumstances.

Racial Externalization

From the analysis of how blacks learn about race, perceive race, experience race, and predict whether race will have a future effect on their lives, we learned about the racial predispositions that can inform blacks' perceptions of actors in social and political contexts. To determine to what extent racially internalized information undergirds attitudes toward groups in specific contexts, chapters 6 and 7 gauged blacks' externalization of race in social and political contexts, respectively.

In chapter 6, we saw how blacks are generally distrusting of others (generalized trust) and more so than all racial groups combined. With closer inspection of comparative analyses of specific racial groups, we learned that blacks and Latinos are equally distrusting of others in general, and only whites and Asians are more socially trusting than blacks are in others in general (generalized trust). Through contextualized analysis of the extent to which blacks are more or less trusting in others in social spaces—neighborhoods, shopping places, workplaces, and religious institutions—we ascertained that blacks are less trusting in each of these contexts in comparison to all nonblack racial groups combined. This is especially surprising given the centrality of religion in many blacks' lives and the racial homogeneity of many of their religious institutions, wherein we might think blacks would be more trusting than other racial groups.

Of all contexts, blacks also are least trusting in shopping places, where they express more distrust in shopping clerks than other racial groups do. On the other hand, blacks are, in fact, most trusting of others in the context of religious institutions. However, through analyzing blacks' trust compared to other racial groups' trust in these contexts, Latinos actually express the same level of distrust that blacks do in the context of neighborhoods, shopping places, and religious institutions. The exception is in the context of workplaces: blacks are less trusting than each of the nonblack racial groups in the workplace.

Results from the race and contextualized trust experiments illustrate that blacks' shared-minority perceptions are more limited with respect to shopping places and workplaces when it comes to trusting Asian Americans. In these contexts, blacks are more distrusting of this group in ways similar to their distrust of whites. In fact, blacks' having received more emphasis on racial protectiveness messages decreases their trust in Asian actors in neighborhoods, shopping places, and workplaces. Latinos, however, are trusted more as store clerks, when blacks report having received greater emphasis on racial consciousness messages in their racial socialization. Additionally, black linked fate increases blacks' trust in Latinos as store clerks. Socialization about racial uncertainty, however, did not have the predicted effects in the experiments on race and contextualized trust. Thus, we see that race operates differently in blacks' social trust depending on the race of the social actor and the context of the evaluation. Do we also see race operating differently in the political context?

In chapter 7 we examined how race influences blacks' political trust. The first query examined how blacks perceive political propinquity with other blacks, whites, Latinos, and Asian Americans. Unlike the shared minority status that blacks seem to have with Asian Americans as far as their internalized racial knowledge and racial predispositions, with respect to closeness in feelings and ideas about politics, blacks feel the least close to Asian Americans. Interestingly, non–African Americans feel less close to other blacks in their ideas and feelings about politics than African Americans do, the only instance in which African Americans' and non–African Americans' attitudes differ with respect to political proximity. Older blacks feel less close to Latinos in politics than younger blacks do, and having received greater emphasis on racial consciousness messages enhances blacks' feelings of closeness to Latinos. Interestingly, blacks with feelings of stronger partisan ties to the Democratic Party also perceive less closeness to Latinos in ideas and feelings about politics.

In view of blacks' trust in political actors as racial group members and party representatives, blacks in the NPSS do not trust black Democrats more than all of the other racial groups as Democrats. It is notable, however, that they trust black Democrats more than they do white and Latino Democrats. White Democrats and white Republicans have the lowest arithmetic means of trust of all the racial targets with their respective party designations, suggesting the degree of distrust that blacks in the NPSS have in white political actors regardless of their partisanship. In fact, comparing blacks' trust in white Democrats to their trust in black Republicans, white Democrats have lower means than black Republicans. This suggests that perhaps blacks perceive something psychologically different, based on descriptive representation, such that they are less certain that white Democrats can offer substantive representation. As for the effects of racial knowledge and predispositions on blacks' trust in these political actors, having received racial protectiveness messages reduces their trust in Asian American and Latino Democrats and in Asian and Latino Republicans. Feeling greater linkages with other black people decreased blacks' trust in white Democrats; however, interestingly, it did not offer a racially solidarizing influence in increasing their trust in black Democrats. Across the several targets, racial uncertainty did not have the predicted effects.

Turning to trust in levels of government (federal and local), we saw that, in comparison to all nonblack racial groups combined in the SCBS, contrary to expectation, blacks do not trust the federal government more than these other groups do. In comparing blacks' political trust to that of specific groups, in fact, there is no difference in the way that blacks and Latinos trust government. However, whites are less trusting in the federal government than blacks are, and Asian Americans are more trusting than blacks are. When it comes to the local government, as expected, blacks are less trusting in this level of government than are all nonblack racial groups combined. Only whites trust local government more than blacks do, and there are no significant differences in the level of trust in local government between blacks and Asian Americans or blacks and Latinos. In the NPSS, additionally, when determining what effect race has on trust in political actors in the federal or local government to do what is right for blacks' interests, blacks clearly trust other blacks more than they trust any other group to do so. Meanwhile, whites are trusted the least of all racial groups.

In Whom Do We Trust? Black Americans' (Dis)trust

As much of the empirical results suggest, race affects black Americans' generalized social trust, contextualized social trust, and political trust. The extent of their (dis)trust depends on whom they trust as members of racial groups. Additionally, their trust in these racial groups varies depending on the context, and although there is some evidence that race affects contextualized trust, it appears that racial distinctions in blacks' trust based on the race of the actor are most operative in the political context.

Many of the results suggest that blacks are more trusting of other blacks but also of Asian Americans and Latinos, attesting perhaps to a shared minority status that blacks perceive with these two groups. In shopping places, in workplaces, and in the capacity of political representation, blacks trust Asian Americans less than they trust Latinos, however. Blacks trust Latinos more in the context of religious institutions than they do in the political context. Across all contexts, clearly, blacks trust whites less than they trust any other racial group. In political contexts, blacks are even more distrusting of whites.

Greater inculcation of racial consciousness socialization messages appears to enhance trust and relationships with racial and ethnic minority groups, and greater inculcation of racial protectiveness messages appears to detract from the quality of these perceived connections. Blacks' perceived linked fate with other blacks also seems to enhance their perceptions of their relationships with other racial and ethnic minorities; however, it seemingly diminishes their connections with whites. Moreover, many blacks' attitudes toward people in general are mostly consistent with their attitudes toward whites, perhaps suggesting that, when we ask trust questions about "people" only, we miss the nuances of trust variation based on race. Blacks (and other groups, as well), for example, exhibit more (or less) trusting attitudes when trust questions identify the race of the social or political actor in whom to trust. Blacks also have more trust in other racial and ethnic minorities and less trust in whites.

The literature on perceptions of racial discrimination focuses on experiences of racial discrimination. Herein, I have opted to analyze, more specifically, how racial uncertainty (the perceived likelihood of being racially discriminated against in the future) influences intergroup perceptions, because I felt that it was important to control for prospective evaluations in trust assessments as opposed to solely retrospective discrimination experiences. While racial uncertainty did not predict trust in any of the models, nevertheless, the results in chapter 4 reveal that blacks have apprehension about whites and their intentions toward blacks in everyday life experiences and especially (as noted in chapter 7) in politics and the representation of black group interests.

Despite my interest in expanding the analysis of race and trust to include the analysis of blacks' attitudes toward Asian Americans and Latinos, the results here suggest that much of blacks' distrust rests in their assessments of whites. The black-white dichotomy is entrenched in blacks' perceptions, and this is likely due to blacks' racial socialization about the long history of their group's relations with whites, in particular, but also to the consequence of social and political realities that make black-white relations more psychologically salient.

So What about Race and Trust? The Significance of Psychological Injury

Evidence in this book suggests that there is a racial calculus of trust among blacks but also among other racial groups. While all racial group members likely trust other racial groups based on their group-based interests, group experiences in the American racial hierarchy are relative to the racial group's status. For black Americans, the historical entrenchment of opposition, negativity, and disparagement against blackness affects their quality of life. Blacks' learning about blackness facilitates accessible knowledge for navigating American race relations, buoying resiliency and protecting them from the pain, suffering, and psychological shock of unfair treatment in an era of supposed equality.

The fact that race continues to cue black Americans about the quality of their social and political experiences suggests that the vestiges of racial discrimination are ever present for them, not just because they face an uncertain probability of being racially discriminated against but also because their social and political realities involve interacting with people who potentially pose a threat of making their lives reminiscent of historical eras of race relations. Race and racial discrimination experiences, thus, normativize distrust among black Americans. This phenomenon illustrates the injurious nature of racial construction and racial discrimination and, ultimately, the negative effects that they can have by inhibiting the experience of humanity in intergroup relationships and, hence, intergroup coalitions. The evidence herein suggests that race and racial discrimination experiences psychologically injure those who are treated unfairly. As blacks trust sparingly based on race, they also become vulnerable to decision-making that they perceive minimizes their best interests and that may render suboptimal outcomes for them.

Race and Trust in the Age of the First Black President: An Era of Hope or Disillusionment?

In the era after the election of the nation's first African American president, Barack H. Obama, psychological injury from race received a bandage. In a world that only could have been imagined by many blacks as a dream or a racial fantasy, now many blacks have witnessed arguably the ultimate ascension of a black person to political power in the American political system. This election likely renewed faith in the ability of blacks' sociopolitical mobility. It also likely instilled a newfound faith in the ability of the system to accommodate change, despite the race of a person in the system. Evidence from two 2010 Pew Research Center studies (2010b, 2010c) even show an uptick in blacks' political trust, one that uncharacteristically also outpaces whites'.

While we may be witnessing an era of hope and relief from several hundred years of psychological injury from racial discrimination, the effect of President Obama's election has indeterminable effects on the quotidian experiences of individual blacks' lives. Perhaps blacks' racial outlook will change and affect the way they inculcate their children about the effect of race on their lives as blacks in America, as the country has presented a new possibility for black sociopolitical mobility. Nevertheless, the inspirited optimism of blacks over time has been met with the expansion of their equality followed by its retraction.

Sadly, despite the nation's experiencing the momentous political outcome of electing the nation's first African American president, the first two years of President Obama's presidency have been met with much criticism about his competence, power, and implicit racial prejudices against white people. Pundits question the extent to which such criticism is, itself, couched in the "new" modern racism.

One such critique levied against the president charged him with being racist, as conservative talk show host Glenn Beck exclaimed that the president "over and over again" exposes himself as "a guy who has a deep-seated hatred for white people or the white culture": "I don't know what it is. . . . I'm not saying he doesn't like white people, I'm saying he has a problem. This guy is, I believe, a racist" (Beck 2009). Beck, over a year later, retracted his assertion that the president is a racist, yet he noted the effect that President Obama's former pastor, Reverend Jeremiah Wright, may have had on him in preaching about liberation theology (Beck 2010).[1] In other words, in Beck's view, the president still has a biased view of race in favor of black group advancement and implicitly at the expense of broader America's (whites') interests. Nevertheless, we may never know what psychological damage has been done from Beck's influence, encouraging or confirming people's belief that the president is, in fact, a racist.

Initial Tea Party protests of the Obama administration's health care reform also were met with signage depicting the president as a witchdoctor, evoking a historical racial stereotype of blacks' being savage and superstitious. Other signs depicted him as a socialist or a mustache-wearing Nazi, reminiscent of the mustache worn by Nazi leader Adolph Hitler. "Birthers" have charged that the president should not be legally president because they feel that he is not qualified for office because they believe that he was born outside the U.S. territories that would qualify him to be a U.S. citizen.

Equally disconcerting is the fact that "birthers," including billionaire Donald Trump, have requested to see verification of the president's birth certificate, and to quell the controversy, President Obama responded to Trump's request by announcing the public release of his birth certificate in April 2011, two years into his presidency. During the presidential campaign season, Republican congressmember Lynn Westmoreland (GA-Third District) called candidate Obama "uppity," thus evoking the historically and racially charged image of a black person's advancing beyond the level that is allowed for blacks in a white society. Continuing from allegations during the campaign trail, as recently as August 2010, almost one-fifth of Americans in a Pew Research Center poll said they believe that President Obama is a Muslim (Pew Research Center 2010a), allegations that seemingly misconstrue the religion with antipatriotic principles and practices post-9/11 but also that imply the president does not have the nation's best interest at heart.

During summer 2009, President Obama became embattled in a controversy over the arrest of the eminent African American Harvard University professor and African American studies scholar Henry Louis Gates Jr., who also serves as the director of the W. E. B. Du Bois Institute for African and African American Research at Harvard. The president answered a question during a question-and-answer session following his July address about the importance of health care reform. President Obama asserted that Gates's having been arrested in his home after presenting the white police officer, Sgt. James Crawley, with proper identification was a case of the police acting "stupidly." In fact, President Obama remarked about the implications of the ordeal for race and discrimination in criminal justice, jokingly adding that he too may be accosted for the same thing in his own home at the White House but that now he might be shot for it.[2] Due to controversies surrounding whether the president should have interfered and whether he held negative dispositions toward the police and legal authority, President Obama and Vice President Joe Biden later entertained both Gates and Crawley at a "Beer Summit" to spark peaceful discourse between the two and to quell the racial tensions surrounding the event.

In September 2009, unlike the treatment of any U.S. president seemingly witnessed heretofore in recent presidential history, a U.S. congressmember, Joe Wilson (R-SC, Second District), stood up during President Obama's address before the nation and yelled vociferously what seemed to be two simple yet loaded words, as the president described his health care reform plans and coverage of undocumented immigrants: "You lie." The president had already mentioned the fear tactics employed by the Republican Party as a measure of swaying public opinion against his administration's policies and those of the Democratic Party. In a national setting, live on television before the nation, Congressmember Wilson attacked the president's veracity. The words violated congressional decorum, sparking immediate controversy over their appropriateness (Stolberg and Zeleny 2009).

On a lighter note, perhaps some of the sentiments shared by other blacks (and by Obama supporters, in general) about President Obama's treatment were those expressed by Velma Hart, a black woman who stood up during a CNBC town hall meeting with the president in September 2010. She admitted that she voted for him and was tired of defending him, and ultimately, she inquired about the uncertain state of the economy, unemployment, and when the president would bring about the change he envisioned and inspired among millions during his 2008 presidential campaign. More specifically, she stated,

I am one of your middle class Americans and, quite frankly, I'm exhausted. . . . I'm exhausted of defending you. I'm exhausted of defending your administration, defending the mantle of change that I voted for. And I'm deeply disappointed with where we are right now. I have been told that I voted for a man who said he was going to change things in a meaningful way for the middle class. I am one of those people and I'm waiting sir. I'm waiting. I don't feel it yet. And I thought, while it wouldn't be in great measure, I would feel it in some small measure. . . . And quite frankly Mr. President, I need you to answer this honestly: Is this my new reality? (Watkins 2010)

At that moment, the "politics of hope" seemed to hang in the balance, especially as a black American questioned the progression of change with respect to economic stability in Americans' lives. What remains to be seen is how much black Americans perceive that President Obama is being mistreated and disrespected, perhaps, because of his race. With his political power increasingly critiqued and the historic loss for the Democratic Party during the 2010 midterm elections, what President Obama called a "shellacking," blacks who have witnessed and acquired knowledge of racial discrimination becoming an impediment to their success may no longer see the glimmer of hope that they once saw on the days the first African American president was elected and inaugurated. Perhaps they are questioning, if a black person cannot be respected as president of the United States, then what does this imply about the probability of their being treated equally and respectfully as black persons? With respect to trust, such images of the president's treatment can prove deeply troubling for blacks, who by way of many media outlets' racial discourse were thrust into interpretations about America's being a "postracial" society, evidenced by whites' nonresistance to the election of a black president.

On January 20, 2009, I was one of millions of Americans who assembled on the Washington Mall to witness the historic inauguration of the nation's forty-fourth and first African American president. Never before had I witnessed such massive euphoria all at once among thousands of people of all races (with an overwhelmingly large number of black Americans young and old), and I wondered if I would ever see that display of humanity and euphoria ever again. I remember riding on the Metro train and chatting with a young black woman, who expressed how proud she was that she was able to witness the election of a black president. As she stated, not only had "Obama changed the game," but also "he upped the game."

Almost two years later, I wonder if this woman sees the game as "changed" or the game of race as being "the same." Moreover, for millions of other black Americans, I wonder if they still have the renewed faith that racial discrimination will not become an impediment to their personal advancement. Even more, would the stories they share with future generations of blacks characterize that Election Day and Inauguration Day as cherished, unforeseen memories that were matched with continued hope for moving beyond race, or as continued preparation for bias, as the "race game" has perhaps changed yet questionably also remained similar, in that race still matters in ways that can be detrimental to one's life experiences. Only time and more research will tell, but for now, the vestiges of race appear to remain, and we have no choice but to consider what this means for psychological injury and *repair* among black Americans.

On Reconciliation: Repairing Psychological Injuries in Democracy and Trust in the Future

The nation's precedent on race is seemingly indelible in blacks' psyches. As newer generations of blacks replace older cohorts, the experiences of institutionalized racism are less personalized. However, the level of emphasis about racial discrimination experiences and protectiveness socialization messages influence the extent of this indelibility and the continued existence of this racial knowledge in black collective memory. This is the effect of a democratic government and society discriminating against its own citizens. Although more recently, many state and local governments and the U.S. House of Representatives (H.R. 194, 2008) and the U.S. Senate (S.R. 26, 2009) have apologized to blacks for the role of government in facilitating the egregious effects of the institutions of slavery and Jim Crow on their racial group, there is no clear evidence about how such apologetic measures repair the group affected by these experiences (Brophy 2006).

Although many younger, post-civil-rights-generation blacks today were not directly affected by these institutionalized racism experiences of yesteryear, the repair of racial discrimination is less clear, as evidenced by psychological injury and the continued significance of race in blacks' lives and as illustrated in this study regarding race and trust. This is the legacy of race in a democracy: citizens' (and noncitizens') decisions and trust are informed by their group status in the racial hierarchy. At the least, with the acknowledgment of this effect of race on society, scholars should explore more about race and trust, psychological injury, the conceptualization and meaning of repair, and what all this means for public policy and responsiveness to historically injured and underrepresented groups in the United States.

With the enduring effect of race on blacks' lives, race appears to stain the quality of trust relations by the mere conceptualization of what trust involves: retrospective and prospective evaluations of human behavior. Even more, history meets the present when blacks socialize their progeny about racial consciousness and racial discrimination in ways to prepare them for coping with the vagaries of racial construction in America. And when fear of racial discrimination (racial uncertainty) does not affect blacks' prospective assessments of others and their trustworthiness, past personal experiences with race do. Race, thus, is like a Möbius strip that, with repeated twists and attempted changes, nevertheless seems to fall back in place as it once was.

From the analysis herein, we have witnessed the extent to which racial harm and racialized trust seems heightened for blacks particularly in the context of political relations, when resources are meted out and decisions are made in ways that can affect every aspect of Americans' lives. More broadly, through the comparison of blacks' political behavior to that of other racial groups, we have also learned that racialized trust is not a phenomenon unique to black Americans. Rather, race affects various groups' perceptions in American society; how people learn about and experience race can affect how they interact with others and gamble with risks associated with the status of their racial group. Perceptions of distrust are in the eye of the beholder, but we all must behold the historical fact that race inherently institutionalizes distrusting psychological constructs in ways that are both personalized and group oriented and that can affect some groups disproportionately.

Appendix A

NPSS Descriptive Statistics of Survey Sample

Descriptive characteristics	Black respondents % (*n*)	White respondents % (*n*)	Latino respondents % (*n*)
Sex			
Male	42 (216)	48 (122)	42 (105)
Female	58 (301)	52 (130)	58 (147)
N	517	252	252
Ethnicity*a*			
African American	92 (424)	—	—
Caribbean/West Indian	6 (27)	—	—
African	3 (12)	—	—
Other	10 (47)	—	—
N	517		
Region			
South	34 (172)	39 (97)	39 (94)
Non-South	66 (338)	61 (152)	61 (150)
N	510	249	244
Age (mean)	48 years	47 years	39 years
Household income (mean)	$50,000–$74,999	$50,000–$74,999	$35,000–$49,999
Education (mean)	Some college, with associate's degree/ bachelor's degree (10.5)	Some college, with associate's degree/ bachelor's degree (10.7)	Some college, with associate's degree/ bachelor's degree (10.1)

Source: 2007 National Politics and Socialization Survey

a Black ethnicity in the survey reflects the diversity of those who identify as being of African descent. However, as the response "other" indicates, some respondents identify as being other than just of African descent.

Appendix B

Survey Sample and U.S. Census Quota Matching

	In census (in thousands)		In survey	
	N	%	N	%
Overall				
Age				
Total	219,849	100.0	1,021	100.0
18–24	27,964	12.7	128	12.5
25–34	39,481	18.0	203	19.9
35–44	43,121	19.6	191	18.7
45–54	42,797	19.5	231	22.6
55–64	30,981	14.1	185	18.1
65 +	35,505	16.1	83	8.1
Gender				
Total	219,849	100.0	1,021	100.0
Male	106,346	48.4	443	43.4
Female	113,503	51.6	578	56.6
Blacks				
Age				
Total	24,622	100.0	517	100.0
18–24	3,809	15.5	38	7.4
25–34	5,041	20.5	97	18.8
35–44	5,403	21.9	91	17.6
45–54	4,715	19.1	117	22.6
55–64	2,778	11.3	134	25.9
65+	2,876	11.7	40	7.7
Gender				
Total	24,622	100.0	517	100.0
Male	11,004	44.7	216	41.8
Female	13,618	55.3	301	58.2

	In census (in thousands)		In survey	
	N	%	N	%
Whites				
Age				
Total	151,445	100.0	252	100.0
18–24	17,382	11.5	32	12.7
25–34	23,900	15.8	45	17.9
35–44	29,560	19.5	46	18.3
45–54	30,219	20.0	52	20.6
55–64	22,048	14.6	36	14.3
65 +	28,335	18.7	41	16.3
Gender				
Total	151,445	100.0	252	100.0
Male	73,213	48.3	122	48.4
Female	78,232	51.7	130	51.6
Latinos				
Age				
Total	28,366	100.0	252	100.0
18–24	4,866	17.2	58	23.0
25–34	7,851	27.7	61	24.2
35–44	6,465	22.8	54	21.4
45–54	4,398	15.5	62	24.6
55–64	2,470	8.7	15	6.0
65 +	2,315	8.2	2	0.8
Gender				
Total	28,366	100.0	252	100.0
Male	14,621	51.5	105	41.7
Female	13,745	48.5	147	58.3

Sources: Whites and blacks: U.S. Census Bureau, "Current Population Survey, Annual Social and Economic Supplement, 2004," Racial Statistics Branch, Population Division; overall and Latinos: U.S. Census Bureau, "Current Population Survey, Annual Social and Economic Supplement, 2006," Ethnicity and Ancestry Statistics Branch, Population Division.

Note: To ensure that the ending sample is representative in age and gender distributions of the population of each target ethnic group, Luth Research used U.S. Census demographics data to generate corresponding quotas by ethnicity. Quotas were closely monitored throughout the duration of the fielding.

Notes

NOTES TO CHAPTER 1

1. See "Shirley Sherrod," Times Topics, *New York Times*, updated July 22, 2010, http://topics.nytimes.com/top/reference/timestopics/people/s/shirley_sherrod/index.html?scp=1-spot&sq=shirley%20sherrod&st=cse.

2. Breitbart's previous fame linked him to video footage that eventually exposed questionable practices within the ACORN organization, which largely supported efforts to assist low-income Americans in various capacities.

3. See "Shirley Sherrod."

4. I use *black, black American,* and *African American* interchangeably throughout this text, with the exception of specific references to black ethnic groups. I use *black* to refer to people who are African descendants. Much of the literature in black politics assumes that people who are "black" in the United States identify as "African American." However, this nomenclature can be troubling, considering that blacks can have various ethnic backgrounds, such as West Indian, African, and African American, and *African American* may preclude any identification people may have with these ethnicities. In addition, blacks may or may not identify themselves as American, or they may even see themselves as having ethno-histories that are different from American blacks, who more often than not have similar ethno-histories with American slavery, Jim Crow, and various forms of institutionalized racism. See Waters (1999) for more information on West Indian identities.

5. This is not to say that whites do not distrust based on race or perceived "reverse discrimination." For whites, I argue that race operates differently in their trust because historically racial policies benefited their group's interests.

6. Studies of race and mistrust are more abundant in psychology studies, for example. See the research of Wright 1975; Terrell and Terrell 1984; Terrell and Terrell 1981; and Terrell, Terrell, and Taylor 1981, who study blacks' mistrust of whites.

7. See table 15 from the U.S. Census Bureau, "Current Population Survey, Annual Social and Economic Supplement, 2004," Racial Statistics Branch, Population Division: http://www.census.gov/population/socdemo/race/black/ppl-186/tab15.pdf. Additional census data on "black alone" characteristics for 2004 can be found at the following Internet address: http://www.census.gov/population/www/socdemo/race/ppl-186.html.

1. Scholars increasingly note a downward trend in political trust in other democracies worldwide, in Europe, Latin America, and Asia. See Pharr (1997), Dogan (2005), and Adrain and Smith (2006).

2. This anomaly may be occurring because for the first time in American history, an African American has been elected president and is now the "face" and figurehead of America's government. For many blacks, this is a momentous era in America's history, considering that at one time being black precluded one from even running for office or voting. It also can be said that some whites may be resistant to this historical change in blacks' ascendancy to higher office, and thus, they trust an administration led by a black president less.

3. See Shull (1999) for a discussion on twentieth-century American presidents' records on civil rights. Note that critical race theory scholars argue that the judicial system institutionalizes racism through its court decisions (Crenshaw et al. 1995).

4. Voting is one of the most direct, conventional forms of political participation, perhaps other than one's holding an elected or appointed office, which involves one in actual political decision-making. More indirect and unconventional modes of political participation include, for example, wearing political pins, signing petitions, writing representatives, or participating in political protests. See also Rosenstone and Hansen (2003) and Verba, Schlozman, and Brady (1995) for more discussion on various forms of political participation in the United States.

5. Schattschneider (1960) describes how popular sovereignty, in practice, is semi-sovereign because political elites make decisions based on their personal interests, sometimes to the detriment of the masses. For blacks, exclusion from political decision-making and from elite-status circles with whites, thus, limited their input in white, political discourse.

6. Brewer and Brown (1998) contend that social categorizations are used in the psychological dichotomizations between "in-group" and "out-group" members. In-group members are those who have characteristics that make them identifiable with a certain group; those who are not members of the in-group, conversely, are out-group members (Brewer and Brown 1998). In my study, I expect that groups and their "groupness," or "entitativity" (Hamilton, Sherman, and Lickel 1998), affect how people perceive trust in in-group and out-group members. Simply put, group categorizations act as heuristics that group members use to give them information about whom to trust. Race is a heuristic that cues people about the potential of certain behavior in intergroup interactions. The consequence is that people view simultaneously race and behavioral temperament in interpersonal and intergroup interaction.

7. Intergroup psychological research examines how the experiences of individuals are linked to their experiences as members of social groups in society (Tajfel 1982; Tajfel and Turner 1986).

8. Hewstone (1991) extends attribution theory to the analysis of intergroup relations. Considering the conflictual nature of race and race relations, attribution theory (as it relates to intergroup conflict) seems most appropriate as a theoretical approach for analyzing the psychological processes associated with perceptions of race.

9. Racial attributes are those characteristics, or attributes, of race that are either physical, cultural, linguistic, or behavioral and that are racial group specific. Racial attributes function as bits of information that inform people about the racialness of others, including their behavior. In this sense, despite the pseudoscientific construction of race, social norms about racial groups' behaviors assist people in gauging the extent of others' racialness. People's racial attributes furthermore project their racialness in such a way that people perceive their culture and behavior.

10. It must be noted, however, that people can make concerted efforts to conceal their race through what is known as *passing*. Passing, for blacks, involves concealing one's black racial heritage. Traditionally, blacks passed for white in order to avoid mistreatment incurred by being classified as a black racial group member. Because of the "one-drop" laws that defined black racial heritage on the basis of "one drop" of "African" blood, blacks who may have appeared phenotypically white were subsumed into the black racial category and, thus, were treated as black in everyday, exclusionary society, especially before the mid-twentieth century (Davis 1991). While it was possible for a person to pass as black during this era, such passing was disincentivized by the heightened racial discrimination asymmetrically experienced by blacks in the racial hierarchy (Omi and Winant 1994; Bonilla-Silva 2001; Sollors 1999). See John Howard Griffin's (1964) participant-observation of being black in the Jim Crow South, where he transforms himself into a black man and passes for black in order to experience black life in segregation. Passing is distinct from the performance of race via blackface, wherein nonblacks paint themselves black to perform as a black character (Bogle 2001).

11. The figure should not be confused with modeling for a structural equation model. Although the theory behind the structural equation model could be appropriate for these hypothesized relationships, such modeling would not apply to the data in the NPSS, especially given that several measures in the survey are a part of split-sample survey experiments.

NOTES TO CHAPTER 3

1. For more information about the details of Emmitt Till's death, see Till-Mobley and Benson (2003).

2. Jum Nunnally (1978) suggests that the conventionally acceptable Cronbach's alpha coefficient is $\alpha = .70$.

3. Blacks who passed for white were able to do so because of their phenotypic characteristics and their personal decision. Blackness in the United States was defined mostly by the "one-drop rule," the rule explicating that "one drop" of black or African-descended blood made one black in America (Davis 1991). States had different laws that codified the quantum of "African blood" necessary to define one as black. Because blackness often was synonymous with subjugation, whether during slavery or Jim Crow, many blacks who chose to pass did so in order to escape the second-class citizenship and racial discrimination associated with blackness. The denigration of blackness privileged whiteness over blackness, making the aspiration to be white one to which lighter-skinned blacks had more plausible access. "Becoming white" also meant having access to higher social and economic mobility. Once the choice to pass was made, however, living as white involved

one's hiding his or her black identity or black communal connections in order to avoid being forced into living as black.

4. I address some of these generational concerns in Nunnally (2010).

5. To control for the effect that the variable may have on blacks' racial experiences, I include this as a separate variable in the analysis.

NOTES TO CHAPTER 4

1. According to the 2004 "Hate Crime Statistics," data compiled annually by the Federal Bureau of Investigation, racial bias motivated 53.9 percent of 9,021 respondent incidents of single-bias hate crimes (the reason for the hate-crime perpetrator's crime). Of the single-bias offenses (N = 4,863), antiblack bias accounted for the highest percentage of racial bias by the offender.

2. Cronbach's alpha coefficient of reliability for the "effect of knowledge on interactions and feelings" scale is $\alpha = .71$.

3. The scale for positive stereotypes includes an additive scale of the following stereotypes: whether groups are competent, trustworthy, hardworking, honest, and religious. The scale for negative stereotypes includes an additive scale of the following stereotypes: whether groups are lazy, negligent with respect to family caretaking, likely to lie, likely to give up easily, selfish, and bossy.

4. The *frequency of racial discrimination* variable is moderately correlated with the *racial uncertainty* variable: $r = .51$.

5. Blacks with more frequent racial discrimination experiences, furthermore, should perceive more racial uncertainty. However, due to high correlations between this variable and future racial discrimination experiences (r = .43), I exclude this variable in the multivariate analysis to avoid multicollinearity.

NOTES TO CHAPTER 5

1. Putnam conceptualizes trust based on social proximity. Trust is either "thick" or "thin." "Thick trust" is "strong, frequent and nested in wider networks," whereas "thin trust" "can be extended beyond people known very personally" (2000a, 137).

NOTES TO CHAPTER 6

1. Eric Uslaner (2000–2001) argues that trust can be either *generalized* or *particularized*. Generalized trust is "the belief that most people can be trusted"; particularized trust is "faith only in your own kind" (573). Here, I distinguish generalized trust based on trust in people in general. I develop a separate conceptualization of trust, what I refer to as *contextualized trust*, to account for specific contexts of social trust: neighborhoods, shopping places, workplaces, and religious institutions. While I am concerned about the extent to which blacks distinguish trust in their fellow group members from trust in persons of other racial groups, I do not use particularized trust as a reference because I want to focus particularly on the social contexts as sites of distinctive social trust in which racial actors' bodies are interpreted differently.

2. I discuss later in the methods sections additional variables of interest specific to the determination of trust in each social context.

NOTES TO CHAPTER 7

1. Several acts of Congress described the means by which states would become a part of the United States through a rubric for admission as "free" or "slave" states. See the Wilmot Proviso (1848), the Missouri Compromise (1820), the Missouri Compromise (1850), and the Kansas-Nebraska Act (1854).

2. The number of representatives in the House of Representatives from each state is determined by the population in the state. The Electoral College comprises the total number of electors who cast votes for the president. Electors per state are determined based on the sum of representatives in the House of Representatives and the Senate for the state. States with more numerous populations, thus, have a greater influence on the election of the president.

3. Cook, Hardin, and Levi (2005) discuss "institutionalized distrust" as a practical expectation of "healthy skepticism" of government operations. In the case of blacks in America, this is not the character of "institutionalized distrust" that I am describing. Instead, here, I am suggesting that government-sponsored discrimination induces levels of distrust that are "unhealthy" as a psychological response. Such distrust takes the form of apathy and withdrawal from political participation because of political disillusionment and reduced faith in the ability of the political system to operate fairly.

4. This measure was asked to black, white, and Latino respondents based on their perception that the targets of the experiment who served in the levels of government would represent the interests of their respective racial group. The analysis here features only the responses of blacks.

5. King-Meadows (2010) describes the complex nature of racial and partisan considerations in Steele's campaign for U.S. senator in the state of Maryland during the 2006 senatorial election. Steele's election depended heavily on the support of black voters, who were mostly Democrats, in part, because of his need to get support across party lines to make up for lackluster support among white Republicans in the state. Steele lost the race against the white Democratic candidate, Benjamin L. Cardin.

6. Fauntroy (2007) discusses additional historical examples that illustrate political maneuvers that may be viewed as oppositional to black electoral support because of their racial overtones.

NOTES TO CHAPTER 8

1. Liberation theology advocates for the advancement of blacks beyond oppression, seeking liberation through collective, spiritual awareness. During the 2008 presidential campaign, candidate Obama distanced himself from Reverend Jeremiah Wright, who was the former pastor of his church in Chicago, when allegations were made that Wright's sermons were antipatriotic and prejudicial against whites.

2. More specifically, the president stated, "I don't know, not having been there and not seeing all the facts, what role race played in that [Gates case]. But I think it's fair to say,

number one, any of us would be pretty angry; number two, that the Cambridge police acted stupidly in arresting somebody when there was already proof that they were in their own home; and, number three, what I think we know separate and apart from this incident is that there's a long history in this country of African Americans and Latinos being stopped by law enforcement disproportionately. That's just a fact." (See McPhee and Just 2009 for more details about the press conference.)

References

Abelmann, Nancy, and John Lie. 1995. *Blue Dreams: Korean Americans and the Los Angeles Riots*. Cambridge: Harvard University Press.

Aberbach, Joel D., and Jack L. Walker. 1970. The Meanings of Black Power: A Comparison of White and Black Interpretations of a Political Slogan. In *American Political Science Review* 64:367–388.

Abramson, Paul R. 1972. Political Efficacy and Political Trust among Black School Children: Two Explanations. *Journal of Politics* 34:1243–1275.

———. 1977. *The Political Socialization of African Americans: A Critical Evaluation of Research on Efficacy and Trust*. New York: Free Press.

Adrain, Charles F., and James T. Smith. 2006. *Political Democracy, Trust, and Social Justice*. Boston: Northeastern University Press.

Alford, John R. 2001. We're All in This Together: The Decline of Trust in Government, 1958–1996. In *What Is It about Government That Americans Dislike?*, ed. John R. Hibbing and Elizabeth Theiss-Morse, 237–252. Cambridge: Cambridge University Press.

Allen, Richard L., Michael C. Dawson, and Ronald E. Brown. 1989. A Schema-Based Approach to Modeling an African American Racial Belief System. *American Political Science Review* 83 (June): 421–441.

Allport, Gordon. 1954. *The Nature of Prejudice*. Reading, MA: Addison-Wesley.

Alvarez, R. Michael, and Charles H. Franklin. 1994. Uncertainty and Political Perceptions. *Journal of Politics* 56 (3): 671–688.

Alvarez, R. Michael, Robert P. Sherman, and Carla VanBeselaere. 2003. Subject Acquisition for Web-Based Surveys. *Policy Analysis* 11 (1): 23–43.

Anyon, Jean. 1997. *Ghetto Schooling: A Political Economy of Urban Educational Reform*. New York: Teachers College Press.

Assensoh, Akwasi B. 2000. Conflict or Cooperation? Africans and African Americans in Multiracial America. In *Black and Multiracial Politics in America*, ed. Yvette M. Alex-Assensoh and Lawrence J. Hanks, 113–130. New York: NYU Press.

Avery, James M. 2006. The Sources and Consequence of Political Mistrust among African Americans. *American Politics Research* 34 (5): 653–682.

———. 2009. "Political Mistrust among African Americans and Support for the Political System." *Political Research Quarterly* 62:132–145.

Bacharach, Michael, and Diego Gambetta. 2001. Trust in Signs. In *Trust in Society*, ed. Karen S. Cook, 148–184. New York: Russell Sage Foundation.

Barber, Bernard. 1983. *The Logic and Limits of Trust*. New Brunswick: Rutgers University Press.

Bay, Mia. 2000. *The White Image in the Black Mind: African American Ideas about White People, 1830–1925*. New York: Oxford University Press.

Beck, Glenn. 2009. Fox Host Glenn Beck: Obama Is a "Racist." Video. *Huffington Post*, 28 July. http://www.huffingtonpost.com/2009/07/28/fox-host-glenn-beck-obama _n_246310.html.

———. 2010. Beck Amends "Obama Is a Racist" Charge, Questions President's Belief in "Collective Salvation." *Fox News*, 29 August. http://www.foxnews.com/politics/ 2010/08/29/beck-amends-obama-racist-comment-questions-belief-collective -salvation/.

Bell, Tyronn J., and Terence J. G. Tracey. 2006. The Relation of Cultural Mistrust and Psychological Health. *Multicultural Counseling and Development* 34:2–14.

Bennett, Stephen Earl. 2001 Were the Halcyon Days Really Golden? An Analysis of Americans' Attitudes about the Political System, 1945–1965. In *What Is It about Government That Americans Dislike?*, ed. John R. Hibbing and Elizabeth Theiss-Morse, 47–58. Cambridge: Cambridge University Press.

Berstein, Jeffrey. 2001. Linking Presidential and Congressional Approval during Unified and Divided Governments. In *What Is It about Government That Americans Dislike?*, ed. John R. Hibbing and Elizabeth Theiss-Morse, 98–117. Cambridge: Cambridge University Press.

Bianco, William T. 1994. *Trust: Representatives and Constituents*. Ann Arbor: University of Michigan Press.

Blackburn, Simon. 1998. Trust, Cooperation, and Human Psychology. In *Trust and Governance*, ed. Valerie Braithwaite and Margaret Levi, 28–45. New York: Russell Sage Foundation.

Bledsoe, Timothy, Susan Welch, Lee Sigelman, and Michael Combs. 1995. Residential Context and Racial Solidarity among Black Americans. *American Journal of Political Science* 39 (May): 434–458.

Blendon, Robert J., John M. Benson, Richard Morin, Drew E. Altman, Mollyann Brodie, Mario Brossard, Matt James. 1997. Changing Attitudes in America. In *Why Americans Don't Trust Government*, ed. Joseph S. Nye, Philip D. Zelikow, and David C. King, 205–216. Cambridge: Harvard University Press.

Bobo, Lawrence, and Franklin D. Gilliam. 1990. Race, Sociopolitical Participation, and Black Empowerment. *American Political Science Review* 84 (2): 377–393.

Bobo, Lawrence, and Vincent L. Hutchings. 1996. Perceptions of Racial Group Competition: Extending Blumer's Theory of Group Position to a Multiracial Social Context. *American Sociological Review* 61 (December): 951–972.

Bobo, Lawrence, and James R. Kluegel. 1993. Opposition to Race-Targeting: Self-Interest, Stratification Ideology, or Racial Attitudes? *American Sociological Review* 58 (4): 443–464.

Bobo, Lawrence, and Camille L. Zubrinsky. 1996. Attitudes on Residential Integration: Perceived Status Differences, Mere In-Group Preference, or Racial Prejudice? *Social Forces* 74 (3): 883–909.

Bogle, Donald. 2001. *Toms, Coons, Mulattos, Mammies, and Bucks: An Interpretive History of Blacks in American Films*. New York: Continuum.

Bok, Derek. 1997. Measuring the Performance of Government. In *Why People Don't Trust Government*, ed. Joseph S. Nye, Jr., Philip D. Zelikow, and David C. King, 55–75. Cambridge: Harvard University Press.

Bonilla-Silva, Eduardo. 2001. *White Supremacy and Racism in the Post–Civil Rights Era.* Boulder, CO: Lynne Rienner.

Boulware, L. Ebony, Lisa A. Cooper, Lloyd E. Ratner, Thomas A. LaVeist, Neil R. Powe. 2003. Race and Trust in the Health Care System. *Public Health Reports* 118 (4): 358–365.

Bowler, Shaun, and Jeffrey A. Karp. 2004. Politicians, Scandals, and Trust in Government. *Political Behavior* 26 (3): 271–287.

Bowman, Phillip J., and Cleopatra S. Howard. 1985. Race-Related Socialization, Motivation and Academic Achievement: A Study of Black Youths in Three-Generation Families. *Journal of the American Academy of Child Psychiatry* 24 (2): 134–141.

Boykin, A. Wade, and Forrest D. Toms. 1985. Black Child Socialization: A Conceptual Framework. In *Black Children: Social, Educational, and Parental Environments*, ed. H. P. McAdoo and J. L. McAdoo, 33–52. Newbury Park, CA: Sage.

Braithwaite, John. 1998. Institutionalizing Distrust, Enculturating Trust. In *Trust and Governance*, ed. Valerie Braithwaite and Margaret Levi, 343–375. New York: Russell Sage Foundation.

Braithwaite, Valerie. 1998. Communal and Exchange Trust Norms: Their Value Base and Relevance to Institutional Trust. In *Trust and Governance*, ed. Valerie Braithwaite and Margaret Levi, 46–74. New York: Russell Sage Foundation.

Braithwaite, Valerie, and Margaret Levi, eds. 1998. *Trust and Governance*. New York: Russell Sage Foundation.

Brehm, John. 1998. Who Do You Trust? People, Government, Both, or Neither. Paper presented at the Duke University International Conference on Social Capital and Social Networks, 30 October–1 November, Durham, North Carolina.

Brehm, John, and Wendy Rahn. 1997. Individual-Level Evidence for the Causes and Consequences of Social Capital. *American Journal of Political Science* 41 (July): 999–1023.

Brewer, Marilynn B., and Rupert J. Brown. 1998. Intergroup Relations. In *The Handbook of Social Psychology Fourth Edition*, ed. D. Gilbert, S. Fiske, and G. Lindsey, 554–594. New York: McGraw-Hill.

Broman, Clifford L., Roya Mavaddat, and Shu-yao Hsu. 2000. The Experience and Consequences of Perceived Racial Discrimination: A Study of African Americans. *Journal of Black Psychology* 26 (2): 165–180.

Brophy, Alfred L. 2006. *Reparations: Pro and Con*. New York: Oxford University Press.

Brown, R. Khari, and Ronald E. Brown. 2003. Faith and Works: Church-Based Social Capital Resources and African American Political Activism. *Social Forces* 82 (2, December): 617–641.

Brown, Tony N., and Chase L. Lesane-Brown. 2006. Race Socialization Messages across Historical Time. *Social Psychology Quarterly* 69 (2): 201–213.

Browning, Rufus, Dale Rogers Marshall, and David Tabb. 1984. *Protest Is Not Enough: The Struggle of Blacks and Latinos for Equality in Urban Politics*. Berkeley: University of California Press.

Brunson, Rod K., and Jody Miller. 2006. Young Black Men and Urban Policing in the United States. *British Journal of Criminology* 46 (4): 613–640.

Caldwell, Robert, and Stephen D. Jefferson. 2002. An Exploration of the Relationship between the Racial Identity Attitudes and the Perception of Racial Bias. *Journal of Black Psychology* 28 (May): 174–192.

Calhoun-Brown, Allison. 1996. African American Churches and Political Mobilization: The Psychological Impact of Organizational Resources. *Journal of Politics* 58 (4): 935–953.

Canon, David. 1999. *Race, Redistricting, and Representation: The Unintended Consequences of Black Majority Districts.* Chicago: University of Chicago Press.

Carmines, Edward G., and James A. Stimson. 1989. *Issue Evolution: Race and the Transformation of American politics.* Princeton: Princeton University Press.

Carter, Niambi M. 2007. The Black/White Paradigm Revisited: African Americans, Immigration, Race, and Nation. Ph.D. diss., Duke University.

Catterberg, Gabriela, and Alejandro Moreno. 2005. The Individual Bases of Political Trust: Trends in New and Established Democracies. *International Journal of Public Opinion Research* 18 (1): 31–48.

Caughy, Margaret O'Brien, Patricia J. O'Campo, and Suzanne M. Randolph. 2002. The Africentric Home Environment Inventory: An Observational Measure of the Racial Socialization Features of the Home Environment for African American Pre-school Children. *Journal of Black Psychology* 28 (February): 37–52.

Cha-Jua, Sundiata Keita, and Robert E. Weems, Jr. 1994. Coming into Focus: The Treatment of African Americans in Post–Civil War United States History Survey Texts. *Journal of American History* 80 (4): 1408–1419.

Chanley, Virginia A. 2002. Trust in Government in the Aftermath of 9/11: Determinants and Consequences. *Political Psychology* 23 (3): 469–483.

Chanley, Virginia A., Thomas J. Rudolph, and Wendy M. Rahn. 2000. The Origins and Consequences of Public Trust in Government: A Time Series Analysis. *Public Opinion Quarterly* 64 (3): 239–256.

———. 2001. Public Trust in Government in the Reagan Years and Beyond. In *What Is It about Government That Americans Dislike?*, ed. John R. Hibbing and Elizabeth Theiss-Morse, 59–81. Cambridge: Cambridge University Press.

Chatters, Linda M., Robert Joseph Taylor, Karen Lincoln, and Tracy Schroepfer. 2002. Patterns of Informal Support from Family and Church Members among African Americans. *Journal of Black Studies* 33 (1): 66–85.

Chong, Dennis, and Reuel Rogers. 2005. Racial Solidarity and Political Participation. *Political Behavior* 27 (4): 347–374.

Cioffi-Revilla, Claudio. 1998. *Politics and Uncertainty: Theory, Models, and Applications.* New York: Cambridge University Press.

Citrin, Jack. 1974. Comment: The Political Relevance of Trust in Government. *American Political Science Review* 68 (3): 973–988.

Citrin, Jack, and Donald Philip Green. 1986. Presidential Leadership and the Resurgence of Trust in Government. *British Journal of Political Science* 16 (4): 431–453.

Citrin, Jack, and Samantha Luks. 2001. Political Trust Revisited: Déjà Vu All Over Again? In *What Is It about Government That Americans Dislike?*, ed. John R. Hibbing and Elizabeth Theiss-Morse, 9–27. Cambridge: Cambridge University Press.

Citrin, Jack, Herbert McClosky, J. Merrill Shanks, Paul M. Sniderman. 1975. Personal and Political Sources of Political Alienation. *British Journal of Political Science* 5 (1): 1–31.

Cohen, Cathy. 1999. *Boundaries of Blackness: AIDS and the Breakdown of Black Politics.* Chicago: University of Chicago Press.

Coleman, James. 1988. Social Capital in the Creation of Human Capital. *American Journal of Sociology* 94:95–120.

——. 1990. *Foundations of Social Theory.* Cambridge: Harvard University Press.

Combs, Dennis R., David L. Penn, Jeffrey Cassisi, Chris Michael, Terry Wood, Jill Wanner, and Scott Adams. 2006. Perceived Racism as a Predictor of Paranoia among African Americans. *Journal of Black Psychology* 32 (1): 87–104.

Conley, Dalton. 2003. Universal Freckle: How I Learned to Be White. In *Privilege: A Reader*, ed. Michael S. Kimmel and Abbey L. Ferber, 145–212. Cambridge: Cambridge University Press.

Cook, Karen, Russell Hardin, and Margaret Levi. 2005. *Cooperation without Trust?* New York: Russell Sage Foundation.

Cook, Timothy E., and Paul Gronke. 2005. The Skeptical American: Revisiting the Meanings of Trust in Government and Confidence in Institutions. *Journal of Politics* 67 (3): 784–803.

Couper, Mick. 2000. Web Surveys: A Review of Issues and Approaches. *Public Opinion Quarterly* 64 (4, Winter): 464–494.

Crenshaw, Kimberlé, Neil Gotanda, Gary Peller, Kendall Thomas, eds. 1995. *Critical Race Theory: The Key Writings That Formed the Movement.* New York: New Press.

Cross, William E. 1991. *Shades of Black: Diversity in African American Identity.* Philadelphia: Temple University Press.

Cummings, Scott, and Thomas Lambert. 1997. Anti-Hispanic and Anti–Asian American Sentiments among African Americans. *Social Science Quarterly* 78 (2): 338–353.

Damico, Alfonso J., M. Margaret Conway, and Sandra Bowman Damico. 2000. Patterns of Political Trust and Mistrust: Three Moments in the Lives of Democratic Citizens. *Polity* 32 (3): 377–400.

Dasgupta, Partha. 2000. Economic Progress and the Idea of Social Capital. In *Social Capital: A Multifaceted Perspective*, ed. Partha Dasgupta and Ismail Serageldin. Washington, DC: World Bank.

Davis, F. James. 1991. *Who Is Black? One Nation's Definition.* University Park: Pennsylvania State University Press.

Dawson, Michael C. 1994. *Behind the Mule: Race and Class in African-American Politics.* Princeton: Princeton University Press.

——. 2001. *Black Visions in the Mirror: The Roots of Contemporary African American Political Ideologies.* Chicago: University of Chicago Press.

Demo, David H., and Michael Hughes. 1990. Socialization and Racial Identity among Black Americans. *Social Psychology Quarterly* 53 (4): 364–374.

Dennis, Jack. 1973. Major Problems of Political Socialization Research. In *Socialization to Politics: A Reader*, ed. Jack Dennis, 2–27. New York: Wiley.

Diaz-Veizades, Jeannette, and Edward T. Chang. 1996. Building Cross-Cultural Coalitions: A Case Study of the Black-Korean Alliance and the Latino-Black Roundtable. *Ethnic and Racial Studies* 19 (3): 680–700.

Dogan, Mattei. 2005. Introduction: Political Mistrust as a Worldwide Phenomenon. In *Political Mistrust and the Discrediting of Politicians*, ed. Mattei Dogan, 1–8. Leiden: Brill.

Du Bois, W. E. B. [1903] 1990. *The Souls of Black Folk*. New York: Vintage Books/Library of America.

Dyson, Michael Eric. 1996. *Race Rules: Navigating the Color Line*. Reading, MA: Addison-Wesley.

Easton, David. 1965. *A Systems Analysis of Political Life*. New York: Wiley.

Easton, David, and Jack Dennis. 1970. The Child's Image of Government. In *Learning about Politics: A Reader in Political Socialization*, ed. Roberta S. Sigel, 31–49. New York: Random House.

———. 1973. System Relevance. In *Socialization to Politics: A Reader*, ed. Jack Dennis, 32–53. New York: Wiley.

Ellison, Christopher G., and Daniel A. Powers. 1994. The Contact Hypothesis and Racial Attitudes among Black Americans. *Social Science Quarterly* 75 (2): 385–400.

Eyerman, Ron. 2001. *Cultural Trauma: Slavery and the Formation of African American Identity*. Cambridge: Cambridge University Press.

Fanon, Frantz. [1952] 1967. *Black Skin, White Masks*. New York: Grove.

———. 1963. *The Wretched of the Earth*. New York: Grove.

Farley, Reynolds, Charlotte Steeh, Maria Krysan, Tara Jackson, and Keith Reeves. 1994. Stereotypes and Segregation: Neighborhoods in the Detroit Area. *American Journal of Sociology* 100 (3): 750–780.

Fauntroy, Michael K. 2007. *Republicans and the Black Vote*. Boulder, CO: Lynne Rienner.

Feagin, Joe R. 1991. The Continuing Significance of Race: Anti-black Discrimination in Public Places. *American Sociological Review* 56 (February): 101–116.

———. 2000. *Racist America: Roots, Current Realities, and Future Reparations*. London: Taylor and Francis.

Federal Bureau of Investigation. 2004. Hate Crime Statistics 2004. http://www.fbi.gov/ucr/hc2004/tables/HateCrime2004.pdf.

———. 2007. Hate Crime Statistics: Incidents, Offenses, Victims, and Known Offenders by Bias Motivation. http://www.fbi.gov/ucr/hc2007/table_01.htm.

Feldman, Stanley. 1983. The Measurement and Meaning of Political Trust. *Political Methodology* 9 (3): 341–354.

Feldman Barrett, Lisa, and Janet K. Swim. 1998. Appraisals of Prejudice and Discrimination. In *Prejudice: The Target's Perspective*, ed. Janet K. Swim and C. Stangor, 11–36. San Diego: Academic.

Fifield, Adam, and Elise O'Shaughnessy. 2001. Shopping while Black. *Good Housekeeping* 233 (5, November): 129–136.

Franklin, John Hope, and Alfred A. Moss, Jr. 2007. *From Slavery to Freedom: A History of African Americans*. 8th ed. New York: Knopf.

Frymer, Paul. 1999. *Uneasy Alliances: Race and Party Competition in America*. Princeton: Princeton University Press.

Fukuyama, Francis. 1995. *Trust: The Social Virtues and the Creation of Prosperity*. New York: Free Press.

Gaines, Kevin. 1996. *Uplifting the Race: Black Leadership, Politics, and Culture in the Twentieth Century*. Chapel Hill: University of North Carolina Press.

Gay, Claudine. 2002. Spirals of Trust? The Effect of Descriptive Representation on the Relationship between Citizens and Their Government. *American Journal of Political Science* 46 (4): 717–732.

——. 2004. Putting Race in Context: Identifying the Environmental Determinants of Black Racial Attitudes. *American Political Science Review* 98 (4): 547–562.

——. 2006. Seeing Difference: The Effect of Economic Disparity on Black Attitudes toward Latinos. *American Journal of Political Science* 50 (4): 982–997.

Georgakas, Dan, and Marvin Surkin. 1998. *Detroit, I Do Mind Dying: A Study in Urban Revolution*. New York: St. Martin's.

Gilens, Martin. 1999. *Why Americans Hate Welfare: Race, Media, and the Politics of Anti-poverty Policy*. Chicago: University of Chicago Press.

Gillespie, Andra. 2010. Meet the New Class: Theorizing Young Black Leadership in a "Postracial" Era. In *Whose Black Politics? Cases in Post-racial Black Leadership*, ed. Andra Gillespie, 9–42. New York: Routledge.

Glaser, James M. 1995. Black and White Perceptions of Party Differences. *Political Behavior* 17 (2): 155–177.

Gossett, Thomas F. 1997. *Race: The History of an Idea in America*. New York: Oxford University Press.

Green, Melanie C., and Timothy Brock. 1998. Trust, Mood, and Outcomes of Friendship Determine Preferences for Real versus Ersatz Social Capital. *Political Psychology* 19 (3): 527–544.

Greenberg, Edward S. 1970. Black Children and the Political System. *Public Opinion Quarterly* 34:333–345.

Grier, William H., and Price M. Cobbs. 1968. *Black Rage*. New York: Basic Books.

Griffin, John Howard. 1962. *Black Like Me*. New York: Signet.

Griffin, Larry J., and Kenneth A. Bollen. 2009. What Do These Memories Do? Civil Rights Remembrance and Racial Attitudes. *American Sociological Review* 74 (August): 594–614.

Guinier, Lani. 1995. *The Tyranny of the Majority: Fundamental Fairness in American Democracy*. New York: Free Press.

Gurin, Patricia, Shirley Hatchett, and James S. Jackson. 1989. *Hope and Independence: Blacks' Response to Electoral Party Politics*. New York: Russell Sage Foundation.

Guthrie, Patricia, and Janis Hutchison. 1995. The Impact of Perceptions of Interpersonal Interactions in an African American/Asian American Housing Project. *Journal of Black Studies* 25 (3): 377–395.

Hamilton, David, Steven J. Sherman, and Brian Lickel. 1998. Perceiving Social Groups: The Importance of the Entitativity Continuum. In *Intergroup Cognition and Intergroup Behavior*, ed. Constantine Sedikides, John Schopler, and Chester A. Insko, 47–74. Mahwah, NJ: Erlbaum.

Haney López, Ian F. 2006. *White by Law: The Legal Construction of Race*. Rev. and updated ed. New York: NYU Press.

Hardin, Russell. 1998. Trust in Government. In *Trust and Governance*, ed. Valerie Braithwaite and Margaret Levi, 9–27. New York: Russell Sage Foundation.

——. 2001. Conceptions and Explanations of Trust. In *Trust in Society*, ed. Karen S. Cook, 3–39. New York: Russell Sage Foundation.

——. 2002. *Trust and Trustworthiness*. New York: Russell Sage Foundation.

——. 2004. Introduction to *Distrust*, ed. Russell Hardin. New York: Russell Sage Foundation.

——. 2006. *Trust*. Cambridge, UK: Polity.

Harris, David. 1995. Exploring the Determinants of Adult Black Identity: Context and Process. *Social Forces* 74 (September): 227–241.

Harris, Frederick C. 1999. *Something Within: Religion in African American Political Activism*. New York: Oxford University Press.

Harris-Lacewell, Melissa V. 2003. The Heart of the Politics of Race: Centering Black People in the Study of White Racial Attitudes. *Journal of Black Studies* 34 (2): 222–249.

———. 2004. *Barbershops, Bibles, and BET: Everyday Talk and Black Political Thought*. Princeton: Princeton University Press.

Hartman, Saidiya V. 1997. *Scenes of Subjection: Terror, Slavery, and Self-Making in Nineteenth-Century America*. New York: Oxford University Press.

Heider, Fritz. 1944. Social Perception and Phenomenal Causality. *Psychological Review* 51:358–374.

———. 1958. *The Psychology of Interpersonal Relations*. New York: Wiley.

Heimer, Carol. 2001. Solving the Problem of Trust. In *Trust in Society*, ed. Karen A. Cook. New York: Russell Sage Foundation.

Hero, Rodney E. 1992. *Latinos and the U.S. Political System: Two-Tiered Pluralism*. Philadelphia: Temple University Press.

———. 2007. *Racial Diversity and Social Capital: Equality and Community in America*. New York: Cambridge University Press.

Hero, Rodney E., and Christina Wolbrecht. 2005. Introduction to *The Politics of Democratic Inclusion*, ed. Christina Wolbrecht and Rodney E. Hero, 1–14. Philadelphia: Temple University Press.

Hess, Robert D., and Judith Torney. 1967. *The Development of Political Attitudes in Children*. Chicago: Aldine.

Hetherington, Marc J. 1998. The Political Relevance of Trust. *American Political Science Review* 92 (December): 791–808.

———. 2005. *Why Trust Matters: Declining Political Trust and the Demise of American Liberalism*. Princeton: Princeton University Press.

Hetherington, Marc J., and Suzanne Globetti. 2002. Political Trust and Racial Policy Preferences. *American Journal of Political Science* 46 (2): 253–275.

Hetherington, Marc J., and John D. Nugent. 2001. Explaining Public Support for Devolution: The Role of Political Trust. In *What Is It about Government That Americans Dislike?*, ed. John R. Hibbing and Elizabeth Theiss-Morse, 134–155. Cambridge: Cambridge University Press.

Hewstone, Miles. 1983. Attribution Theory and Common Sense Explanations: An Introductory Overview. In *Attribution Theory: Social and Functional Extensions*, ed. Miles Hewstone, 1–26. Oxford, UK: Blackwell.

———. 1991. *Causal Attribution: From Cognitive Processes to Collective Beliefs*. Cambridge, MA: Blackwell.

Hewstone, Miles, and Rupert Brown. 1986. Contact Is Not Enough: An Intergroup Perspective on the Contact Hypothesis. In *Contact and Conflict in Intergroup Encounters*, ed. Miles Hewstone and Rupert Brown. Oxford, UK: Blackwell.

Hibbing, John R., and Elizabeth Theiss-Morse. 2001. Introduction to *What Is It about Government That Americans Dislike?*, ed. John R. Hibbing and Elizabeth Theiss-Morse, 1–7. Cambridge: Cambridge University Press.

Higginbotham, Evelyn Brooks. 1993. *Righteous Discontent: The Women's Movement in the Black Baptist Church, 1880–1920*. Cambridge: Harvard University Press.

Hill, Mark E. 2000. Color Differences in the Socioeconomic Status of African American Men: Results of a Longitudinal Study. *Social Forces* 78 (4): 1437–1460.

Hill, Shirley A. 1999. *African American Children: Socialization and Development in Families.* Thousand Oaks, CA: Sage.

Hochschild, Jennifer L. 1995. *Facing Up to the American Dream: Race, Class, and the Soul of the Nation.* Princeton: Princeton University Press.

———. 2006. When Do People Not Protest Unfairness? The Case of Skin Color Discrimination. *Social Research* 73 (2): 473–498.

Hochschild, Jennifer L., and Vesla Weaver. 2007. The Skin Color Paradox and the American Racial Order. *Social Forces* 86 (2): 643–670.

Hoffman, Aaron M. 2006. *Building Trust: Overcoming Suspicion in International Conflict.* Albany: SUNY Press.

Howell, Susan E., and Deborah Fagan. 1988. Race and Trust in Government: Testing the Political Reality Model. *Public Opinion Quarterly* 52 (3): 343–350.

Huddy, Leonie. 2004. Contrasting Theoretical Approaches to Intergroup Relations. *Political Psychology* 25 (6): 947–967.

Hughes, Diane, and Lisa Chen. 1997. When and What Parents Tell Children about Race: An Examination of Race-Related Socialization among African American Families. *Applied Developmental Science* 1 (4): 200–214.

Hughes, Diane, Deborah Rivas, Monica Foust, Carolin Hagelskamp, Sarah Gersick, and Niobe Way. 2007. How to Catch a Moonbeam: A Mixed-Methods Approach to Understanding Ethnic Socialization Processes in Ethnically Diverse Families. In *Handbook of Race, Racism, and the Developing Child*, ed. Stephen M. Quintana and Clark McKown. Hoboken, NJ: Wiley.

Hunt, Matthew O. 2007. African American, Hispanic, and White Beliefs about Black/White Inequality, 1977–2004. *American Sociological Review* 72 (3): 390–415.

Hunter, Margaret L. 2002. If You're Light You're Alright: Light Skin Color as Social Capital for Women of Color. *Gender and Society* 16 (2): 175–193.

Hyman, Herbert H. 1959. *Political Socialization: A Study in the Psychology of Political Behavior.* Glencoe, IL: Free Press.

Ichilov, Orit. 1990. Introduction to *Political Socialization, Citizenship Education, and Democracy*, ed. Orit Ichilov, 1–8. New York: Teachers College Press.

Jackson, James S. 1991. *Life in Black America.* Thousand Oaks, CA: Sage.

Jackson, John L. 2008. *Racial Paranoia: The Unintended Consequences of Political Correctness.* New York: Basic Civitas.

Jefferson, Stephen D., and Robert Caldwell. 2002. An Exploration of the Relationship between Racial Identity Attitudes and the Perception of Racial Bias. *Journal of Black Psychology* 28 (2): 174–192.

Jennings, M. Kent, and Richard G. Niemi. 1981. *Generations and Politics: A Panel Study of Young Adults and Their Parents.* Princeton: Princeton University Press.

Johnson, James H., Jr., Walter C. Farrell, Jr., and Chandra Guinn. 1997. Immigration Reform and the Browning of America: Tensions, Conflicts, and Community Instability in Metropolitan Los Angeles. *International Migration Review* 31 (4): 1055–1095.

Johnson, James H., Jr., and Melvin Oliver. 1994. Interethnic Minority Conflict in Urban America: The Effects of Economic and Social Dislocations. In *Race and Ethnic Conflict: Contending Views on Prejudice, Discrimination, and Ethnoviolence*, ed. Fred L. Pincus and Howard J. Ehrlich. Boulder, CO: Westview.

Johnson, Walter. 1999. *Soul by Soul: Life inside the Antebellum Slave Market*. Cambridge: Harvard University Press.

Judd, Charles M., and Bernadette Park. 1988. Out-Group Homogeneity: Judgments of Variability at the Individual and Group Levels. *Journal of Personality and Social Psychology* 54 (5): 778–788.

———. 1995. Effects of Racial Stereotypes on Judgments of Individuals: The Moderating Role of Perceived Group Variability. *Journal of Experimental Social Psychology* 32:71–103.

Kahneman, Daniel, and Amos Tversky. 2000. Choices, Values, and Frames. In *Choices, Values, and Frames*, ed. Daniel Kahneman and Amos Tversky. New York: Russell Sage Foundation; Cambridge: Cambridge University Press.

Katznelson, Ira. 2005. *When Affirmative Action Was White: An Untold Story of Racial Inequality in Twentieth-Century America*. New York: Norton.

Keele, Luke. 2005. The Authorities Really Do Matter: Party Control and Trust in Government. *Journal of Politics* 67 (3): 873–886.

———. 2007. Social Capital and the Dynamics of Trust in Government. *American Journal of Political Science* 51 (2): 241–254.

Kelley, Robin D. G. 1994. *Race Rebels: Culture, Politics, and the Black Working Class*. New York: Free Press.

Kessler, Ronald C., Kristin D. Mickelson, and David R. Williams. 1999. The Prevalence, Distribution, and Mental Health Correlates of Perceived Discrimination in the United States. *Journal of Health and Social Behavior* 40 (September): 208–230.

Key, V. O. 1949. *Southern Politics in State and Nation*. New York: Knopf. Reprint, Knoxville: University of Tennessee Press, 1996.

Keyssar, Alexander. 2000. *The Right to Vote: The Contested History of Democracy in the United States*. New York: Basic Books.

Kim, Claire Jean. 2000. *Bitter Fruit: The Politics of Black-Korean Conflict in New York City*. New Haven: Yale University Press.

Kinder, Donald R., and Lynn Sanders. 1996. *Divided by Color: Racial Politics and Democratic Ideals*. Chicago: University of Chicago Press.

Kinder, Donald R., and David O. Sears. 1981. Prejudice and Politics: Symbolic Racism versus Racial Threats to the Good Life. *Journal of Personality and Social Psychology* 40:414–431.

King, David C. 1997. The Polarization of American Parties and Mistrust of Government. In *Why People Don't Trust Government*, ed. Joseph S. Nye, Jr., Philip D. Zelikow, and David C. King, 155–178. Cambridge: Harvard University Press.

King-Meadows, Tyson. 2010. The "Steele Problem" and the New Republican Battle for Black Votes: Legacy, Loyalty, and Lexicon in Maryland's 2006 Senate Contest. In *Whose Black Politics? Cases in Post-racial Black Leadership*, ed. Andra Gillespie, 241–270. New York: Routledge.

Kohatsu, Eric L., Michael Dulay, Cynthia Lam, William Concepcion, Patricia Perez, Cynthia Lopez, and Jennie Euler. 2000. Using Racial Identity Theory to Explore Racial

Mistrust and Interracial Contact among Asian Americans. *Journal of Counseling and Development* 78:334–342.

Kwak, Nojin, Dhavan V. Shah, and Lance Holbert. 2004. Connecting, Trusting, and Participating: The Direct and Interactive Effects of Social Associations. *Political Research Quarterly* 57 (4, December): 643–652.

Laudrine, Hope, and Elizabeth A. Klonoff. 1996. The Schedule of Racist Events: A Measure of Racial Discrimination and a Study of Its Negative Physical and Mental Health Consequences. *Journal of Black Psychology* 22:144–168.

Lawrence, Robert Z. 1997. Is It Really the Economy, Stupid? In *Why People Don't Trust Government*, ed. Joseph S. Nye, Jr., Philip D. Zelikow, and David C. King, 111–132. Cambridge: Harvard University Press.

Lee, Jennifer. 2000. The Salience of Race in Everyday Life: Black Customers' Shopping Experiences in Black and White Neighborhoods. *Work and Occupations* 27 (3, August): 353–376.

Lee, Taeku. 2002. *Mobilizing Public Opinion: Black Insurgency and Racial Attitudes in the Civil Rights Era.* Chicago: University of Chicago Press.

Lesane-Brown, Chase L., Tony N. Brown, Cleopatra H. Caldwell, and Robert M. Sellers. 2005. The Comprehensive Race Socialization Inventory. *Journal of Black Studies* 36 (2): 163–190.

Levine, Jeffrey, Edward G. Carmines, and Paul M. Sniderman. 1999. The Empirical Dimensionality of Racial Stereotypes. *Public Opinion Quarterly* 63:371–384.

Lewis, Earl. 1991. *In Their Own Interests: Race, Class, and Power in Twentieth-Century Norfolk, Virginia.* Berkeley: University of California Press.

Lewis, J. David, and Andrew J. Weigert. 1985a. Social Atomism, Holism, and Trust. *Sociological Quarterly* 26 (4): 455–471.

———. 1985b. Trust as a Social Reality. *Social Forces* 63 (4): 967–985.

Lin, Nan. 2001a. Building a Network Theory of Social Capital. In *Social Capital: Theory and Research*, ed. Nan Lin, Karen Cook, and Ronald S. Burt, 3–29. New York: Aldine De Gruyter.

———. 2001b. *Social Capital: A Theory of Social Structure and Action.* Cambridge: Cambridge University Press.

Lincoln, C. Eric. 1996. "All Niggers Have to Wait": A Child's First Lesson in Jim Crow. *Journal of Blacks in Higher Education* 11 (Spring): 60.

Lincoln, C. Eric, and L. H. Mamiya. 1990. *The Black Church in the African American Experience.* Durham: Duke University Press.

Link, Bruce G., and Jo C. Phelan. 2001. Conceptualizing Stigma. *Annual Review of Sociology* 27:363–385.

Lippmann, Walter. 1922. *Public Opinion.* New York: Macmillan.

Litwack, Leon F. 1998. *Trouble in Mind: Black Southerners in the Age of Jim Crow.* New York: Knopf.

Logan, Rayford W. 1965. *The Betrayal of the Negro, from Rutherford B. Hayes to Woodrow Wilson.* New York: Collier Books.

Lublin, David. 1997. *The Paradox of Representation: Racial Gerrymandering and Minority Interests in Congress.* Princeton: Princeton University Press.

Luhmann, Niklas. 1979. *Trust and Power.* New York: Wiley.

Luhmann, Niklas. 1988. Familiarity, Confidence, Trust: Problems and Alternatives. In *Trust*, ed. Diego Gambetta, 94–107. Oxford, UK: Blackwell.

Lupton, Deborah. 1999. *Risk*. London and New York: Routledge.

Mangum, Maurice. 2003. Psychological Involvement and Black Voter Turnout. *Political Research Quarterly* 56 (1, March): 41–48.

Mannheim, Karl. [1928] 1952. The Problem of Generations. In *Essays on the Sociology of Knowledge*. New York: Oxford University Press.

Mansbridge, Jane M. 1997. Social and Cultural Causes of Dissatisfaction with the U.S. Government. In *Why People Don't Trust Government*, ed. Joseph S. Nye, Jr., Philip D. Zelikow, and David C. King, 133–153. Cambridge: Harvard University Press.

———. 1999. Should Blacks Represent Blacks and Women Represent Women? A Contingent "Yes." *Journal of Politics* 61 (3): 628–657.

Marschall, Melissa J., and Dietlind Stolle. 2004. Race and the City: Neighborhood Context and the Development of Generalized Trust. *Political Behavior* 26 (2): 125–153.

Martin, Pamela P., and Harriette Pipes McAdoo. 2007. Sources of Racial Socialization: Theological Orientation of African American Churches and Parents. In *Black Families*, ed. Harriette Pipes McAdoo, 125–142. Thousand Oaks, CA: Sage.

Massey, Douglas, and Nancy Denton. 1993. *American Apartheid: Segregation and the Making of the Underclass*. Cambridge: Harvard University Press.

McAdam, Doug. 1982. *Political Process and the Development of Black Insurgency, 1930–1970*. Chicago: University of Chicago Press.

McAdoo, Harriette Pipes. 2007. Introduction to *Black Families*, ed. Harriette Pipes McAdoo. Thousand Oaks, CA: Sage.

McClain, Paula D. 1993. The Changing Dynamics of Urban Politics: Black and Hispanic Municipal Employment—Is There Competition? *Journal of Politics* 55 (2, May): 399–414.

———. 2006. Presidential Address: Racial Intergroup Relations in a Set of Cities: A Twenty-Year Perspective. *Journal of Politics* 68 (4): 757–770.

McClain, Paula D., Niambi M. Carter, Victoria M. DeFrancesco Soto, Monique L. Lyle, Jeffrey D. Grynaviski, Shayla C. Nunnally, Thomas J. Scotto, J. Alan J. Kendrick, Gerald F. Lackey, and Kendra Davenport Cotton. 2006. Racial Distancing in a Southern City: Latino Immigrants' Views of Black Americans. *Journal of Politics* 68 (3, August): 571–584.

McClain, Paula D., and Albert K. Karnig. 1990. Black and Hispanic Socioeconomic and Political Competition. *American Political Science Review* 84 (June): 535–545.

McClain, Paula D., Monique Lyle, Niambi M. Carter, Victoria M. DeFrancesco Soto, Gerald Lackey, Kendra Davenport Cotton, Shayla C. Nunnally, Thomas J. Scotto, Jeffrey D. Grynaviski, and J. Alan Kendrick. 2007. Black Americans and Latino Immigrants in a Southern City: Friendly Neighbors or Economic Competitors? *Du Bois Review* 4 (1): 1–21.

McClain, Paula D., Monique L. Lyle, Efrén O. Perez, Niambi M. Carter, Jessica Johnson Carew, Eugene Walton, Candis Watts, Gerald F. Lacke, Dianelle Cleland, and Shayla C. Nunnally. 2009. Black and White Americans and Latino Immigrants: A Preliminary Look at Attitudes toward Latino Immigration in Three Southern Cities. Paper presented at the 2009 annual meeting of the Southern Political Science Association, 8–10 January, New Orleans, Louisiana.

McClain, Paula D., and Joseph M. Stewart. 2006. *"Can We All Get Along?" Racial and Ethnic Minorities in American Politics.* Boulder, CO: Westview.

McCormick, Joseph P., and Charles E. Jones. 1993. The Conceptualization of Deracialization. In *Dilemmas of Black Politics,* ed. Georgia Persons, 66–84. New York: HarperCollins.

McDaniel, Eric. 2008. *Politics in the Pews: The Political Mobilization of Black Churches.* Ann Arbor: University of Michigan Press.

McDermott, Monika. 1998. Race and Gender Cues in Low-Information Elections. *Political Research Quarterly* 51:895–918.

McGarty, Craig, Vincent Y. Yzerbyt, and Russell Spears. 2002. *Stereotypes as Explanations: The Formation of Meaningful Beliefs about Social Groups.* Cambridge: Cambridge University Press.

McHale, Susan M., Ann C. Crouter, Ji-Yeon Kim, Linda M. Burton, Kelly D. Davis, Aryn M. Dotterer, and Dena P. Swanson. 2006. Mothers' and Fathers' Racial Socialization in African American Families and Implications for Youth. *Child Development* 77 (5): 1387–1402.

McPhee, Michelle, and Sara Just. 2009. Obama: Police Acted "Stupidly" in Gates Case. *ABC News,* 22 July. http://abcnews.go.com/US/story?id=8148986&page=1.

Mendelberg, Tali. 2001. *The Race Card: Campaign Strategy, Implicit Messages, and the Norm of Equality.* Princeton: Princeton University Press.

Merelman, Richard M. 1972. The Adolescence of Political Socialization. *Sociology of Education* 45 (2): 134–166.

Messick, David M., and Roderick M. Kramer. 2001. Trust as a Form of Shallow Morality. In *Trust in Society,* ed. Karen S. Cook, 89–118. New York: Russell Sage Foundation.

Miller, Alan S., and Tomoko Mitamura. 2003. Are Surveys on Trust Trustworthy? *Social Psychology Quarterly* 66 (1, March): 62–70.

Miller, Arthur H. 1974. Political Issues and Trust in Government: 1964–1970. *American Political Science Review* 68 (3): 951–972.

Miller, Arthur H., Patricia Gurin, Gerald Gurin, and Oksana Malanchuk. 1981. Group Consciousness and Political Participation. *American Journal of Political Science* 25 (3): 494–511.

Miller, David R. 1999. Racial Socialization and Racial Identity: Can They Promote Resiliency for African American Adolescents? *Adolescence* 34 (134): 493–501.

Miller, David R., and Randall MacIntosh. 1999. Promoting Resilience in Urban African American Adolescents: Racial Socialization and Identity as Protective Factors. *Social Work Research* 23 (3): 159–169.

Mindiola, Tatcho, Jr., Yolanda Flores Niemann, and Nestor Rodriguez. 2002. *Black-Brown Relations and Stereotypes.* Austin: University of Texas Press.

Mohl, Raymond A. 2003. Globalization, Latinization, and the Nuevo New South. *Journal of American Ethnic History* 22 (4): 31–66.

Morales, Dana Ables. 1999. Racial Attitudes and Partisan Identification in the United States, 1980–1992. *Party Politics* 5:191–198.

Morris, Aldon. 1984. *The Origins of the Civil Rights Movement: Black Communities Organizing for Change.* New York: Free Press.

Morris, Irwin L. 2000. African American Voting on Proposition 187: Rethinking the Prevalence of Interminority Conflict. *Political Research Quarterly* 53 (1): 77–98.

Mutisya, P. Masila, and Louie E. Ross. 2005. Afrocentricity and Racial Socialization among African American College Students. *Journal of Black Studies* 38 (3): 235–247.

Myrdal, Gunnar. 1944. *An American Dilemma: The Negro Problem and Modern Democracy.* New York: Harper and Brothers.

Neustadt, Richard E. 1997. The Politics of Mistrust. In *Why People Don't Trust Government,* ed. Joseph S. Nye, Jr., Philip D. Zelikow, and David C. King, 179–201. Cambridge: Harvard University Press.

Niemi, Richard G., and Mary A. Hepburn. 1995. The Rebirth of Political Socialization. *Perspectives on Political Science* 24 (1): 7–17.

Nilson, Douglas C., and Linda Burzotta Nilson. 1980. Trust in Elites and Protest Orientation: An Integrative Approach. *Political Behavior* 2 (4): 385–404.

Nunnally, Jum C. 1978. *Psychometric Theory.* 2nd ed. New York: McGraw-Hill.

Nunnally, Shayla C. 2008. Zero-Sum Politics as a Trust Dilemma: How Race and Gender Affect Blacks', Whites', and Latinos' Trust in Obama's and Clinton's Representation of Group Interests. Unpublished paper.

———. 2009. Racial Homogenization and Stereotypes: Black American College Students' Racial Stereotypes. *Journal of Black Studies* 40 (2): 252–265.

———. 2010. Learning Race, Socializing Blackness: A Cross-Generational Analysis of Blacks' Racial Socialization Experiences. *Du Bois Review* 7 (1): 185–217.

Nye, Joseph S. 1997. Introduction: The Decline of Confidence in Government. In *Why People Don't Trust Government,* ed. Joseph S. Nye, Jr., Philip D. Zelikow, and David C. King, 1–18. Cambridge: Harvard University Press.

Offe, Claus. 1999. How Can We Trust Our Fellow Citizens? In *Democracy and Trust,* ed. Mark E. Warren, 42–87. Cambridge: Cambridge University Press.

Oliver, J. Eric, and Tali Mendelberg. 2000. Reconsidering the Environmental Determinants of White Racial Attitudes. *American Journal of Political Science* 44 (3): 574–89.

Oliver, J. Eric, and Janelle Wong. 2003. Intergroup Prejudice in Multiethnic Settings. *American Journal of Political Science* 47 (4): 567–582.

Omi, Michael, and Howard Winant. 1994. *Racial Formation in the United States: From the 1960s to the 1980s.* New York: Routledge.

Orey, B. D'Andra. 2004. Explaining Black Conservatives: Racial Uplift or Racial Resentment? *Black Scholar* 34 (1): 18–22.

Orr, Marion. 1999. *Black Social Capital: The Politics of School Reform in Baltimore, 1986–1998.* Lawrence: University Press of Kansas.

Orren, Gary. 1997. Fall from Grace: The Public's Loss of Faith in Government. In *Why People Don't Trust Government,* ed. Joseph S. Nye, Jr., Philip D. Zelikow, and David C. King, 77–107. Cambridge: Harvard University Press.

Ostrom, Elinor, and James Walker. 2003. Introduction to *Trust and Reciprocity: Interdisciplinary Lessons from Experimental Research,* ed. Elinor Ostrom and James Walker, 3–18. New York: Russell Sage Foundation.

Owen, Diana, and Jack Dennis. 2001. Trust in Federal Government: The Phenomenon and Its Antecedents. In *What Is It about Government That Americans Dislike?,* ed. John R. Hibbing and Elizabeth Theiss-Morse, 207–226. Cambridge: Cambridge University Press.

Parker, Frank R. 1990. *Black Votes Count: Political Empowerment in Mississippi after 1965.* Chapel Hill: University of North Carolina Press.

Parker, Suzanne L., and Glenn R. Parker. 1993. Why Do We Trust Our Congressman? *Journal of Politics* 55 (2): 442–453.

Pattillo-McCoy, Mary. 1999. *Black Picket Fences: Privilege and Peril among the Black Middle Class*. Chicago: University of Chicago Press.

Peng, Yali. 1994. Intellectual Fads in Political Science: The Cases of Political Socialization and Community Power Studies. *PS: Political Science and Politics* 27 (March): 100–108.

Peters, Marie F. 1985. Racial Socialization of Young Black Children. In *Black Children: Social, Educational, and Parental Environments*, ed. H. P. McAdoo and J. L. McAdoo, 159–173. Newbury Park, CA: Sage.

Pew Research Center. 2005. *Huge Racial Divide over Katrina and Its Consequences*. 8 September. http://people-press.org/reports/pdf/255.pdf.

———. 2007. *Americans and Social Trust: Who, Where, and Why*. Social Trends Report. 22 February. http://pewresearch.org/assets/social/pdf/SocialTrust.pdf.

———. 2010a. *Growing Number of Americans Say Obama Is a Muslim*. 19 August. http://pewresearch.org/pubs/1701/poll-obama-muslim-christian-church-out-of-politics-political-leaders-religious.

———. 2010b. *The People and Their Government: Distrust, Discontent, Anger, and Partisan Rancor*. 18 April. http://people-press.org/reports/pdf/606.pdf.

———. 2010c. *A Year after Obama's Election: Blacks Upbeat about Black Progress, Prospects*. 12 January. http://pewresearch.org/pubs/1459/year-after-obama-election-black-public-opinion.

Pharr, Susan J. 1997. Public Trust and Democracy in Japan. In *Why People Don't Trust Government*, ed. Joseph S. Nye, Jr., Philip D. Zelikow, and David C. King, 237–252. Cambridge: Harvard University Press.

Philpot, Tasha S. 2004. A Party of a Different Color? Race, Campaign Communication, and Party Politics. *Political Behavior* 26 (3): 249–270.

Phinney, J. S. and V. Chavira. 1995. Parental Ethnic Socialization and Adolescent Coping with Problems Related to Ethnicity. *Journal of Research on Adolescence* 5:31–54.

Pickering, Michael. 2001. *Stereotyping: The Politics of Representation*. New York: Palgrave.

Pinar, William F. 2001. *The Gender of Racial Violence in America: Lynching, Prison Rape, and the Crisis of Masculinity*. New York: Peter Lang.

Pitkin, Hanna. 1967. *The Concept of Representation*. Berkeley: University of California Press.

Powers, Daniel A., and Christopher G. Ellison. 1995. Interracial Contact and Black Racial Attitudes: The Contact Hypothesis and Selectivity Bias. *Social Forces* 74 (1): 205–226.

Price, Melanye T. 2009. *Dreaming Blackness: Black Nationalism and African American Public Opinion*. New York: NYU Press.

Putnam, Robert. 1993. *Making Democracy Work: Civic Traditions in Modern Italy*. Princeton: Princeton University Press.

———. 1995. Tuning In, Tuning Out: The Strange Disappearance of Social Capital in America. *PS: Political Science and Politics* 28 (4): 664–683.

———. 2000a. *Bowling Alone: The Collapse and Revival of American Community*. New York: Simon and Schuster.

———. 2000b. Social Capital Benchmark Survey Executive Summary. Saguaro Seminar, Civic Engagement in America, Harvard University. http://www.cfsv.org/communitysurvey/results_pr.html.

Rahn, Wendy M. 1993. The Role of Partisan Stereotypes in Information Processing about Political Candidates." *American Journal of Political Science* 37 (2): 472–496.

Rahn, Wendy, and John Transue. 1998. Social Trust and Value Change: The Decline of Social Capital in American Youth, 1976–1995. *Political Psychology* 19:545–566.

Rayner, Steve. 1992. Cultural Theory and Risk Analysis. In *Social Theories of Risk*, ed. Sheldon Krimsky and Dominic Golding, 83–115. Westport, CT: Praeger.

Reese, Laura A., and Ronald E. Brown. 1995. The Effects of Religious Messages on Racial Identity and System Blame among African Americans. *Journal of Politics* 57 (1): 24–43.

Renshon, Stanley Allen. 1977. Assumptive Frameworks in Political Socialization Theory. In *Handbook of Political Socialization*, ed. Stanley Allen Renshon, 3–44. New York: Free Press.

Richardson, Lilliard E., Jr., David J. Houston, and Chris Sissie Hadjiharalambous. 2001. Public Confidence in the Leaders of American Governmental Institutions. In *What Is It about Government That Americans Dislike?*, ed. John R. Hibbing and Elizabeth Theiss-Morse, 83–97. Cambridge: Cambridge University Press.

Ritterhouse, Jennifer. 2006. *Growing Up Jim Crow: The Racial Socialization of Black and White Southern Children, 1890–1940*. Chapel Hill: University of North Carolina Press.

Roberts, Dorothy E. 1997. *Killing the Black Body: Race, Reproduction, and the Meaning of Liberty*. New York: Pantheon Books.

Rodriguez, Marnie Salupo. 2008. Perceived Discrimination: Multiple Measures and the Intersections of Race and Gender. *Journal of African American Studies* 12:348–365.

Rogers, Reuel R. 2000. Afro-Caribbean Immigrants, African Americans, and the Politics of Group Identity. In *Black and Multiracial Politics in America*, ed. Yvette M. Alex-Assensoh and Lawrence J. Hanks, 15–59. New York: NYU Press.

———. 2006. *Afro-Caribbean Immigrants and the Politics of Incorporation: Ethnicity, Exception, or Exit*. Cambridge: Cambridge University Press.

Rohrmann, Bernd, and Ortwin Renn. 2000. Risk Perception Research—An Introduction. In *Cross-Cultural Risk Perception: A Survey of Empirical Studies*, ed. Ortwin Renn and Bernd Rohrmann, 11–53. Dordrecht, Netherlands: Kluwer.

Rosenstone, Steven J., and John Mark Hansen. 2003. *Mobilization, Participation, and Democracy in America*. New York: Longman.

Rudolph, Thomas J., and Jillian Evans. 2005. Political Trust, Ideology, and Public Support for Government Spending. *American Journal of Political Science* 49 (3): 660–671.

Rusch, Lara. 2009. Rethinking Bridging: Risk and Trust in Multiracial Community Organizing. *Urban Affairs Review* 45 (4): 483–506.

Russell, Kathy, Midge Wilson, Ronald Hall. 1992. *The Color Complex: The Politics of Skin Color among African Americans*. New York: Anchor/Doubleday.

Sanders Thompson, Vetta L. 1992. A Multifaceted Approach to the Conceptualization of African American Identification. *Journal of Black Studies* 23 (September): 75–85.

———. 1994. Socialization on Race and Its Relationship to Racial Identification among African Americans. *Journal of Black Psychology* 20:175–188.

———. 1996. Perceived Experiences of Racism as Stressful Life Events. *Community Mental Health Journal* 32:223–233.

———. 1999. Factors Affecting African American Racial Identity Salience and Racial Group Identification. *Journal of Social Psychology* 139:748–761.

Sapiro, Virginia. 2004. Not Your Parents' Political Socialization: Introduction for a New Generation. *Annual Review of Political Science* 7:1–23.

Schattschneider, E. E. 1960. *The Semi-sovereign People: A Realist's View of Democracy in America*. Chicago: Holt, Rinehart, and Winston.

Schneider, Mark, Paul Teske, Melissa Marschall, Michael Mintrom, Christine Roch. 1997. Institutional Arrangements and the Creation of Social Capital: The Effects of Public School Choice. *American Political Science Review* 91 (1): 82–93.

Schneider, Mark, Paul Teske, Christine Roch, Melissa Marschall. 1997. Networks to Nowhere: Segregation and Stratification in Networks of Information about Schools. *American Journal of Political Science* 41 (4): 1201–1221.

Schnittker, Jason. 2004. Social Distance in the Clinical Encounter: Interactional and Sociodemographic Foundations for Mistrust in Physicians. *Social Psychology Quarterly* 67 (3): 217–235.

Schuman, Howard, Charlotte Steeh, Lawrence Bobo, Maria Krysan. 1997. *Racial Attitudes in America: Trends and Interpretations*. Cambridge: Harvard University Press.

Scott, Lionel D. 2003. The Relation of Racial Identity and Racial Socialization to Coping with Discrimination among African American Adolescents. *Journal of Black Studies* 33 (4): 520–538.

Sears, David O. 1990. Whither Political Socialization Research? The Question of Persistence. In *Political Socialization, Citizenship Education, and Democracy*, ed. Orit Ichilov, 69–97. New York: Teachers College Press.

Sears, David O., Jim Sidanius, and Lawrence Bobo. 2000. *Racialized Politics: The Debate about Racism in America*. Chicago: University of Chicago Press.

Seligman, Adam B. 1997. *The Problem of Trust*. Princeton: Princeton University Press.

Sellers, Robert M., Cleopatra H. Caldwell, Karen H. Schmeelk-Cone, and Marc A. Zimmerman. 2003. Racial Identity, Racial Discrimination, Perceived Stress, and Psychological Distress among African American Young Adults. *Journal of Health and Social Behavior* 44 (3): 302–317.

Sellers, Robert M., and J. Nicole Shelton. 2003. The Role of Racial Identity in Perceived Racial Discrimination. *Journal of Personality and Social Psychology* 84 (5): 1079–1092.

Shah, Dhavan. 1998. Civic Engagement, Interpersonal Trust, and Television Use: An Individual-Level Assessment of Social Capital. *Political Psychology* 19 (3): 469–496.

Shingles, Richard D. 1981. Black Group Consciousness and Political Participation: The Missing Link. *American Political Science Review* 75 (1): 76–91.

Shirley Sherrod. 2010. Times Topics. *New York Times*. 22 July. http://topics.nytimes.com/top/reference/timestopics/people/s/shirley_sherrod/index.html?scp=1-spot&sq=shirley%20sherrod&st=cse.

Shull, Steven A. 1999. *American Civil Rights Policy from Truman to Clinton: The Role of Presidential Leadership*. Armonk, NY: M. E. Sharpe.

Sigel, Roberta S. 1970. An Exploration into Some Aspects of Political Socialization: School Children's Reactions to the Death of a President. In *Learning about Politics: A Reader in Political Socialization*, ed. Roberta S. Sigel, 152–172. New York: Random House.

———. 1989. Introduction: Persistence and Change. In *Political Learning in Adulthood: A Sourcebook of Theory and Research*, ed. Roberta S. Sigel, vii–xvi. Chicago: University of Chicago Press.

Sigelman, Lee, and Steven A. Tuch. 1997. Metastereotypes: Blacks' Stereotypes about Whites' Stereotypes about Blacks. *Public Opinion Quarterly* 61 (1, Spring): 87–101.

Sigelman, Lee, and Susan Welch. 1991. *Black Americans' Views of Racial Inequality: A Dream Deferred.* Cambridge: Cambridge University Press.

Simien, Evelyn M. 2006. *Black Feminist Voices in Politics.* Albany: SUNY Press.

Simpson, Andrea. 1998. *The Tie That Binds: Identity and Political Attitudes in the Post–Civil Rights Generation.* New York: NYU Press.

Sniderman, Paul M., Richard A. Brody, and Philip E. Tetlock. 1991. *Reasoning and Choice: Explorations in Political Psychology.* Cambridge: Cambridge University Press.

Sniderman, Paul M., and Thomas Piazza. 2002. *Black Pride and Black Prejudice.* Princeton: Princeton University Press.

Sollors, Werner. 1999. *Neither Black nor White yet Both.* Cambridge: Harvard University Press.

Solomon, Robert C., and Fernando Flores. 2001. *Building Trust in Business, Politics, Relationships, and Life.* Oxford: Oxford University Press.

Stevenson, Howard C. 1994. Validation of the Scale of Racial Socialization for African American Adolescents: Steps toward Multidimensionality. *Journal of Black Psychology* 20 (4): 445–469.

Stevenson, Howard C., Jocelyn Reed, Preston Bodison, and Angela Bishop. 1997. Racism and Stress Management: Racial Socialization Beliefs and the Experience of Depression and Anger in African American Youth. *Youth and Society* 29 (2): 197–223.

Stolberg, Sheryl Gay, and Jeff Zeleny. 2009. Obama, Armed with Details, Says Health Plan Is Necessary. 9 September. http://www.nytimes.com/2009/09/10/us/politics/10obama.html.

Swain, Carol. 1993. *Black Faces, Black Interests: The Representation of African Americans in Congress.* Cambridge: Harvard University Press.

Tajfel, Henri. 1982. Social Psychology of Intergroup Relations. *Annual Review of Psychology* 33:1–30.

Tajfel, Henri, and Turner, John C. 1986. The Social Identity Theory of Intergroup Behaviour. In *Psychology of Intergroup Relations*, ed. Stephen Worchel and William G. Austin, 7–24. Chicago: Nelson.

Tate, Katherine. 1993. *From Protest to Politics: The New Black Voters in American Elections.* New York: Russell Sage Foundation.

———. 2003. *Black Faces in the Mirror: African Americans and Their Representatives in the U.S. Congress.* Princeton: Princeton University Press.

Taylor, Robert Joseph, Linda M. Chatters, Rukmalie Jayakody, and Jeffrey S. Levin. 2001. Black and White Differences in Religious Participation: A Multi-sample Comparison. *Journal for the Scientific Study of Religion* 35 (4): 403–410.

Taylor, Robert Joseph, Michael C. Thornton, and Linda M. Chatters. 1987. Black Americans' Perceptions of the Sociohistorical Role of the Church. *Journal of Black Studies* 18 (2): 123–138.

Taylor, Shelly E., Susan T. Fiske, N. L. Etcoff, and Audrey J. Ruderman. 1978. Categorical and Contextual Bases of Person Memory and Stereotyping. *Journal of Personality and Social Psychology* 36:778–793.

Terrell, Francis, and Sandra L. Terrell. 1981. An Inventory to Measure Cultural Mistrust among Blacks. *Western Journal of Black Studies* 5 (3): 180–184.

———. 1984. Race of Counselor, Client Sex, Cultural Mistrust Level, and Premature Termination from Counseling among Black Clients. *Journal of Counseling Psychology* 31 (3): 371–375.

Terrell, Francis, Sandra L. Terrell, and Jerome Taylor. 1981. The Effects of Race of Examiner and Cultural Mistrust on the WAIS Performance of Black Students. *Journal of Consulting and Clinical Psychology* 49 (5): 750–751.

Thompson, C. Patricia, Louis P. Anderson, and Roger A. Bakeman. 2000. Effects of Racial Socialization and Racial Identity on Acculturative Stress in African American College Students. *Cultural Diversity and Ethnic Minority Psychology* 6 (2): 196–210.

Thornton, Michael C., Linda M. Chatters, Robert Joseph Taylor, and Walter R. Allen. 1990. Sociodemographic and Environmental Correlates of Racial Socialization by Black Parents. *Child Development* 61 (2): 401–409.

Thornton, Michael C., and Yuko Mizuno. 1999. Economic Well-Being and Black Adult Feelings toward Immigrants and Whites. *Journal of Black Studies* 30 (1): 15–44.

Tillery, Alvin B. 2005. Diversity within and across Groups. In *The Politics of Democratic Inclusion*, ed. Christina Wolbrecht and Rodney E. Hero, 15–18. Philadelphia: Temple University Press.

Till-Mobley, Mamie, and Christopher Benson. 2003. *Death of Innocence: The Story of the Hate Crime That Changed America.* New York: One World.

Tilly, Charles. 2005. *Trust and Rule.* Cambridge: Cambridge University Press.

Timberlake, Jeffrey M., and Sarah Beth Estes. 2007. Do Racial and Ethnic Stereotypes Depend on the Sex of Target Group Members? Evidence from a Survey-Based Experiment. *Sociological Quarterly* 48:399–433.

Tomz, Michael, Jason Wittenberg, and Gary King. 2003. Clarify. *Journal of Statistical Software* 8 (1).

Torres, Kimberly, and Camille Z. Charles. 2004. Metastereotypes and the Black-White Divide: A Qualitative View of Race on an Elite College Campus. *Du Bois Review* 1:115–149.

Tuch, Steven A., Lee Sigelman, Jason A. MacDonald. 1999. The Polls—Trends: Race Relations and American Youth, 1976–1995. *Public Opinion Quarterly* 63:109–148.

Turner, Margaret. 2005. *Race, Gender, and the Politics of Skin Tone.* New York: Routledge.

Tyler, Tom R. 2001. The Psychology of Public Dissatisfaction with Government. In *What Is It about Government That Americans Dislike?*, ed. John R. Hibbing and Elizabeth Theiss-Morse, 227–242. Cambridge: Cambridge University Press.

U.S. Census Bureau. 2004. Census Report on Black Americans: The American Community—Blacks: 2004. http://www.census.gov/prod/2007pubs/acs-04.pdf.

Uslaner, Eric M. 2000–2001. Producing and Consuming Trust. *Political Science Quarterly* 115 (4): 569–590.

———. 2001. Is Washington Really the Problem? In *What Is It about Government That Americans Dislike?*, ed. John R. Hibbing and Elizabeth Theiss-Morse, 118–133. Cambridge: Cambridge University Press.

———. 2002. *The Moral Foundations of Trust.* Cambridge: Cambridge University Press.

Verba, Sidney, Kay Lehman Schlozman, and Henry E. Brady. 1995. *Voice and Equality: Civic Voluntarism in American Politics.* Cambridge: Harvard University Press.

Walton, Hanes. 1985. *Invisible Politics: Black Political Behavior.* Albany: SUNY Press.

Walton, Hanes, and Robert C. Smith. 2008. *American Politics and the African American Quest for Universal Freedom*. New York: Longman.

Warren, Mark E. 1999. Introduction to *Democracy and Trust*, ed. Mark E. Warren. Cambridge: Cambridge University Press.

Washington, Harriet A. 2006. *Medical Apartheid: The Dark History of Medical Experimentation on Black Americans from Colonial Times to Present*. New York: Harlem Moon.

Waters, Mary. 1994. Ethnic and Racial Identities of Second Generation Black Immigrants in New York City. *International Migration Review* 20:795–820.

———. 1999. *Black Identities: West Indian Immigrant Dreams and American Realities*. Cambridge: Harvard University Press.

Watkins, Boyce. 2010. Black Woman Tells Obama, "I'm Exhausted of Defending You & Disappointed": Should We All Be? *Black Voices*, 21 September. http://www.bvonmoney .com/2010/09/21/woman-exhausted-by-defending-obama-should-we-all-be/.

Weathers, Monica D., Elaine M. Frank, Leigh Ann Spell. 2002. Differences in the Communication of Affect: Members of the Same Race versus Members of a Different Race. *Journal of Black Psychology* 28:66–77.

Weiss, Nancy J. 1983. *Farewell to the Party of Lincoln: Black Politics in the Age of F.D.R.* Princeton: Princeton University Press.

Weitzer, Ronald, and Steven A. Tuch. 2004. Race and Perceptions of Police Misconduct. *Social Problems* 51:305–325.

———. 2006. *Race and Policing in America: Conflict and Reform*. Cambridge: Cambridge University Press.

Welch, Susan, Lee Sigelman, Timothy Bledsoe, Michael Combs. 2001. *Race and Place: Race Relations in an American City*. Cambridge: Cambridge University Press.

Whaley, Arthur L. 1998. Cross-Cultural Perspective on Paranoia: A Focus on the Black American Experience. *Psychiatric Quarterly* 69 (4): 325–343.

———. 2001. Cultural Mistrust: An Important Psychological Construct for Diagnosis and Treatment of African Americans. *Professional Psychology: Research and Practice* 32 (6): 555–562.

Whitby, Kenny J. 1997. *The Color of Representation: Congressional Behavior and Black Interests*. Ann Arbor: University of Michigan Press.

White, Ismail K. 2007. When Race Matters and When It Doesn't: Racial Group Differences in Response to Racial Cues. *American Political Science Review* 101 (2): 339–354.

White, Joseph L. 1984. *The Psychology of Blacks: An Afro-American Perspective*. Englewood Cliffs, NJ: Prentice Hall.

Wielhouwer, Peter. 2000. Releasing the Fetters: Parties and the Mobilization of the African-American Electorate. *Journal of Politics* 62 (1): 206–222.

Williams, Jerome D., Geraldine R. Henderson, and Anne-Marie Harris. 2001. Consumer Racial Profiling: Bigotry Goes to Market. *Issues and Views*, November–December, 22–24.

Williams, Melissa S. 1998. *Voice, Trust, and Memory: Marginalized Groups and the Failings of Liberal Representation*. Princeton: Princeton University Press.

Willie, Sarah S. 2003. *Acting Black: College, Identity, and the Performance of Race*. New York: Routledge.

Wilson, William Julius. 1987. *The Truly Disadvantaged: The Inner City, the Underclass and Public Policy*. Chicago: University of Chicago Press.

———. 1996. *When Work Disappears: The World of the New Urban Poor*. New York: Knopf.

Wong, Paul, Chienping Faith Lai, Richard Nagasawa, Tieming Lin. 1998. Asian Americans as a Model Minority: Self-Perceptions and Perceptions by Other Racial Groups. *Sociological Perspectives* 41 (1): 95–118.

Woodson, Carter G. [1933] 1999. *The Mis-education of the Negro*. Trenton, NJ: Africa World.

Woodward, C. Vann. [1951] 1999. *Origins of the New South: 1877–1913*. Baton Rouge: Louisiana State University Press and the Littlefield Fund for Southern History.

———. 1974. *The Strange Career of Jim Crow*. 3rd ed. New York: Oxford University Press.

Wright, Wilbert. 1975. Relationships of Trust and Racial Perception toward Therapist-Client Conditions during Counseling. *Journal of Negro Education* 44 (2): 161–169.

Wynes, Charles E. 1961. *Race Relations in Virginia, 1870–1902*. Charlottesville: University of Virginia Press.

Yamagishi, Toshio. 2001. Trust as a Form of Social Intelligence. In *Trust in Society*, ed. Karen S. Cook, 121–147. New York: Russell Sage Foundation.

Index

Abramson, Paul R., 13, 34

Accountability, of government, 191

Acculturative stress, 60

ACORN, 245n2

Acting white, 59

Affective judgments, 48, 53

African American culture, 58

African American ideologies, 129, 222

African American studies programs, 68

African-centered culture, 43, 67

Africans, 22, 117, 120, 245n4; political trust and, 198–99; racial socialization and, 64, 65, 78, 81

African worldview, 60

Afrocentric identity, 43, 68

Afro hairstyle, 67

Age: cohorts, 35; distrust and, 89, 91, 95, 134–35; divisions, 22, 77, 85; political trust and, 199, 208, 216; racial discrimination and, 111; racial knowledge and, 98; racial socialization and, 79; social trust and, 165, 177, 187–88; trust and, 146; trustworthiness and, 124

Agency, individual, 156, 158

AIDS, 130

Allen, Richard L., 37

American Community Survey Report, 18

American dream, 161–62

American Indians, 62, 92

American racial hierarchy, 90

Anderson, Louis P., 60

Antiblack attitudes, 9–10

Antimiscegenation practices, 61

Appearance, 122–25

"Appropriate" black behavior, 64, 77–78, 85

Arithmetic Means for Blacks' Positive and Negative Stereotypes, 102

Arithmetic Means of Blacks' Contextualized Trust, 178

Arithmetic Means of Racial Groups' Contextualized Social Trust, 171

Asian Americans, 11, 20–22; black Americans and, 42, 48, 51, 59, 82, 87, 94–95, 98, 133–37; *Blacks' Feelings of Political Closeness to Black, White, Latino, and Asian Groups*, 200; colorism among, 62; *Determinants of Blacks' Racial Trust in Black, White, Latino, and Asian Groups*, 145; *Determinants of Groups' Racial Trust in Black, White, Latino, and Asian Groups*, 144; as political actors, 36; political trust and, 198–99, 203–9, 212–16, 218–23; racial discrimination against, 80; racial trust by, 142–47; racial uncertainty and, 113–14, 117, 119–20; social trust and, 163–67, 169–78, 181–83, 187–89; stereotypes about, 110

Attitudes: antiblack, 9–10; "color-blind," 12; on immigration, 135, 137–38, 143, 146–47, 150, 161, 165, 177; interracial, 93–94; projection of, 146; racial attitudes, of black Americans, 23, 40–41, 53, 133–37; risk-averse, 93, 113; *Univariate Results for Black Attitudes in the Racial Uncertainty Survey Experiment*, 116

Attribution: positive or negative, 96; of racism, 94; of stereotypes, 100–101

Attribution theory, 47–48, 246n8

Avery, James, 32–33

Bags, for purchases, 57

Bakeman, Roger A., 60

Baptist tradition, 162

Beauty, 65, 76

Messages, of racial socialization, 46, 50, 53, 58–60; black identity and, 92; *Categorical Emphases of Racial Socialization Messages, 73*; cautious/defensive, 59; individualistic-universalistic, 59; integrative/assertive, 59; *Ordered Probit Regression Models of Black Americans' Racial Socialization Messages, 74–75*; on racial consciousness, 87–88, 92, 100, 111, 117, 228; on racial protectiveness, 87–88, 92, 96, 100, 111, 114–15, 117, 228; *Racial Socialization Messages Received among Black Americans, 70–72*; stereotypes and, 105; "whites not all racist" message, 84, 88, 99, 100, 114

Metastereotypes, 131

Miller, Alan, 190

Missouri Compromises (1820 and 1850), 249n1

Mitamura, Tomoko, 190

Mizuno, Yuko, 134

Mobility, social, 86–87

Mobility, sociopolitical, 235

Model of Effect of Racial Discrimination Knowledge on Interracial Feelings and Interactions, 99

Models of Trust in Federal and Local Governments to Do What Is Right, 214

Morris, Irwin, 136

Morrison, Toni, 223

Multivariate Models of Black Americans' Racial Uncertainty, 118

Multivariate Models of Blacks' Racial Discrimination Perceptions: Experienced Racial Discrimination and Racial Uncertainty, 112

NAACP. *See* National Association for the Advancement of Colored People

The Nadir, 9, 193–94

National Association for the Advancement of Colored People (NAACP), 3–4

National Black Election Study, 134

Nationalist racial ideology, 93

National Politics and Socialization Survey (NPSS), 16–22, 49, 133, 138; political trust and, 201–3, 205–11, 218–21, 223; racial discrimination and, 97; racial knowledge and, 117–19; racial socialization and, 63,

69, 77, 78, 87; racial uncertainty and, 115–17; risk and, 96; SCBS and, 149–51, 230; social trust and, 165, 177–89; stereotypes and, 97, 100–110, 127

National Survey of Black Americans (NSBA), 17, 19, 39; racial socialization and, 58, 59, 63, 66

Neglectfulness, 102

Negrophiles, 9

Negrophobes, 9

Neighborhoods, 51, 98–99, 114, 115, 155; associations, 164; racial discrimination in, 159–60

Neighbors: *Comparisons of Arithmetic Means for Racial Groups' Trust in Neighbors, 179*; *OLS Regression Model of Blacks' Contextualized Trust in Neighbors, 180*; social trust and, 166–67, 169, 171, 173, 178, 187

Networks: of racial knowledge, 121, 128, 147, 213; racially diverse, 212; social, 44, 125, 194, 226

Niemi, Richard G., 38

"Nigger lovers," 9

Nigrescence, stages of, 43, 88

Non-Afrocentric identity, 43

Nonverbal racial communication, 94

Nonwhites, and white Americans, 92

Normative judgments, 24

Normative theories, of trust, 12–13, 226

Normative values, 37

Normativization, of distrust, 9, 16

NPSS. *See* National Politics and Socialization Survey

NSBA. *See* National Survey of Black Americans

Obama, Barack H., 3, 4, 23, 217, 223–25; race and, 235–39, 249–50n2

Obama administration, 246n2

Offe, Claus, 127

Old-fashioned racism, 101

OLS Models of Blacks' Contextualized Trust in Co-congregants, 186

OLS Models of Blacks' Contextualized Trust in Co-workers, 184

OLS Models of Blacks' Contextualized Trust in Store Clerks, 182

OLS Regression Model of Blacks' Contextualized Trust in Neighbors, 180

One-drop laws, 247n3, 247n10
Ordered Probit Models of Blacks' Subscription to Racial Stereotypes, 108–9
Ordered Probit Regression Models of Black Americans' Racial Socialization Messages, 74–75
Ordered Probit Regressions of Blacks' Contextualized Trust, 174–75
Ordered Probit Regressions of Racial Groups' Contextualized Trust, 172–73
Orr, Marion, 86
Outcomes, 25, 125

Paranoia: cultural, 130–31; racial, 131–32
Partisanship, 30, 52; political closeness and, 198–201; race and partisanship trust experiment, *207, 210–11*; racial, 205–11, 232–33
Passing for white, 76, 247n3, 247n10
Peer relations, 44, 67
People in general (control group perceptions), 101–2, 104–5; distrust of, 148–49; political trust and, 205–6, 218; racial discrimination and, 119–20, 229; racial uncertainty and, 115–17; stereotypes and, 127–38
Personal knowledge, about racial discrimination, 97–100
Personal rights, 30
Pew Research Center, 29–30, 125, 133, 235; polls of, 217, 236
Pew Social Trends Survey, 158–59
Phenotypic characteristic, race as, 50, 247n3, 247n10
Picketing, 33
Pitkin, Hanna, 196
Police, 91
Political activism, 61–62, 162–63
Political actors, 36, 191–92, 203–5
Political closeness, 198–201; *Blacks' Feelings of Political Closeness to Black, White, Latino, and Asian Groups, 200*; racial consciousness and, 199, 232
Political context, 60, 158, 191–225
Political distrust, 196–98
Political learning, 37–38
Political participation, 33–34, 246n4
Political proximity. *See* Political closeness
Political representation: of black Americans, 31–32, 191–96; descriptive, substantive or

symbolic, 196–97, 201–3, 220; trust and, 201–3
Political scandals, 27
Political science, 132–33
Political socialization, 33; generational model of, 37–38, 40; life-cycle model of, 37–38; lifelong openness model of, 37–38; lifelong persistence model of, 37; racial socialization and, 39–40
Political spaces, dual, 51
Political system: disequilibrium in, 26–27; trust in, 31
Political trust, 14–15, 17, 22–23, 101; Africans and, 198–99; age and, 199, 208, 216; Asian Americans and, 198–99, 203–9, 212–16, 218–23; black consciousness and, 191, 209; black linked fate and, 199, 208, 209, 221; decline in, 25–28, 246n1; Democratic Party and, 201–9, 220–24; income levels and, 209, 215; Latino Americans and, 198–201, 203–9, 212, 215–23; NPSS and, 201–3, 205–11, 218–21, 223; people in general and, 205–6, 218; race and, *219*, 219–25; racial consciousness and, 199, 208; racial protectiveness and, 208–9, 220, 232; racial uncertainty and, 208, 209; *Regression Models of Blacks' Political Trust Based on the Race and Partisanship Experiment, 210–11*; Republican Party and, 202–9, 220–23; SCBS and, 192, 212–15, 217; white Americans and, 198–99, 203–9, 212–23
Poverty, 33
Powell, Colin, 223
Predicted Probabilities of Trust in Federal and Local Governments, 215
Pride: racial, 44, 58; racial socialization scale on black pride, 64, 69, 76, 85
Probit Models of Generalized Trust in Others, 168
Productivity, 125
Projection, of attitudes, 146
Proposition 187, 136
Protests, 33, 38
Psychology, 41–54, 129; psychological conditions of black Americans, 130–31; psychological development, of black Americans, 40; psychological injury, 234–35, 239–40; psychological processing of race, 7, 43, 245n6; social psychology literature, 40.

See also Discriminative racial-psychological processing

Psychotic disorders, 131

Public accommodations, 160–61

Public good, 26

Public-opinion literature, 121

Public opinion studies, 28–29, 35, 41

Putnam, Robert, 10, 26, 125, 126, 248n1

Quality of life, 164, 177, 217

Race: construction of, 34; democracy and, 8–13, 126, 137, 239; historical race relations, 45; mattering less, 60, 64, 83–85, 88, 92, 114, 203; mattering less, racial socialization scale on, 83–85; medicine and, 129–30; Obama and, 235–39, 249n2; as phenotypic characteristic, 50, 247n3, 247n10; political trust and, *219*, 219–25; psychological processing of, 7, 43, 245n6; race and contextualized trust experiments, 177–87; race and partisanship trust experiment, *207, 210–11*; race and social trust experiments, *178, 179, 180, 181, 182, 183, 184, 185*; race and trust experiment, 138, 139, *140*, 147–48; "race traitors," 9; risk and, 3–7, 92–96, 226–27; as social construct, 6; socially desirable responses on, 147–48; social trust and, 139–41, 187–90; trust and, 234–35; vestiges of, 226–28

Racelessness (race mattering less), 60, 64, 83–85, 88, 92, 114, 203

Racial actors, social trust in, 177–87, 189

Racial attitudes, of black Americans, 23, 40–41, 53, 133–37

Racial attributes, 47–48, 247n9; with causal links, 48; context of, 52, 79

Racial communication, nonverbal, 94

Racial competition, 52, 189, 223

Racial consciousness: black linked fate and, 94, 96, 110; messages about, 87–88, 92, 100, 111, 117, 228; political closeness and, 199, 232; political trust and, 199, 208; racial protectiveness and, 120; social trust and, 183, 187

Racial-contextual perception, and discriminative racial-psychological processing, 51–53, 227

Racial discrimination, 3–23; age and, 111; against Asian Americans, 80; beliefs about, 32; black, 86, 115; black linked fate and, 111, 115; contemporary experiences of, 14, 19–21, 31, 38, 86, 90, 96, 110–13, *112*, 120, 141, 228; de jure and de facto, 34, 39, 79, 123, 132, 188; experiences of, and discriminative racial-psychological processing, 50–51, 227; frequency of, 111; future, 113–15; gender and, 91; historical experiences of, 15, 68–69, 86–87, 97, 110, 127, 228; housing and, 91, 114; income levels and, 90; against Latino Americans, 80; *Model of Effect of Racial Discrimination Knowledge on Interracial Feelings and Interactions, 99; Multivariate Models of Blacks' Racial Discrimination Perceptions: Experienced Racial Discrimination and Racial Uncertainty, 112;* in neighborhoods, 159–60; NPSS and, 97; ongoing, 32; people in general and, 119–20, 229; personal knowledge about, 97–100; racial identity and, 91, 115; racial knowledge and, 114–15; racial protectiveness and, 119; reverse, 3, 132; risks of, 5–6, 49–50, 92–93; stereotypes and, 47–49, 53, 94–95, 101–2, 229; trustworthiness and, 88; in workplaces, 161–62

Racial epithets, 91, 236

Racial etiquette, 79–80

Racial externalization, 19, 21–23, *54*, 227, 230–33

Racial homogenization, 14; discriminative racial-psychological processing and, 47–49, 53, 227; in-group and out-group perceptions and, 100; racial socialization and, 92; stereotypes and, 100–110

Racial identity: constructs, 59; racial discrimination and, 91, 115

Racial inequality, codification of, 10

Racial internalization, 19–21, *54*, 218, 227, 228–30

Racialized distrust, 131–33; interracial, racial socialization scale on, 64, 82; intraracial, racial socialization scale on, 64, 81–82

Racialized reputations, 41–42

Racialized social capital, 125–26

Racialized trust, 13, 121–22, 148–51, 240; discriminative racial-psychological processing and, 51, 53, 227; trustworthiness and, 141–42

About the Author

SHAYLA C. NUNNALLY is Associate Professor of Political Science and African American Studies at the University of Connecticut.